D1523358

ONE CHINA, MANY TAIWANS

ONE CHINA, MANY TAIWANS

The Geopolitics of Cross-Strait Tourism

Ian Rowen

CORNELL UNIVERSITY PRESS   ITHACA AND LONDON

First published 2022 by Cornell University Press

Library of Congress Cataloging-in-Publication Data

Names: Rowen, Ian, author.
Title: One China, many Taiwans : the geopolitics of cross-strait tourism / Ian Rowen.
Description: Ithaca, NY : Cornell University Press, 2022. | Includes bibliographical references and index.
Identifiers: LCCN 2022005845 (print) | LCCN 2022005846 (ebook) | ISBN 9781501766930 (hardcover) | ISBN 9781501767692 (paperback) | ISBN 9781501766947 (pdf) | ISBN 9781501766954 (ebook)
Subjects: LCSH: Tourism—Political aspects—Taiwan. | Tourism—Social aspects—Taiwan. | Taiwan—Relations—China. | China—Relations—Taiwan.
Classification: LCC DS799.63.C6 R69 2022 (print) | LCC DS799.63.C6 (ebook) | DDC 327.51249051—dc23/eng/20220429
LC record available at https://lccn.loc.gov/2022005845
LC ebook record available at https://lccn.loc.gov/2022005846

For Asher Zeno and his many worlds

Contents

Illustrations

Acknowledgments

This book owes immeasurably to the keen and generous eyes of Scott Writer, Lev Nachman, and Lauren Dickey, who each looked over the full manuscript at various stages of completion, sometimes more than once, and to Daniel Kao for his beautiful map of Taiwan. Painstakingly thorough reviews from Jenny Chio and Marc Moskowitz and two more anonymous referee reports greatly strengthened the manuscript. Emily Yeh, John O'Loughlin, and especially Tim Oakes were instrumental to the development of this work. Thanks are due as well to Catherine Chou, Shu-mei Huang, Chris Horton, Jamie Rowen, and Max Farrell, who kindly read portions of the manuscript and offered helpful comments. I also owe a debt of gratitude to Yang Yang, Amelia Schubert, Sam Tynen, and Tan Shi Ying for help with finding sources.

My fieldwork and writing benefited immensely from my time affiliated at Academia Sinica in Taipei, including the gracious hosting of Maukuei Chang at the Institute of Sociology and Peng Jen-yu at the Institute of Ethnology. Field research was supported by the Fulbright Commission and Foundation for Scholarly Exchange, the US National Science Foundation, the Taiwan Foundation for Democracy, and the University of Colorado Boulder Geography Department. Ideas were further refined during a delightful summer as a visiting scholar at the European Research Center on Contemporary Taiwan at Tübingen University and in countless conferences and workshops. I thank Gunther Schubert, Dafydd Fell, and other Taiwan studies colleagues for their hospitality and support.

Portions of chapter 6 appeared in "Chinese Tourism as Trigger and Target of the Sunflower and Umbrella Movements" in the 2020 book *Sunflowers and Umbrellas: Social Movements, Expressive Practices, and Political Culture in Taiwan and Hong Kong*, edited by Thomas Gold and Sebastian Veg, published by the Institute of East Asian Studies, University of California, Berkeley. Portions of chapter 3 appeared in "Touring in Heterotopia: Travel, Sovereignty, and Exceptional Spaces in Taiwan and China" in *Asian Anthropology* 16 (1), published in 2017.

Thanks are owed to my editor Jim Lance for seeing the book through with the press and to Nanyang Technological University, Singapore, for use of the balance of my start-up research funds to support open-access electronic publication of this book.

Finally, thanks to Guy Rubin at Imperial Tours in Beijing for a yearlong whirlwind tour of the travel industry capped by excellent career advice, and to Titi for seeing the book through with my psyche.

Abbreviations

ADS	Approved Destination Status
ARATS	Association for Relations Across the Taiwan Straits (People's Republic of China)
CCP	Chinese Communist Party
DPP	Democratic Progressive Party
ECFA	Economic Cooperation Framework Agreement
FISU	International University Sports Federation
KMT	Chinese Nationalist Party
MAC	Mainland Affairs Council (Republic of China, Taiwan)
NGO	nongovernmental organization
PFP	People's First Party
PRC	People's Republic of China
ROC	Republic of China
SEF	Straits Exchange Foundation (Republic of China, Taiwan)
TAO	Taiwan Affairs Office (People's Republic of China)
TIRA	Taiwan Independence Revolutionary Army
WHA	World Health Assembly
WHO	World Health Organization

Note on Transliteration

Taiwan's place and personal names continue to be romanized in dazzlingly in-consistent ways, reflecting and reproducing the cultural tensions traced in this book. When I first resided in Taipei in 2001, a walk north from National Tai-wan University took me past signs for Xinsheng S. Road, Hsin-sheng S. Road, and Shin-sheng S. Road, all on the same road. Even today, years after China's standard Hanyu Pinyin was adopted by Taipei City under the leadership of then mayor Ma Ying-jeou, it is still common to see the same places, persons, or prod-ucts written differently depending on where one stands.

In general, this book uses the most prevalent romanization for places within Taiwan (i.e., Taitung, not Taidong), while Hanyu Pinyin is used for mainland Chinese place-names. Personal names of well-known figures are written in what-ever romanization appears most commonly in news reports or official docu-ments. My named informants are written in their preferred romanization. For pseudonymous informants, Hanyu Pinyin is used if they are from China, and a quasi–Wade Giles spelling is used if they are from Taiwan. For Chinese-language words with polysemic or questionable English glosses, Hanyu Pinyin is included in parentheses for additional clarity.

MAP 0.1. Map of Taiwan and surrounds.

ONE CHINA, MANY TAIWANS

INTRODUCTION

In 2008, as the People's Republic of China (PRC) pointed thousands of missiles toward Taiwan, it started sending millions of tourists the same way. The tourists were welcomed by a travel industry eager for new sources of revenue as well as by President Ma Ying-jeou, who was elected earlier that year. President Ma claimed that the opening would strengthen the economy and improve Taiwan's relations with what he called "mainland China." The tourists, said Ma's administration, might return home with a positive impression of Taiwan's democracy, which would lead to mutual understanding and maybe even political reconciliation. Still, despite the growing flow of leisure travelers and the social, economic, and political connections that they facilitated, citizens and officials on both sides of the Taiwan Strait did not quite agree on the cultural character or spatial definition of the territories they were traveling between. It turned out that tourism deepened the difference.

As far as most Chinese tourists were concerned, they were traveling in a part of China, culturally familiar if undeniably distinct politically. Indeed, Taiwan, an archipelago of twenty-three million people, with the western shore of its main island about 160 kilometers away across a heavily militarized strait, was listed as a province on all PRC maps and passports. As for Chinese authorities, the ultimate goal of all cross-strait policy, including tourism, was political control and ultimately annexation—euphemistically referred to as "unification" and defined as a "national core interest." Some China-friendly leaders in Taiwan also hoped for territorial unification, even if they had a different vision of what that future "China" would look like and how it would be governed.

However, many people in Taiwan had a different idea—that these "mainland guests" (*lu ke*), as they called them, were entering a different country entirely, where they were welcome to spend their money, have a good time, mind their own business, and then go home. For those concerned about PRC irredentism, tourism looked like another one of several weapons aimed at Taiwan's sovereignty. As it happened, at the same time that cross-strait tourism accelerated, so did Taiwanese national identification and pro-independence sentiment, leading to unprecedented protests and electoral shifts against PRC-friendly politicians.

A potential for tension should have been clear, for 2008 was not the first time that Taiwan had received a rapid influx of arrivals from China. Sixty-odd years earlier, at the close of World War II, Taiwan was overwhelmed by weary and desperate soldiers serving the Chinese Nationalist Party (KMT), who were then retreating from the military advance of the Chinese Communist Party (CCP). These soldiers and the KMT-dominated state apparatus they propped up, the Republic of China (ROC), occupied Taiwan in 1945 with the support of the United States after imperial Japan was forced to end its half century of colonization. Many Taiwanese saw the military men as uncouth and unhygienic (Kerr 1965), qualities not so dissimilar from those later attributed to twenty-first-century tourists. But unlike today's visitors, these soldiers had nowhere to return to after the CCP consolidated its control and established the PRC in Beijing. They instead were pressed to enforce the repressive and often murderous rule of the émigré ROC in Taiwan and sometimes also suffered violence themselves under the authoritarian KMT regime (Yang 2020). Even after the lifting of martial law in 1987, Taiwanese have continued to live under the ever-present threat of a new Chinese military invasion, this time from the PRC, whose leaders have pledged to eventually "reunify" Taiwan by any means necessary.

Subtly written into the practice of tourism, then, amid the rhetoric of reconciliation, was the recapitulation of a past military occupation and the foreshadowing of a future assault. Such semiotic excess evokes Jacques Derrida's meditation on the etymological entwinement and transmutable tension between hospitality and hostility, in which he suggests that "for the invited guest as much as for the visitor, the crossing of the threshold always remains a transgressive step" (2000, 75).

Taiwan's thresholds are tense, tangled, and constructed through a series of transgressions. Here, tourism animates guests, hosts, and guides in a turbulent dance of difference and identity, making plain that travel is no mere leisure activity. Rather, it is a stage for struggle over ethnic identity and national borders, a geopolitical instrument and event that performs and transforms state territory.

Tourism, I will demonstrate, has been one of several strategies aimed at achieving the political control of Taiwan for the PRC. But how has it worked in practice? And what does this case have to say to the claims of many tourism scholars and industry and political leaders that tourism can promote peace and mutual under-standing? This book argues that contrary to the PRC's efforts to incorporate Tai-wan as part of an undivided "One China," tourism actually aggravated tensions between the two polities, polarized Taiwanese society, and pushed Taiwanese popular sentiment farther toward support for national self-determination.

In the process, Taiwan's staging of state sovereignty bifurcated into what could be described as "two Taiwans"—the Taiwan performed as a part of China for group tourists versus the Taiwan experienced as a site of everyday life by local residents and some independent tourists. The split corresponded with a grow-ing fissure of the domestic political economy, amplifying a conflict between those business, civil society, and state actors that had an interest in sustaining a PRC-oriented tourist industry and those that did not. These tourism-inflected two Tai-wans are among the most vivid manifestations of inconsistent nationalisms spanning a territory that was already realizing a distinct, and distinctively in-clusive, subjectivity. Indeed, Taiwan's identity is increasingly predicated on a plu-ralistic civic nationalism in which not just one or two but *many* Taiwans coexist more or less comfortably, even as it is existentially threatened.

Although the transformations of Taiwan and China are the focus of this study, attention to their unusual features can illustrate the role of everyday practices—such as the use of national flags, maps, names, and travel permits—in the con-duct of tourism and the production of political spaces elsewhere. Looking at everyday practices of state administration and interpersonal encounter in con-tested states sheds light on the peculiarity of normative sovereignties more gen-erally (Navaro-Yashin 2012; Friedman 2015; Mälksoo 2012).

Likewise, looking at exceptional and even world-shattering moments can shed light on peculiar practices long taken for granted. By traveling along such spatial and temporal edges of sovereignty, one can witness the instability of the center—in this case, the notion of exclusive state territory, an elusive yet persistent phan-tasm that haunts the gaps and fissures of the world system, its incomplete suture to international representative bodies like the United Nations rupturing violently into view through the COVID-19 pandemic of 2020, which imploded global mobility and illuminated the geopolitical stakes of tourism.

Tourism and Territory

"This is all just for show!" shouted a Chinese tourist during the routine chang-ing of the guards at Sun Yat-sen Memorial Hall in Taipei, a scene pictured in figure I.1. I observed him complain loudly to whoever would listen before he stormed outside. He was not wrong. Of course, the military guards, wearing

FIGURE I.1. Changing of the guards at Sun Yat-sen Memorial Hall, Taipei.

starched uniforms and marching with bayonets in precisely timed drills, were giving a show. The monument, with its grandiose, if now slightly dilapidated, facade and gigantic statue of Sun Yat-sen, the founder of the ROC, was designed for show. Likewise, the tourist's loud public dismissal was a kind of show. But blatant theatricality makes such phenomena no less powerful or productive—these phenomena are powerful and productive precisely because they are performances. The performance with both the soldiers *and* the tourist, like the tourist's prior encounter with a border guard on his arrival to Taiwan and his application for a travel permit to enter Taiwan in the first place, produced the tourist and the toured as national subjects. In so doing, it produced, reproduced, and troubled the state and interstate system.[1] The unsettling and uncanny aspects of such spaces and practices point not only to the fragility of contested states but also to the general instability of states and state subjects, which require constant work to maintain.

Although cross-strait tourism may seem in many ways to be an extraordinary case, contoured as it is by clashing territorial claims, it is precisely its extraordinariness that makes it valuable for building theory about the geopolitics of tourism in general. So much is taken for granted in the scholarship and practice of tourism that the study of an extraordinary situation may uncover what, through repetition, has come to seem ordinary—a world split into nation-states with mutually exclusive territories, a global mobility regime of visas and passports, of embassies and border guards, and so on—but which is in fact an unlikely and unstable configuration of spaces, bodies, and practices.

Pandemic punctuations notwithstanding, millions of tourists cross borders every year. Passports in hand, these tourists act as the citizen-subjects of the various nation-states of the world. They travel for any number of reasons. When they cross borders from their own country into another and then return home, they not only carry memories and souvenirs—they, along with border agents and airlines, travel agents and tour operators, are performing, effectively enacting, and potentially transforming the borders that they are crossing and the territories that they are traversing.

The central conceptual proposition of this book is that tourism performs and can transform state territory. This argument is informed by Michel Foucault's analytics of government, which attends to points of "contact between the technologies of domination of others and those of the self" (Foucault 1988, 17). These social and political technologies produce temporarily durable but never finished subjects and objects (Foucault 2009; Lemke 2007; Rose and Miller 2012). Seen this way, states and citizens are not a priori political agents, and territories are not passive spatial containers, but rather are effects of power-laden relationships—always-already in a state of flux, of becoming, of change, contradiction, rupture, and reformation (Mitchell 1991; Abrams 1988). To put the point concisely, tourism can and should be theorized as a technology of state territorialization.

What does it mean to perform state territory, and how might tourism transform it? Let us begin with territory, which is "better conceived as an act or practice rather than an object or physical space" (Brighenti 2010, 53). I treat territory as a political practice and pattern of relations that names, claims, calculates and bounds space. More specifically, I use state territorialization to refer to the particular practices by which space is rendered or configured as belonging to and bounded by a collective actor imagined as a particular state, "in whose name individuals are interpellated (implicitly or explicitly) as citizens or subjects, aliens or foreigners, and which is imagined as the source of central political authority for a national territory" (Painter 2006, 758). However this collective actor is imagined, "the practices, mechanisms and institutions through which processes of interpellation take place are very real" and often violent (758).

Territories acquire spatial definition through the production and reproduction of borders, which establish constitutive divisions between what is inside and what is outside. These borders are not simply lines on a map, but social and discursive practices that take place in time (Paasi 1998). To name the processes by which people become attached to particular state or national territories, I take the term "territorial socialization" from the political geographer David Newman (1999), who has observed that places just outside effective administrative borders but still within other imagined boundaries often become cast as crucial to the integrity of a territorial unit, amplifying potential for physical and symbolic conflict.

Boundaries are both legitimated and contested in cultural, civic, ethnic, biological, and other terms that extract and enforce singular identities from a multiplicity of possibilities. Among the most persistent of these formations has been the nation, succinctly defined by Benedict Anderson (2006) as an "imagined political community," on whose behalf the modern territorial state claims a basis for legitimacy. With most of contemporary global space represented and subdivided such that every putative nation is implied to have a state territorial roof (Gellner 1983), state territory in this normative sense "is the coordinate space occupied by a nation-state . . . with each piece a part of one or another nation-state's territory" (Wainwright and Robertson 2003, 201). Of course, the real world is far messier, with Taiwan as a case in point.

State sovereignty and national citizenship are enacted whenever a traveler proffers a passport and submits to the authority of a border guard. In this way, the borders of the nation-state are socially produced and reproduced, and sometimes transgressed and transformed, when they are crossed by mobile actors, including tourists and migrants (Cresswell 2010; Richardson 2013; Salter 2013; Sheller and Urry 2006).

Territorial socialization occurs inside borders as well, during moments of everyday life in which routine and even banal performances of nation, state, and region take place. Displayed in museums and monuments, inscribed into maps and other cartographic devices, representations of borders circulate in print, speech, and social media. They appear in books and newspapers, and in shows and at sites, often popular with tourists, where state and national heroes are celebrated and collective yet selective memory transmutes to myth (Balibar 2002; Paasi 1998, 2000; Billig 1995).

Performing Guests and Hosts

If territoriality pivots on the constitutive distinction between inside and outside, tourism theory pivots on the constitutive distinction between guest and host. The guest received the spotlight in the groundbreaking analysis of Dean Mac-Cannell (1976), who posited that "the tourist" was emblematic of the modern subject's search for meaning and authenticity. Subsequent contributions, including the influential edited book *Hosts and Guests* (Smith 1977), examined both sides of the equation by attending to tourism's impacts on receiving areas and communities. Extending these insights to examine tourism's effects on ways of sensing and knowing, John Urry's later work on the "tourist gaze," loosely following Foucault, suggested that tourism generated a distinctive way to make the world legible for tourists and everyone they implicate, with potentially limitless effects (Urry and Larsen 2011).

These early works tend to treat "the tourist" as a typical, or even the quintessential, modern subject in search of a sense of authenticity and difference from "home." Although they provide useful reference points for the present case, their empirical basis in Euro-American leisure tourism limits their geographical scope and theoretical purchase. Later waves of tourism research by Asian and Asia-focused scholars, inspired in part by postcolonial and post-structural theory, both built on and pushed back against these conceptual foundations to argue that tourism elsewhere can operate, and therefore needs to be theorized, in radically different ways (Winter, Teo, and Chang 2009; Edensor 2008; Teo and Leong 2006; T. Chang 2021; Adams 2021).

China received a significant amount of this scholarly attention due both to the superlative size of its market as well as the theoretical provocations it provides. After considering how the Chinese party-state has used tourism to support foreign policy aims (Richter 1983a), to articulate a sense of modernity (Oakes 1998), and to project authority over cultural interpretation, it becomes difficult to characterize tourism primarily as a search for meaning by adrift modern subjects. Speaking directly back to earlier such theories, Pál Nyíri (2006, 2010) has argued that unlike the idealized Western tourist in search of the exotic, many Chinese travelers are not necessarily interested in pursuing an experience of cultural authenticity or *difference*—in many cases, it is actually a space of *identification* and familiarity that is desired by visitors and produced by the tourism industry and state agencies that cater to them.

Studies of ethnic tourism in China's diverse southwestern regions offer suggestive hints for how to more carefully consider tourism's capacity to produce spaces and practices of identification and difference. Such ethnographies emerged together with other studies of social difference, including work on the stereotyping of minority populations as gendered, fetishized, disliked, backward, harmless, or nearly indistinguishable from the dominant Han majority, who relationally construct themselves in opposition as rational and modern subjects (Blum 2001). Scholars observed that many such quasi-colonial tropes and stereotypes were in turn incorporated into the products and landscapes, both physical and imaginary, of ethnic tourism (Schein 2000; Oakes 1998; Chio 2014). These theoretically sophisticated studies are as important for what they can anticipate about Chinese tourism to Taiwan as for what they cannot account for:

the peculiar cross-strait case in which Han Chinese guests identify with Taiwanese hosts as fellow ethnonational subjects, albeit under a distinct political regime they are themselves implicated in transforming, yet with limited recognition that their sense of ethnonational fellowship is seldom shared by their hosts.

In Taiwan, such tricky gaps between senses and spaces of identity and difference are mediated through the personage of the guide, a professional specialist who interprets for and translates between guests and hosts. As we will see in chapter 4's ethnography of a Chinese group tour, the translational work of guides, whether fulfilled with faithful or fraudulent intent, is not mimetic, but creative and productive. Through their skillful sequencing and staging, tour guides, together with their manifold props and supporting actors, not only smoothen social difference but also actively reassemble the worlds they translate between (Satsuka 2015; Bunten 2015; Salazar 2006).

Tourism scholars long ago anticipated the sentiment shouted by the Chinese tourist recounted above, "This is all just for show!" Early analysis in this vein drew from Erving Goffman's pioneering dramaturgical theory of social roles to profitably treat much of what goes on in destinations as a series of performances. This usually relied on distinguishing between the front stage performed by locals for tourists and the (presumably stable) backstage in which locals actually live and which tourists may hope to penetrate (MacCannell 1976). Guides, in Taiwan or anywhere, can blur these putative distinctions.

Tourists perform and blur these distinctions as well, as observed by Tim Edensor (2000), who suggested that tourists engage in self-conscious displays of realization and liberation, aspirational and ironic role-playing, and "unreflexive, habitual, unintentional" repetitions (Edensor 2001, 60). Attending to the way these performances unfold in different spaces, be they in the enclavic, "purified" spaces of theme parks and resort hotels or more heterogeneous public squares and markets, reveals how "tourism as performance can both renew existing conventions and provide opportunities to challenge them" (78). For even as the routines of commercial tourism can flatten cultural difference, they can also "open up the world, invade the everyday, and expand the repertoire of performative options and the range of stages upon which tourists may perform" (79).

Given the fact that touring selves are constituted in territorial terms—and that these terms can be contested—my analysis draws further from theories of "performativity" (Butler 1993; McKinlay 2010), which emphasize the capacity of performance to produce, reproduce, and disrupt subject positions and spaces of power (Gregson and Rose 2000).

Treating tourism through a performative lens affords an exploration of how territories are not only performed but also *enacted* by tourists. Like all good theater, tourist performance depends on props and pageantry, continuity, and consistency. Performative props for international travel include passports, visas, and other devices that claim citizenship and confer the right to travel. At moments of border crossing, and during discussions about places of origin, state and nation are cited, iterated, and further articulated through choices of dress, patterns of speech, and other multisensory modalities, with enduring effects. These devices and practices constitute and communicate the division between inside and outside that delimit the territories of sending and receiving states, contested or otherwise (Torpey 2000; Navaro-Yashin 2012). Circulating as components of tourism's "hybrid assemblages," along with a wide variety of other material and discursive practices, they represent, enact, and suffuse national and international divisions of space (Franklin 2004; Salter 2013; Franklin and Crang 2001).

Contingent on citation and iteration, performative practices harbor the possibility of a failure of repetition (McKinlay 2010). These failures can open up new and previously unimaginable possibilities. Furthermore, when tourism is subject to changing constraints, prohibitions, and taboos—when the contours of state territory and national identity are as vague, shifting, and contested as they are in the case of China and Taiwan—possibilities for breakdowns, ruptures, or novelty multiply in fascinating ways.

To briefly summarize the book's conceptual framework, I have proposed that state territories are composed and challenged through shifting sets of social and spatial practices. Tourism, managed through a mobility regime that includes border crossing and requires the citation of state and national symbols, can constitute, reproduce, and subvert state territory and citizens. For these reasons, tourism should be treated as a mode of territorial socialization and a political technology of state territorialization.

Tourism and Territory in Taiwan

Scholarship on cross-strait tourism has usually assumed an affect and effect of reconciliation and rapprochement. This is symptomatic of much of tourism studies' assumptions about peace and borders, which usually elide the unpleasantries of politics. The typical treatment is one in which Taiwan and mainland China are partitioned states expected to "reconcile" and even unify in part through the promotion of cross-strait tourism (L. Yu 1997; Guo et al. 2006; Zhang 2013, 2017). As for Chinese-language scholarship, most accounts from both sides of the strait also assume a telos of reconciliation and focus largely on economic impacts or destination marketing (Ho, Chuang, and Huang 2012; Liu W.-T. 2009; L. Wang 2011).

One China, Many Taiwans speaks back to this body of scholarship and aims to open up new trajectories for tourism studies and the social sciences more broadly.

What has been missing in these past studies, apart from a more critical discussion of Taiwan's territoriality, is an appreciation that tourism does not necessarily promote reconciliation or rapprochement, but can serve opposing interests and produce unpredictable effects. Apart from the ideological or institutional commitments and constraints of individual researchers, previous cross-strait tourism scholarship perhaps lacked opportunity to find theoretical resources with which to pose sharper geopolitical questions. Although there have been some scholarly examinations of the role of borders in encouraging or restricting tourism (Timothy 1995, 2001; Sofield 2006), the potential instrumentality of tourism for peace and reconciliation or even unification between nation-states (Guo et al. 2006; Kim, Timothy, and Han 2007; D'Amore 1988; Jafari 1989), and the use of tourism as an instrument of foreign policy (Richter 1983b; Arlt 2006) or nation building (Oakes 1998; Johnson 1999; Light 2001; Gillen 2014), less read but no less important are studies that examine tourism as a modality of state violence, domination, and difference-making (Stein 2008; Lisle 2016).

While it might feel gratifying to imagine that tourism can produce peace, the evidence for such hopes remains thin at best (Farmaki 2017). Sometimes, the relationship often works the opposite way claimed by industry cheerleaders (Litvin 1998). Tourism in many cases has been targeted precisely to undermine peacemaking efforts, as seen in threats to or even kidnappings of tourists. And even within relatively settled borders, state deployment of tourism as a tool for producing national solidarity can exacerbate ethnic and economic tensions (Adams 1998).

Korea provides a useful case for comparison. Although early 2000s tourism between South and North Korea produced feelings of internationalization and deterritorialization for a few participants, it often produced the opposite effect of "retrenchment of identity in a territory" (Park 2005, 116). This makes tourism "an arena of contestation and cooperation where different states compete, negotiate, manipulate, and maneuver cultural meanings and representations to find their places in the complex and changing international political order" (116). However, unlike the situation in Korea, which both states characterized as intranational tourism (with each side pointing to the other as a false state), or which Christian J. Park suggests is "inter-state tourism where two states, however hostile, belong to one nation" (125), in Taiwan authorities stopped seriously claiming sovereignty over China long before they permitted inbound tourism. Moreover, according to public opinion polls, a clear and increasingly large majority of the people in Taiwan did not identify as "Chinese"—even ethnically, well before the rise of cross-strait tourism (National Chengchi University Election Study Center 2019). Given such complexity, rather than assume the inevitability of "reconciliation," analysts might have considered the possibility that tourism could aggravate contention.

Taiwan's management of inbound Chinese tourism has been shaped as much by cross-Strait contention as it has by shifts in its own political administration. Although Taiwan's then authoritarian leadership first permitted ROC citizens to visit China in 1987, and PRC citizens were permitted to enter Taiwan for family visitation the following year, the PRC did not allow for mass leisure tourism until 2008, following the election of Ma Ying-jeou, who promised economic growth by pursuing closer ties with China. After millions of tourists flooded in, the president often touted the opening of the gates as a spectacular achievement.

This tourism was conducted under the rhetorical cover of the so-called 1992 Consensus, the supposed outcome of a meeting between KMT and CCP officials in 1992, during which both sides were said to agree that there was but "one China," with the KMT insisting that its formulation allowed for each side to uphold "different interpretations" about what "China" meant. Given the intrinsic ambiguity of such a diplomatic device, even as the purported social benefits of tourism were propounded by both the PRC and the Ma administration, the contradiction between both sides' territorial claims later created an uncanny sense of multiple, distinctive, yet overlapping sensations of stateness for Chinese tourists and Taiwanese residents alike, affecting Taiwan's domestic politics and self-definition, as discussed in chapters 3 and 6. It has also offered opportunity for some tourists to reflect deeply, and sometimes uncomfortably, on Chinese politics, culture, and society, as related in chapter 5.

Contention characterizes many of these encounters, belying undemonstrated claims that tourism would ameliorate conflict. Although it is difficult to draw a direct causal arrow between the growth in inbound tourism from China and the sharpening of protest against Ma's China policy, their tandem acceleration is striking. Tourism was championed by Ma's administration as an economic boon that only the KMT could deliver, but its implementation fueled opposition from a variety of actors: independence advocates eager to reduce Taiwan's reliance on China, populists who complained that the benefits of cross-strait trade were felt only by people with elite KMT or PRC connections, and social activists who claimed that the costs were therefore displaced onto the Taiwanese public. The following is a characteristic example: "They [Chinese] create their own market—they fly their own airlines, they hire their own buses, eat and live at their own hotels—but they are using our land and our scenery, to make money. Our scenic hotspots such as Sun Moon Lake and Kenting are now filled with Chinese. We are left with their trash. Allowing Chinese tourists into the country costs more than we gain" ("Bohmann von Formosa," quoted in Tsai and Chung 2014).

There is precious little reliable data about Taiwan's aggregate economic gain from tourism during the Ma years. Tourism Bureau figures, both published publicly and reconfirmed to me in my interviews with officials, were rough estimates based on self-reported tourist guesses of per-day spending multiplied by total arrivals, instead of a careful audit of actual revenues. With economic benefits unclear, unseen, and immaterial for the vast majority of Taiwanese, my interview data suggests that it was precisely the perception of tourist behavior, rather than faith in the claim of economic benefits that ostensibly derive from them, that proved most salient to Taiwanese people.

Chinese tourists in Taiwan, like those in nearby Hong Kong, were frequently depicted as rude, loutish, noisy, smelly, and unhygienic. Reports both on social media and in the popular press include tourists defacing greenery on the east coast (Zhuang 2013), tourists bathing in their underwear in the popular southern beach town of Kenting (Tsai and Chung 2014), and public urination (Ramzy 2014). Similar sentiment was expressed even by an academic colleague: "I don't go to the beach at Kenting anymore. There are too many mainlanders there now. It's like going to China."[2] While there is an element of "othering" at play here, arguably with racist or discriminatory overtones, this reaction is situated in the uncomfortable historical context of repeated waves of invasion and colonization and the unrealized promise of tangible or widely shared gains from the tourism trade. Like the tourists, Ma's KMT came from China, and his China-centric policies—of which tourism was particularly prominent—failed to deliver many of their promised economic and political benefits.

By 2013, discontent about the material failures of these policies, and the rhetorical and political compromises necessary to pursue them, had earned Ma an approval rating as low as 9 percent. In 2014, Ma's China agenda sparked the Sunflower Movement, "the greatest episode of collective contention in Taiwan's history" (Ho 2015, 91), during which thousands of student and civic activists occupied the area inside and around the Legislative Yuan (parliament) to protest a trade deal that would liberalize cross-strait economic exchanges, including the tourism industry, and further open up Taiwan to PRC-controlled capital. The movement was in part populated by people who entered as concerned passersby, tourists in a way, who were transformed into a new kind of subject, Sunflower activists, who went on to realize new ways of being Taiwanese. In my own case, after climbing a ladder into the Legislative Yuan on the second day of the occupation, I found myself transformed into a Sunflower action researcher, which both risked and revitalized my relationship with my field of study. Suddenly, Taiwan's seemingly inexorable drift toward political capitulation to the PRC, propelled by the economic inducements of tourism, no longer appeared a fait accompli.

The movement precipitated the KMT's landslide defeat by the Democratic Progressive Party (DPP), whose roots lay in earlier democratic, social justice, and independence movements, first in the November 2014 local elections and then in the 2016 presidential and legislative elections. The incoming DPP president,

Tsai Ing-wen, disavowed the "1992 Consensus" and instead emphasized the need for Taiwan's future to be determined by its twenty-three million people. The PRC responded by cutting most tourism to Taiwan, but this tactic proved insufficient to sway subsequent elections or stifle the long-term rise in those claiming an exclusively Taiwanese identity and, to a lesser degree, support for de jure independence. This shift is significant not only for Taiwan and its allies but also for the rest of the world, because Taiwan's position outside China's de facto borders heightens its salience for PRC discourses of national humiliation, which prop up party-state patriotism and aggressive foreign policy postures (Callahan 2009).

Although the Sunflower Movement was certainly the most domestically explosive expression of Taiwan's geopolitical drama recounted in this book, other extraordinary displays of tourist-oriented nascent nation-state theater took place during my field research period. As I recount in chapter 3, pro-Taiwan independence and pro-China activists regularly demonstrated under the landmark Taipei 101 skyscraper, hoisting ROC, PRC, and Taiwan independence flags and shouting at each other in front of audiences of Chinese tourists, attracting concern from passersby and politicians alike. Only two years later, when the PRC slashed tourism as a retaliatory measure, many members of the tourism industry staged an unprecedented protest, marching through the heart of Taipei to demand that President Tsai accept the 1992 Consensus to restore PRC tourism and save their jobs, as I recount in chapter 6.

Cross-strait tourism spurred many such strange scenes, but it also yielded hopeful and perhaps even instructive lessons for other polities. Sheltered between and spurred by the shadow dance of contending US and Chinese hegemonies, Taiwan's liminal polity continues experimenting with new forms of representative democracy and international representation. If the Sunflower Movement in its time represented the "most important rethinking of 21st Century democratic politics" (Harrison 2015), then it is appropriate to think with it about new modes of mobility and territoriality. It is hard to imagine another place where student and civil society activists could occupy a parliament, earn the support of a majority of polled citizens, develop a functional decision-making process, and exit peacefully more or less on their own terms after twenty-four days. Likewise, raucous gatherings of protesters and counterprotesters waving and claiming allegiance to contradicting flags at a national landmark or tourism industry leaders demanding their president abandon a popular position on the nation's sovereignty are idiosyncratic forms of political expression, to say the least. Yet Taiwan's very exceptionality makes it a perfect site for a study of emergent political practice. In an archipelago where the contours of the nation and the structure of the state appear up for grabs by both "external" and "domestic" forces (their distinction blurry anywhere, but all the more obviously so in Taiwan), and in which an unresolved history of colonial state violence seethes under a usually placid and polite surface, different political mentalities contend in spaces charged with the affective potencies of life-and-death struggle.

The COVID-19 pandemic thrust Taiwan's nascent nation-state theater to the center of world attention. The pandemic is also of course a story of Chinese tourism, as travelers unwittingly spread the novel coronavirus domestically and abroad. Well before the PRC and the World Health Organization (WHO) acknowledged human-to-human transmission, weeks before China was locked down, Taiwan was the first country to send investigators to the epicenter in Wuhan, the first to conduct medical checks on incoming flights from China, and the first to provision masks to protect its people. Taiwan's early and effective public health management action made it one of the only places in the world to avoid an epidemic surge and maintain socioeconomic normalcy throughout 2020, in large part precisely because it is a contested state, wary of the PRC, and excluded from global health bodies. Taiwan's exclusion quite likely endangered other places—the WHO ignored Taiwan's early inquiries and conflated its caseloads with those of the PRC. Taiwan's leadership used this opportunity to press for further recognition, even as the rest of the world fell into disarray, raising further questions about the durability of state territory and the fragility of the interstate order, to which I return in the epilogue.

Itinerary

Taiwan's contemporary condition—administered domestically and represented internationally by the ROC, claimed and threatened by the PRC, and imagined and lived as a free and democratic Taiwan—is so unusual that this introduction is followed by a general overview of Taiwan's political history in chapter 1. Chapter 2 covers mobility within and between Taiwan and China, as well as the baroque institutional arrangements and exotic rhetorical formulations that regulated it. Together, these historical chapters set the stage to understand the post-2008 rise of Chinese tourism to Taiwan.

The ethnographic section begins with chapter 3's tour of Taiwan's most visited sites, which pays particular attention to their geopolitical characteristics. The reader is then invited to hop on the bus for chapter 4's eight-day Chinese group tour of Taiwan, to see just how meticulously Taiwan can be performed as a part of China. Chapter 5 then turns to the far more varied experiences and interpretations of independent tourists, unleashed as they are from the political and economic imperatives that determine group tour management. Fieldwork for these chapters was conducted at the height of the cross-strait tourism trade, between 2011 and 2015.

The remainder of the book picks up chronologically where the ethnographies leave off, to examine the role of tourism in the end of the "1992 Consensus" under which Taiwan's Ma administration had engaged with the PRC. It traces a line between the 2014 Sunflower Movement, a massive protest against a trade agreement that included tourism provisions, and the subsequent electoral collapse of the KMT. With an eye toward Hong Kong, it considers the PRC's use of the tourism industry as a political weapon against the new DPP administration, which disavowed the KMT's "one China" policy and looked to strengthen ties with the United States, Japan, and other regional neighbors. The book concludes by addressing the COVID-19 pandemic and contemplates the crisis's implications for tourism and territory in Taiwan and beyond.

HOW TAIWAN BECAME AN EXCEPTIONAL TERRITORY

"Taiwan is not a country. Please present an identity document from a country recognized by the UN," said the officer at the entrance to the Geneva headquarters of the United Nations High Commissioner for Human Rights to a Taiwanese student in 2017. Before arriving in Switzerland, the student's professor had successfully applied for her and her team of students to enter the office's public gallery. However, each of them was treated differently when they presented their passports to the various staff at the office's registration counter. The professor's passport was rejected, but she was allowed to enter after presenting her international driver's license. Another student was initially allowed to enter after presenting his international student card, but he was ejected after another "very rude" staffer, in the words of the professor, rejected the same card from another student (Tong 2017).

This account is but one of many from frustrated Taiwanese travelers who are frequently misrecognized as nationals of the People's Republic of China (PRC) at border crossings or subject to inconsistent reception or outright rejection from international venues, even from those that nominally champion human rights, such as the offices of the UN. Taiwanese travelers and tourists have long dealt with such arbitrary and capricious treatment, which results from the incongruency of Taiwan's limited international recognition with its reality as a de facto independent polity (H. Wang 2004). Yet, it is not only in their border crossings and overseas declarations of citizenship that senses of national identity and territory have been contested and blurred but also in their everyday engagements in their home territory, which is administered and internationally represented by the Republic of China (ROC), threatened and claimed by the PRC, and lived and imagined as an independent Taiwan.

Changes to the design of Taiwan's passport, as well as its changing representation within international bodies like the UN, can be read as indexes of the various ways its territory has been staged as a colony, a province, a nation-state, or otherwise. In 2002, when the Chen Shui-bian administration added the word "Taiwan" to a green-colored document that previously printed only "Republic of China" on its cover, ROC loyalists denounced what they perceived as a perilous step toward de jure independence. The Chen administration said that it was simply facilitating ease of movement for passport holders who had long complained of being misrecognized as PRC nationals when crossing borders. However, as devices that allow national subjects to move between state-occupied territories, such paper plays can go only so far. As seen in the above anecdote, passports require reciprocal recognition, and not only from states, to realize their efficacy.

Taking these passport changes as a point of departure, this chapter provides a historical account of Taiwan's changing political geography. I present contemporary Taiwan's territoriality as emerging from and forming against clashing colonial and national projects within Taiwan. Taiwan's ways of staging territory are further subject to changing relations with political entities and representative bodies beyond it, producing uneven modes of ethnic, national, and state identification.

My approach draws from several histories, including Evan N. Dawley's study of ethnogenesis in the port town of Keelung, which argues that "Taiwanese forged their ethnic consciousness in contradistinction to two nationalisms, Japanese and Chinese, both of which were imposed on Taiwan in the guise of intentional projects to modernize, civilize, and deterritorialize or reterritorialize the place and its people" (2019, 21). Similarly, Arif Dirlik, following Leo T. S. Ching, suggests that contemporary Taiwanese identification has been shaped as "a product of the interplay between an emerging 'Chinese' identity on the Mainland, the affiliation with Japan under colonialism, and a resistant local identity" (Dirlik 2018, 9).

Taiwan's "resistant local identity" requires unpacking. The islands of Taiwan witnessed Austronesian migration, Dutch colonial incursions, Han Chinese settlement sanctioned by the Qing empire, Japanese imperial occupation, authoritarian Chinese Nationalist Party (KMT) rule, and finally the contemporary condition of national autonomy and democratic governance. Providing this historical context, along with an account of Taiwan's changing international relations and contemporary political society, situates the following chapters, which examine how cross-strait tourism grew in the wake of these longer-term shifts in national identification and territorial representation.

Tracing Taiwan's Political History

Although Taiwan was studied as a proxy for China by a generation of Sinologists shut out of the PRC, feted as "Free China" by cold warriors, and often acclaimed as "the first Chinese democracy" following the end of martial law in 1987 (Chao and Myers 1994), its richly layered history of multiple colonial, national, and territorial projects has resisted scholarly efforts toward neat ethnonational characterization. These layers also complicate efforts to narrate Taiwan for tourists, Chinese or otherwise.

Taiwan's effective administrative borders have been unchanged since 1949. That said, its performance of territory, in terms of everyday life, state definition, and international recognition, has shifted dramatically. These shifts took place even as the territory remained governed under the transplanted ROC, whose rule was enforced with a great deal of violence and whose constitution was progressively amended to focus on the governance of Taiwan, without an explicit territorial redefinition. These shifts have been both constrained and facilitated by domestic decolonization and democratization projects, as well as changing relations with the PRC, Japan, the United States, and international representative bodies such as the United Nations.

An archipelago whose main island is about 160 kilometers off the coast of southeast China's Fujian Province, Taiwan was inhabited for millennia by diverse Austronesian populations and refashioned violently by waves of European, Chinese, and Japanese settlers, making it a site of "hybrid colonialisms managed by statist organizations that relied on a frontier that shifted over time" (Eskildsen 2005, 285). When European explorers arrived in the seventeenth century to claim land and develop trading posts, Han Chinese settlers came in search of economic opportunity, collaborating in a co-colonial scenario of "Chinese settlement under Dutch rule" centered in present-day Tainan (Andrade 2008, 2).

The Dutch were soon expelled by the military of the Ming loyalist warlord Koxinga. His descendants were defeated decades later by naval forces of the Qing empire, a conquest dynasty originating in Manchuria that expanded to rule all of present-day China as well as Mongolia and other territories, which provided the ROC and later the PRC the basis for most of their territorial claims. The Qing governed Taiwan in a piecemeal fashion with an inconsistent immigration policy and limited control or claim over the main island's mountainous interior and east coast (Shepherd 1993). Qing cartographers drew a dividing line between Taiwan's "civilized" west and "savage" and patchily charted east. This border figured its uncolonized parts as "quite literally 'off the map'" (Jacobs 2005, 17). During this period, Taiwan was imagined by literati as an exotic and even barbaric travel destination that served as a site of exile for troublemaking scholar-officials (Teng 2004). Immigration and trade continued nonetheless, and soon a majority of the population was composed of Chinese settlers and the offspring of mixed Fujianese, Hakka, and indigenous parentage.

Starting in the late nineteenth century, a modern Taiwanese consciousness began to congeal and spread, spurred in response to the next phase of colonization, this time from Japan (M. Chang 2003; Dawley 2019). The turning point came in 1895, when the Qing, beset by both domestic instability and external incursions, lost a war with Japan and ceded its claims to Taiwan in perpetuity as part of a settlement in the Treaty of Shimonoseki. A short-lived Republic of Taiwan was declared by local elites, who even raised a flag of their own design, but it was quickly put down by the Japanese occupying forces.

In contrast to the Qing's inconsistent administration, Japan aggressively administered Taiwan as an economically valuable colony without explicitly designating it as such. The colonial project proved useful for Japan's performance of parity with, but munificent distinction from, European imperial powers. In the more urban and agricultural western plains, which were already dominated by the descendants of Han settlers, the regime implemented a centralized system of taxation and trade, partly built on top of district divisions and tithing practices held over from the Qing period (Barclay 2017). This funded a transportation, education, and sanitation infrastructure that rapidly eclipsed anything in China. During this time, tourism from Japan to Taiwan was promoted to valorize the supposedly civilizing and modernizing contributions of the imperial venture (McDonald 2017).

The landscape was dramatically different in the east coast and central mountains, home to valuable camphor forests. To stabilize its rule and secure access to resources, the Japanese administration conducted extensive mapping, ethnic classification, and "pacification" campaigns, effectively reconstituting the "civilized" west and "savage" east into "regularly administered" and "specially administered" zones with very different political economies. The east was largely left out of agricultural and manufacturing projects, and much of its land was nationalized for resource extraction. As the activities of timber merchants intensified and impinged on the so-called savage border, the colonial administration brutally quelled indigenous resistance movements. Meanwhile, indigenous people were classified, driven into reserves, conscripted into the military, or "museumized" as tourist attractions. This set the "terms of engagement" for post-Japanese administrations, which maintained ethnically differentiated governance models and state forestry management of lands, much of which is now contested as indigenous sovereign territory (Barclay 2017, 249).

Meanwhile, across the strait, the Qing empire ultimately collapsed after multiple uprisings. It was followed by the establishment of the ROC in 1911. The

ROC, like the PRC that succeeded it, staked most of its territorial claims on those of the Qing. Sun Yat-sen, a longtime anti-Qing activist who served as the first president of the ROC, proved unable to assert control over a vast landscape riven by warlords and factions, despite his drive to establish a central, unitary state.

The KMT (short for Zhongguo Guomindang, literally translated as Chinese National People's Party), which grew out of earlier revolutionary organizations, was formally founded in 1912 by Sun. After he passed away in 1925, authority over the KMT eventually passed into the hands of military strongman Chiang Kai-shek, who shared Sun's conviction that the Chinese people, defined in part by the boundaries of (Qing-claimed) territory as well as including diasporic emigrants, should "constitute not only one nation, but one race" (Fitzgerald 1995, 88).

Chiang received support from the Soviet Union and he reorganized the KMT along Leninist lines (although he and the KMT later received considerable US support for adopting a staunch anticommunist stance). Chiang faced warlords, a Japanese invasion, and the emergence of the rival Chinese Communist Party (CCP), also a Leninist organization, led by Mao Zedong. Although Chiang, as the head of the ROC, was eventually able to assert control over much of China, his administration proved notoriously corrupt and unstable. It was further challenged by occupation and invasions from Japan in the run-up to World War II. The KMT and the CCP cooperated at times throughout this chaotic period, but ultimately fought each other viciously in what became known as the Chinese Civil War, in which the United States backed the KMT and the Soviet Union backed the CCP.

Neither the KMT nor the CCP showed significant interest in Taiwan itself until the 1943 signing of the Cairo Declaration, a document that expressed the aligned US, UK, and ROC position against Japan. Prior to that, Taiwanese people were variously described by leaders of both parties as belonging to a distinct nationality (*minzu*), potentially sovereign or at least possessing the right to self-govern. However, after the Cairo Declaration called for Taiwan to be "restored" to the ROC (which had in fact never ruled Taiwan), both KMT and CCP leaders claimed that Taiwan had been an integral part of Chinese territory all along (Hsiao and Sullivan 1979).

Two years later, in 1945, the ROC, led by the KMT, occupied Taiwan with US support after Japan surrendered at the close of World War II. Some Taiwanese elites were cautiously optimistic that the ROC's takeover of Taiwan, euphemistically referred to as "retrocession," would lead to some kind of conational self-rule after the generally efficient but unquestionably colonial Japanese administration, which imposed a campaign of assimilation and "imperialization" on the population. This campaign included Japanese-language education and military conscription that accelerated under wartime conditions (Ching 2001). However, KMT leaders quickly alienated Taiwanese by centralizing power under a brutal and un-accountable administration, dismissing local people as colonized and even en-slaved by Japan, and pillaging resources to support their failing war effort on the mainland.

Feelings of cultural if not national difference were also accentuated by the fact that many of the first KMT arrivals were desperate, battle-weary soldiers who had never seen modern amenities such as streetcars, railroads, or indoor plumb-ing. Their disorderly conduct shocked the relatively prosperous and urbane Tai-wanese. As put by the historian Steven E. Phillips, "The Taiwanese considered both the Chinese and Japanese regimes exploitative, but deemed the new gov-ernment particularly dishonest, incompetent, unpredictable and inefficient" (2003, 57). Some Taiwanese, nostalgic for the relatively stable rule of Japan, felt that one colonial administration had been traded for another, and many pre-ferred the former (Kerr 1965).

Widespread discontent exploded in what later became known as the 228 In-cident, a seminal event in the formation of a modern Taiwanese subjectivity that emerged against and through authoritarian KMT rule and that is marked in vari-ous memorial sites around Taiwan that are studiously avoided by China-savvy tour guides. The 228 Incident is named for February 28, 1947, the day after po-lice struck a female cigarette vendor and killed a bystander in a crowd that had formed to defend the woman. On the twenty-eighth, the KMT administration declared martial law as Taiwanese formed loosely organized brigades, occupied government buildings, and articulated increasingly ambitious demands for self-rule. Some mainlanders were also beaten up by small groups of Taiwanese. Early indications that the local KMT leadership might pursue a compromise were dashed when military reinforcements arrived from China and quickly crushed the uprising with an overwhelming show of force. In the following weeks, KMT forces killed approximately ten thousand people and wounded per-haps another thirty thousand, many of them educated elites.

In 1949, the KMT was finally forced out of mainland China by the CCP, which established the PRC. Led by Chiang, the KMT retreated completely to Taiwan with 1.5 million refugees in tow. To consolidate ROC rule as an émigré regime with an eye toward retaking China, state and party organs favored arrivals from mainland Chinese over anyone born in Taiwan. All travel between Taiwan and China was banned for the next several decades.

Facing a restive population, the KMT intensified its surveillance apparatus and attempted to further legitimize it with anticommunist rhetoric and purges. Later known as the White Terror, this 38-year period of martial law saw thou-sands more killed or imprisoned. As with the 228 Incident, the party-state vio-lence of the White Terror was aimed both at alleged communist conspirators and at Taiwanese independence advocates. It wiped out an entire generation of intellectuals—native-born Taiwanese and mainland Chinese exiles alike were imprisoned, tortured, and executed. For nascent Taiwanese nationalists, the 228 Incident and the White Terror definitively established the KMT-ROC party-state as an illegitimate "alien regime." Along with institutional discrimination against native-born Taiwanese, who officially constituted roughly 80 percent of the population, this set the stage for decades of tension, fueling an initially illegal but increasingly vigorous independence movement (Makeham and Hsiau 2005).

KMT rule transformed Taiwan's politics, economy, and culture. Taiwan was administered as the only part of the ROC under KMT authority. A new provincial government headquarters was built in central Nantou County, augmented by a highly paid national assembly of pensioned officials appointed to represent their "home" provinces in China. Political society became stratified between Taiwanese (*benshengren*, or "people of this province") and mainlanders (*waishengren*, or "people from outside this province"), with party, military, police, and educational positions reserved for the latter.

Economically, the KMT implemented land and other policy reforms, converting landowners into industrial capitalists and financing the creation of small- and medium-scale businesses. These reforms, along with the infrastructure remaining from the Japanese colonial period (much of which was directly appropriated by the KMT), preferential trade policies with the United States, and the hard work of people across Taiwan, eventually resulted in the so-called Taiwan miracle, a booming export-driven economy that raised the standard of living for all social classes, however unevenly (Tu 1996).

Culturally, the KMT implemented a "Sinicization" campaign to inculcate Chinese values into the Taiwanese, whom the KMT claimed to liberate from Japanese colonial exploitation. Native-born Taiwanese, who had been under Japanese rule for fifty years, were forcibly "reeducated" as Chinese subjects. The Hoklo (southern Fujianese) language spoken by most Taiwanese was suppressed in favor of Mandarin, the official language of the ROC. Textbooks emphasized Chinese history and gave little if any attention to Taiwan (Chang 2015). Streets and public spaces were renamed after places in China, for Sun Yat-sen and Chiang Kai-shek, or for Confucian or other classical Chinese values. KMT outposts were set up in every indigenous township. Advocacy for Taiwanese independence, or any mention of a distinct Taiwanese nationality or identity, was strictly prohibited. This project was not just a simple transfer of Chinese cultural practices, but a wholesale reinvention of them to serve the KMT regime. As put by the anthropologist Allen Chun: "The government in effect played an active role (as author) in writing culture (by constructing discourses on tradition, ethnicity, ethical philosophy and moral psychology). It also inculcated these reconstructed notions of tradition (as culture) through the 'normative' machinery of the school, media, family and military in order to construct disciplinary lifestyles and ritual patterns of behaviour compatible with the underlying ethos of the State" (1994, 54).

The KMT's ethos, etched in its name and extended through its policies, relied on representing Taiwan as part of China while preparing to retake the mainland. But as the PRC consolidated its rule, the impossibility of reconquering the mainland became increasingly clear to the KMT leadership. The point was made even clearer after a series of diplomatic crises, including the expulsion of the ROC from the United Nations, the United States' normalization of relations with the PRC, and the partial readmission of the ROC to other international bodies under a variety of confected names, such as "Chinese Taipei." The KMT was forced to localize and liberalize not only in response to these international crises but also due to pressure from within Taiwan. These reforms, spurred by continual grassroots pressure, ultimately led to the lifting of martial law in 1987 and the permitting of people to travel to China.

After Chiang Kai-shek's death in 1975, leadership of the KMT and the ROC eventually passed to his son, Chiang Ching-kuo, who pragmatically recognized the need to bring members of the non-mainlander majority into the party in order to maintain its rule. Still, a vigorous grassroots human rights and democracy movement challenged the legitimacy of the regime. Led primarily by ethnic Taiwanese and strengthened considerably by ties with Taiwanese activists in Japan and North America, this movement was known as the *dangwai*, meaning "outside the [KMT] party". Violent government response to several rallies led to the arrest and trial of many *dangwai* activists (Jacobs 2005).

Facing popular pressure and continued hemorrhaging of international diplomatic support, President Chiang Ching-kuo initiated a number of electoral and administrative reforms. These were stewarded and accelerated by his Taiwan-born successor, Lee Teng-hui. Taiwan's first multiparty presidential election followed in 1991, when Lee was easily elected in a contest against the new Democratic Progressive Party (DPP). The DPP had grown out of the *dangwai* movement (Rigger 1999) and initially had a plank calling for de jure independence in its 1991 party charter, until it was later removed to reposition the party to appeal to voters concerned about political stability (Clark 2008). This election led some scholars to acclaim Taiwan as "the first Chinese democracy" (Chao and Myers 1994), but Taiwan's "Chineseness" should not be taken for granted.

With a democratic political culture supplanting Chinese ethnic nationalism, Lee garnered widespread electoral support by promoting the idea of the "new

Taiwanese." This category encompassed both Taiwanese and mainlanders, many of whom who had by then spent most of their lives and raised children in Taiwan, and downplayed historical animosity between the two groups.[1] Crucially, *democracy* was presented by Lee as a key component of the new Taiwanese identity, set in opposition to the authoritarianism of the PRC (S. Tsai 2005). Underscoring the distinct "new Taiwanese" identity was the social, cultural, and political gulf between Taiwan and China, which had developed along very different paths, as became immediately evident to anyone who traveled to China from Taiwan (H. Wang 2009; Shih 1995).

In 1991, Lee's government proclaimed an end to the war with the CCP and acknowledged that another regime did indeed rule most of China. This move indicated a profound shift in the ROC's state territorial program. For the first time, rather than claim to rule or promise to retake territory undeniably administered by the PRC, ROC leadership formally committed to pursue political unification under the auspices of the newly established National Unification Council, which was set up to negotiate with China through quasi-official channels (Jacobs and Ben Liu 2007).

Although Lee began his presidency by declaring support for unification, he gradually moved toward a stance of supporting national self-determination for Taiwan, even if it was still administered by the ROC. His more provocative ideas were often floated in international venues. In June 1995, Lee was issued a US visa for a "private visit" to his alma mater, Cornell University, enraging the PRC, which argued that the head of a "separatist" government should not be given permission to enter the United States. During his visit, Lee delivered a speech in which he referred nine times to the "Republic of China on Taiwan," provoking further consternation from PRC leadership. In response, the PRC cut off all talks with ROC agencies, and PRC premier Zhu Rongji made a televised address warning Taiwanese against voting for Lee in the 1996 presidential election. The PRC also conducted missile tests in the Taiwan Strait, prompting the United States to briefly send in naval forces to show support for Taiwan (Romberg 2004). These threats backfired, foreshadowing further such blunders to come, when Lee was comfortably reelected with 54 percent of the vote.

Lee further pushed the envelope in an interview with Radio Deutsche Welle in 1999, when he famously called for "a state-to-state relationship or at least a special state-to-state relationship" (Leifer 2001). This was a profound statement to come from the leader of the KMT, which had long stubbornly claimed to be the true legitimate leader of an undivided China. Lee's "two-state theory" was predictably denounced by the PRC and publicly criticized by US president Bill Clinton's administration, which maintained its support for the "status quo." Lee went on to abolish the Taiwan provincial government, calling it an administra-

tive redundancy, effectively redrawing the boundaries of the national administration to be congruent with its territorial extent. This move was infuriating to
KMT traditionalists, more or less in line with mainstream public opinion, and
not far from the stance of the more moderate wing of the DPP.

Taiwan's party politics turned upside down in 2000 when Lee's successor as
head of the KMT, Lien Chan, lost a three-way presidential race to Chen Shui-
bian, the DPP standard-bearer and former mayor of Taipei. The KMT retained
the legislature, but this marked the first time it did not rule the executive branch.
As part of his election campaign, Chen had agreed to "five nos," including no
declaration of independence, no change to the ROC's official name, and no inclusion of Lee's "special state-to-state relations" terminology in the ROC constitution. Despite this, and his conciliatory inauguration speech, the PRC, wary
of Chen's affiliation with a traditionally pro-independence party, reacted by
freezing communications with the ROC.

The Chen administration instituted a number of "Taiwanization" (*bentuhua*)
cultural initiatives, which included expanding Hoklo, Hakka, and Austronesian
"mother tongue" language education. It also produced new maps that represented
Taiwan as closer to other Pacific nations than to China (Callahan 2009). Seen in
the light of these moves to recenter Taiwan, the 2002 passport changes appear
part of a larger shift, implemented from the top down but more representative
of a long-repressed and now rebounding Taiwanese consciousness.

Despite Chen's "five nos" promise and substantial Taiwanese investment in
the PRC, Chen's administration made assertive gestures to promote Taiwan's autonomy during the challenging 2004 election season. These included a failed
effort to hold a national referendum on formal independence (Bedford and
Hwang 2006). After barely winning reelection, Chen moved to abolish the by
then moribund National Unification Council, but this did not effect further
change to already icy relations (Clark 2008). This period also saw the renaming
of a number of monuments and spaces dedicated to the cult of Chiang Kai-shek
(Taylor 2010).

The KMT regained the presidency with the 2008 election of Ma Ying-jeou,
who had beat Chen in the 2000 mayor's race. Ma, the Hong Kong–born son of a
high-level KMT official, came from an elite mainlander background and had
served as Chiang Ching-kuo's secretary in the 1970s after earning a law degree
at Harvard University.[2] He promised and delivered tighter political and economic
cooperation, including the expansion of tourism, with the PRC, which was much
more amenable to him than to Chen. Ma went on to win a tight reelection race
against the DPP's Tsai Ing-wen in 2012, before the pendulum swung furiously
back in the next cycle, which receives a fuller treatment in chapter 6.

Taiwan's Shifting Territorial Designations

Taiwan's anomalous territoriality can be approached as a question of statehood or alternately as a question of international law. While each is important to consider, answering either question would still not resolve the "Taiwan problem," because satisfaction of conditions for statehood or even an airtight legal case does not necessarily clear a path to universal recognition, especially when there are powerful territorial counterclaimants (Kolstø 2006; Rich 2009). For these and other reasons, scholars have variously classified Taiwan as occupying "an intermediate position between a quasi-state and a recognized state" (Kolstø 2006), as an unrecognized state (Caspersen 2012), as a de facto state (Callahan 2004b; Long and Urdinez 2021), and finally as a contested state (Bouris and Fernández-Molina 2018), which is the term I will generally adopt when discussing the problematic of Taiwan's external recognition.

The question of statehood is often posed against one of the earliest and mostly widely accepted definitions as written in the 1933 Montevideo Convention on the Rights and Duties of States, which includes five criteria: a permanent population, an effective government, the capacity to enter into relations with other states, independence, and a defined territory. Taiwan easily satisfies the first four, having maintained diplomatic relations with a number of countries, however dwindling (fourteen as of the end of 2021). The final criterion was a confusing one between 1945 and 1994, the year when the ROC mostly stopped claiming mainland China as its territory (Bush 2005; Charney and Prescott 2000).

The question of Taiwan's status under international law remains difficult to answer. In 1951, as part of a World War II settlement signed with fifty-one Allied powers in San Francisco, Japan formally renounced the claim to Taiwan established in its 1895 Treaty of Shimonoseki signed with the Qing. The San Francisco treaty, however, did not specify to which entity sovereignty over Taiwan would be transferred, and neither the ROC nor the PRC was a signatory. The following year, Japan and the ROC signed a treaty in which Japan renounced sovereignty over Taiwan, but this treaty also did not explicitly specify to which entity sovereignty was being transferred (Charney and Prescott 2000). Taiwan's status under international law is therefore often characterized as undetermined, even if it has been effectively ruled by the ROC since 1945, because the Qing claimant state that preceded the ROC no longer exists and because the PRC has never administered Taiwan.

Despite such indeterminacy, and despite the consolidation of the PRC in Beijing and the successful expansion of its international diplomatic space, the ROC on Taiwan has maintained official and unofficial bilateral relations with a number of countries. Even many of the countries that have established formal relations with the PRC, which demands derecognition of the ROC as a precondition, maintain de facto embassies within Taiwan and host de facto Taiwan embassies in their own capitals, usually named as trade or cultural representative offices.

Taiwan's most important bilateral relationship has long been with the United States, even after the United States normalized relations with the PRC and formally derecognized the ROC in 1979. With continued support for Taiwan still a concern of Cold War–era domestic US politics, the Taiwan Relations Act was signed into law that year by President Jimmy Carter. The act provided nonbinding assurance for the military defense of Taiwan, including arms sales, which have been a continual target of PRC protest.

Apart from maintaining such key bilateral ties, participation in multilateral bodies has been key to the ROC's external legitimation strategy. The UN is a particularly salient arena, as China, at the time represented by the ROC, had been a founding charter member and is the only non-Euro-American permanent member of the UN's powerful Security Council. This status gave the ROC the authority to veto draft resolutions and made its representation a matter of global importance. With the support of the United States and its anticommunist allies, ROC representatives continued to perform within the UN as if they governed all of China, even after they were displaced to Taipei. They exercised their veto power exactly one time, in 1955, to block the UN's admission of Mongolia, which they claimed as their own territory.

The expulsion of the ROC from the UN in 1971 proved to be a crucial tipping point in the transition from the ROC's fantastical domestic and international claim to represent all of China (and then some) to contemporary Taiwan's condition as a coherent if contested entity. UN General Assembly Resolution 2758 recognized the PRC as the sole representative of China and expelled "the representatives of Chiang Kai-shek from the place which they unlawfully occupy at the United Nations and in all the organizations related to it."[3] The UN's expulsion of the ROC produced a domino effect of derecognition of the ROC in other international bodies, including the World Bank and the International Monetary Fund (Hickey 1997).

Although Resolution 2758 said nothing specifically about Taiwan or its place within China, it has frequently been cited by PRC representatives as evidence of international support for a "one China" policy that includes Taiwan as part of its territory. With the PRC's growing international influence precluding participation by any entity named the "ROC" or "Taiwan," Taipei's pursuit of participation in various bodies involved a variety of creative and often nonconsensual name changes. "Chinese Taipei" first appeared in 1979, after the PRC was admitted to the International Olympic Commission. The ROC delegation, which had previously represented China in the Olympics, was readmitted as the "Chinese Taipei Olympic Committee" and banned from using ROC flags and anthems (J. Yu 2008). The "Chinese Taipei" designation proliferated elsewhere, a confusing situation that still characterizes the contemporary spectacle of Taiwan's participation in international events and bodies, both inside and outside of Taiwan, including the World Health Assembly (WHA).

Other formulations found their way into various economic and trade bodies, including the Asian Development Bank, where the ROC had also been a founding member. When the PRC was admitted to the bank in 1986, the ROC was relisted against its own protestations as "Taipei, China." In 1992, the World Trade Organization admitted both China and Taiwan, listing the latter as the "Separate Customs Territory of Taiwan, Penghu, Kinmen, and Matsu" (Li 2006).

Although Taiwan prospered economically throughout this time, it was increasingly shut out from international bodies or forced to participate under a name not of its leaders' or its people's choosing. Finding this intolerable, Lee's administration declared its intention to rejoin the UN in 1993. Seemingly subscribing to the Montevideo notion of statehood, he acknowledged that the PRC exerted de facto authority over mainland China, while insisting that the ROC was still an "independent sovereign state" (Hickey 1997; Bush 2005).

With full admission to the UN an unlikely prospect, Taiwan attempted to rejoin the international community by specifically targeting the WHA, a UN agency, which oversees the World Health Organization (WHO) as a steppingstone to renewed external recognition and legitimacy (Herington and Lee 2014). This made some degree of practical sense because, unlike the UN, the WHA allows a variety of entities to participate as "observers," should they be invited by the director general of the WHO. In practice, such observers have included the Holy See, Palestine, and the International Committee of the Red Cross (P.-K. Chen 2018).

Between 1997 and 2008, Taiwan unsuccessfully bid to join the WHA under various names, including "Taiwan (Republic of China)," "Taiwan," and "Health Authorities of Taiwan." The drive to join received increased impetus with the 2003 SARS (sudden acute respiratory syndrome) epidemic, a particularly damaging episode for Taiwan, which suffered the world's third-highest number of casualties when the WHO only sent a team of experts fifty days after Taiwan requested help. Although the PRC eventually permitted the WHO to afford Taiwan a limited degree of access to its communication systems, with the 2020 outbreak of COVID-19, Taiwan's inability to fully participate in the WHA would have serious repercussions not only for Taiwan's territoriality but also for global health and the governance of tourism, as I discuss in the epilogue.

Party Politics and National Identity

For tourists, Taiwan's democratic politics proffer an obvious and unavoidable distinction from China. Taiwan's most significant domestic political cleavage is in fact defined by differing stances toward China and Chineseness, which are conveniently color coded for the blue of the KMT flag and the green of the DPP flag. The flag of the KMT depicts a blue sky with a white sun and was originally designed by an ally of Sun Yat-sen for an anti-Qing revolutionary society. This design was later incorporated into the ROC flag, which retains the blue sky and white sun and surrounds it with block red, representing the earth. Even after the KMT lost the presidency in 2000, the overlap of the KMT and the ROC flag remained a source of contention for non-KMT politicians and civil society actors concerned about the residue of the party-state.

The flag of the DPP centers a graphic image of Taiwan's main island inside a green and white cross. The party's "democratic" name evokes its origins as a party that emerged from the *dangwai* democracy movement that opposed one-party KMT rule. Much of the DPP's early leadership and support drew from the Hoklo-speaking majority, especially in the south, who had been politically marginalized by the KMT's administrative privileging of mainland Chinese, as well as by Sinicization campaigns that portrayed Taiwanese as unreconstructed Japanese colonial subjects.

These two major parties have been bolstered or constrained via alliances with smaller parties, such as the New Party, the People's First Party, and the Taiwan Solidarity Union, which waxed and waned through the 1990s and 2000s, forming "pan-blue" and "pan-green" blocs with distinct emphases on national identity and territory.[4] Although the DPP initially contained a plank in its platform that called for de jure independence, it (and the wider pan-green camp) harbors a variety of stances on the mode and time frame of independence. These can roughly be divided into two camps: *huadu* (the *hua* being the short form for *Zhonghua Minguo*, e.g., ROC), who feel that the ROC is already independent and sovereign and therefore there is no need for further declarations or name changes, and *taidu* (the *tai* being the short form for Taiwan), who advocate for de jure independence and the renaming of the ROC as Taiwan. The former approach is often presented as a pragmatic response to PRC external pressure, while the latter is preferred by more assertive Taiwanese nationalists. Both the *huadu* and *taidu* camps are spanned by the so-called *tianrandu* generation of "natural-born independents," who grew up after the end of martial law, have only known a democratic and de facto independent Taiwan, and may not explicitly advocate any particular stance beyond defense from PRC encroachment.

Changes in Taiwan's political culture have been driven not only by domestic dynamics, including social movements and electoral reform, but also by the complicated ways that Taiwanese and ROC actors have participated in China's political and economic transformations. As PRC leaders pursued market reforms under the reform and opening policy in the 1980s, Taiwan offered a proximate source of investment capital, business expertise, and linguistic affinity. Tens of thousands of people moved to the PRC to establish businesses. Known as Taishang (Taiwanese businesspeople), they became major nodes of economic and social contact, and sometimes political pressure across the strait, and also helped drive China's capitalist transformation (Hsing 1998). As business elites took advantage of economic opportunity across the strait, the vigorous anticommunist rhetoric of the Cold War slipped away. For some politicians and businesspeople, it was replaced by the far more profitable performance of pan-Chinese nationalist sentiment and an emphasis on familial ties and cultural affinities that could help lubricate the wheels of industry. In this way, state and capital on both sides briefly converged on a mutually acceptable fashion for framing Taiwan's status vis-à-vis mainland China, which also helped to spur a growing tourism industry. At the same time, as PRC elites began to legitimize their governance in terms of economic growth rather than adherence to Marxist or Maoist principles, Chinese ethnonationalism increasingly filled the ideological breech, often expressed through an aggressive stance toward Taiwan (Zhao 2013).

In some ways, the ethnonational malleability of Taishang is reminiscent of the anthropologist Aihwa Ong's treatment of diasporic Chinese as exemplary practitioners of "flexible citizenship," a condition produced by "the cultural logics of capitalist accumulation, travel, and displacement that induce subjects to respond fluidly and opportunistically to changing political-economic conditions" (1999, 6). Still, despite such fluidity, and the economic opportunity represented by deeper integration with the PRC, Taiwanese national identification and independence sentiment continued to rise steadily.

The most extensive longitudinal polls on Taiwan's "core political attitudes" have been measured by the National Chengchi University Election Study Center since 1992, shortly after the end of martial law and the liberalization of the speech environment. In the first year of polling, 17.6 percent of respondents identified as Taiwanese, versus 25.5 percent as Chinese and 46.4 percent as Taiwanese and Chinese. By 2008, 48.4 percent identified as Taiwanese, versus 4.5 percent as Chinese and 45.1 percent as Taiwanese and Chinese. These trends corresponded with changes in reported sentiment for independence versus unification with the PRC: In 1992, 20 percent supported unification immediately or at a later date, while the remainder supported indefinitely maintaining the status quo or moving toward de jure independence. By 2008, only 10.4 percent supported immediate or eventual unification (National Chengchi University Election Study Center 2019). These shifts accelerated through the following decade, as I discuss in chapter 6, and are even more pronounced when analyzed according to age, with more young people identifying as Taiwanese and supporting independence with every passing generation. If considered only against the financial opportunity represented by China's massive market and inducements, this counterintuitive result makes more sense in light of Taiwan's longer-term cultural trends, further primed by cross-strait political and military tension and the threat to sovereignty represented by economic overreliance on China (S. Lin 2016).

"Chinese Taipei" and Its Discontents

Taiwan's contemporary territoriality, in its color and confusion, contradiction and contestation, is vividly illustrated through its awkward representation in sporting events both at home and abroad. In a widely circulated tweet that pithily summarized Taiwan's ambiguities, the writer Chris Horton (2017) included an image from the 2019 Summer Universiade, an international sporting event held in Taipei, along with the following text: "Why reporting on Taiwan isn't easy, in one photo: Taiwanese audience in Republic of China afro wigs cheer the arrival of team Chinese Taipei."[5] Translated into analytic terms, a people with a consolidated national identity are administered by a dislocated state apparatus that anachronistically shares the territorial referent of the irredentist power that replaced it, symbolically figured by a nationality ("Chinese") to which only a dwindling minority subscribes, and imagined to live in a city (Taipei) not inhabited by a majority of the island's residents. The so-called status quo is a strange kind of status, indeed.

Wherever athletes and fans may fall along the blue-green divide, the "Chinese Taipei" formula has proved to be a sore spot. During the 2012 London Olympics, the ROC flag disappeared without explanation from a prominent international display in the Regent Street commercial district. A few days later, Taiwan's Tourism Bureau instructed Taiwan nationals not to carry ROC flags into the Olympic events. Rather, they were to carry, if anything at all, "Chinese Taipei" flags. A number of Taiwanese across London responded by flying their ROC flags higher, thumbing their noses at *both* the ROC and the PRC, demonstrating the disconnect between the states that claim to represent them and the ambiguous nations they so tensely navigate between (Loa 2012).

Five years later, a similar thing happened at the 2017 Summer Universiade, an international sporting event held *in* Taiwan, which the sponsoring organization referred to as Chinese Taipei. As the biggest sporting competition ever held in Taiwan, with more than ten thousand athletes and delegates, this event was meant as a major tourist draw. Unable to reconcile its rules with the reality on the ground, the English-language guide produced by the Switzerland-based International University Sports Federation (FISU), referred not only to Taiwan's sporting team but also to the island itself as "Chinese Taipei": "Chinese Taipei is a special island and its capital Taipei is a great place to experience Taipei's culture." A subsection, "Introduction of Our Island," said that "Chinese Taipei is long and narrow that lies north to south [sic]" (Horton 2017).

Following a public uproar, FISU explained its choice of terminology in the following way: "As a member of the Olympic Movement, FISU is generally bound by the resolution to refer to Taiwan as Chinese Taipei." But, it conceded, "the term Taiwan Island is clearly more appropriate in cases that refer to geography by itself." Still, six months after the end of the event, FISU's website introduced the host city Taipei as part of "Chinese Taipei," not Taiwan: "Located in the northern part of Chinese Taipei in the heart of the Asia-Pacific region, Taipei is a vibrant and strategically important economic and cultural center." Writing for the *New York Times*, Horton (2017) observed, "Imagine if the United States were to hold a major international event, but one of the conditions was for it to call itself 'British Washington.'"

One final anecdote, from a pop culture event, illustrates how Taiwan's contested territoriality can explode into visibility in surprising, dramatic, and colorful ways. While opening for Madonna on February 4, 2016, at the Taipei Arena, a DJ shouted "I love Taiwan!" and was cheered by the crowd. He followed this up with "I love China!" According to the personal communication of an eyewitness, "The stadium, filled mostly with young people, went nearly silent. No booing. Just a polite, albeit pregnant, silence. . . . Said DJ has since apologized."[6] Madonna wrapped herself in the ROC flag to close the show, repeating a maneuver performed by the star Katy Perry a year earlier in Taipei (both of them received opprobrium for this from Chinese netizens). Days earlier, Madonna's online promotional campaign featured an image of her face on the blue-and-white sun flag of the KMT, which is embedded in the corner of the ROC. The image did not sit well with some Taiwanese fans who saw it as a reminder of the old party-state apparatus. The top Facebook commenter (with thirty-five hundred likes) pointed out that Madonna was (unintentionally) conflating the KMT regime with Taiwan: "OMG this is not Taiwan or Taipei's symbol, this is the symbol of the party KMT that kills so many Taiwanese. please correct this ridiculous mistake. show some respect to this island," according to a February 5, 2016, report in *The Shanghaiist*. In the meantime, Madonna was also attacked online by Chinese netizens for wearing the ROC flag. Even America's pop queen proved unable to navigate the cross-strait territorial vortex.

What these episodes should make clear is that despite its political autonomy, its stable and publicly accountable institutions, and an increasingly consolidated national self-consciousness, Taiwan's performances of territory—and its peoples' identities and mobilities—are contested, constrained, and confused due not only to the external pressures of the PRC but also to the lasting impacts of past decisions by China-centric KMT elites and the actions of international government and nongovernmental organizations. It is in this cauldron that the cross-strait tourism industry developed after 2008, adding new ingredients and further stirring the pot.

2

THE RISE OF CROSS-STRAIT TRAVEL AND TOURISM

"One China, each with its own interpretation." This phrase performatively constituted the so-called 1992 Consensus, which was the rhetorical basis for China-Taiwan political relations, including the regulation and facilitation of tourism, during the 2008–16 presidency of Chinese Nationalist Party (KMT) leader Ma Ying-jeou. A diplomatic fiction, it referred to the apocryphal outcome of a series of meetings between quasi-official People's Republic of China (PRC) and Republic of China (ROC) on Taiwan representatives in 1992. These meetings did not actually result in any jointly written statements, but ROC representatives, all of whom belonged to the KMT, later claimed they had agreed with their counterparts that both sides of the Taiwan Strait belong to one country called "China," with each side allowed a different interpretation of what that China is (Saunders and Kastner 2009). The PRC, for its part, never acknowledged the "each with its own interpretation" clause, even as it was frequently cited by KMT leaders.

If the Ma administration's steadfast invocation of the 1992 Consensus temporarily maintained the actually exceptional "status quo" of Taiwan's de facto independence, it also fueled popular suspicion that forces on both sides of the strait planned to use state and market mechanisms to enact political unification with or annexation by the PRC. The 2008 opening of direct flights and an explosion in tourism, in terms of both capital investment and human traffic, were among the most visible outcomes of cross-strait political cooperation (or conniving, depending on one's point of view). By 2010, Chinese tourists surpassed Japanese to become the top inbound tourist segment in Taiwan, and their numbers continued to rise throughout the Ma administration. Muddling the usual foreign/domestic binaries of the nation-state, this wave of tourism wrought profound effects on Taiwan's cultural politics and political culture.

Tourism's broad instrumentality was on display when it was used as a justification to establish the first reciprocal state offices of any kind. In May 2010, the Beijing-based Cross-Strait Tourism Association set up office in Taipei, and the Taipei-based Taiwan Strait Tourism Association set up office in Beijing. In Taiwan, this was presented as a nonpolitical and purely functional arrangement to facilitate tourism. Said Tourism Bureau director general Janice Seh-jen Lai, "The new offices will focus on promoting cross-Strait tourism, assisting tourists and resolving emergency situations. Issues relating to politics and foreign affairs will not be involved," as noted in a report on February 26, 2010 (*China Times* 2010b). However, Chinese officials had already expressed hope for broader significance from the office openings. Fan Liqing, spokeswoman for China's Taiwan Affairs Office (TAO), stated, "The move is conducive to facilitating future cross-Strait development," as quoted in a report on February 11, 2010 (*China Times* 2010a). The political operation of tourism, it seemed, was wrapped in its nonpolitical appearance.

That tourism was the rationale for the establishment of the first cross-strait quasi-state reciprocal offices underscores its political importance, from which its economic impact cannot be divorced. The interplay between, and relative importance of, the political and the economic is a long-standing concern of cross-strait researchers. For example, Karen M. Sutter has argued for the primacy of economic interests, suggesting that there is a "dynamic of business interests pulling government policy along as policy makers struggle to keep apace with commercial reality" (2002, 522). Following the failure of the more aggressive cross-strait policies of Chinese president Jiang Zemin, many scholars maintained that the primary political tactic of his successor, Hu Jintao, was to use economic leverage to increase Taiwan's dependence on China. Such a tact was exemplified by the slogan *Yi shang cu zheng, yi min cu guan*, meaning "peddle politics through business, to influence government through the people" (S. Kastner 2006, 336) It should not be forgotten that this economic tactic came in tandem with a military buildup targeting Taiwan (Shambaugh 2004), and a 2005 anti-secession law that provided a legal basis for invasion. Given such militarization, skepticism might have been warranted about arguments that economic integration initiatives, including tourism development, would necessarily precipitate peaceful relations.

Tourism as Tool of State Power

Long before the 2008 opening of cross-strait flights and travel offices, tourism had been a political battleground of the PRC and the ROC in their contest for international recognition and support from overseas Chinese. During the Cultural Revolution, when China effectively closed its borders and persecuted citizens with ties to overseas Chinese, the ROC in Taiwan enticed visitors to their rendition of "Free China." During that period, the sympathies and capital of a majority of overseas Chinese communities aligned with the ROC and away from the PRC (Arlt 2006, 33). The ROC used this position to shore up its international diplomatic support and to finance major infrastructure projects.

Soon after China reopened its borders in 1978, overseas Chinese were targeted as sources of capital and international support, which were to be key to the Chinese Communist Party's (CCP) modernization and development campaign under the leadership of Deng Xiaoping. The CCP endeavored not just to profit from foreign currency inflows (a major goal of inbound non-Chinese tourism) but also to strengthen links with overseas Chinese sources of investment capital and to use transnational Chinese cultural affinities to strengthen the regime. This campaign was successful—as inbound tourism and foreign direct investment increased, overseas Chinese visitation and financial support began moving from Taipei to Beijing (Arlt 2006, 30). All China inbound tourist numbers went up following 1978, but overseas Chinese arrivals dwarfed the rest—over the following seven years, annual foreign arrivals grew sixfold to 1.37 million, while annual overseas Chinese arrivals grew tenfold to 16.48 million. By 1985, China had nearly fifteen times more overseas Chinese visitors than foreign visitors. Overseas Chinese (classified as "compatriots") became the major source for foreign direct investment, with 76 percent coming from Hong Kong and Macao between 1978 and 1993 and 9 percent from Taiwan. Simultaneously, China's tourism policy also called for outcompeting the ROC in the game of international recognition and support, "especially by parading the economic success of China vis-à-vis Taiwan" to overseas Chinese visitors (Arlt 2006, 37).

Economic incentives and the cultural draw of China's role as an ancestral home were deployed in the PRC's campaign to expand its influence over Hong Kong, Macao, and Taiwan, and to deepen ties with overseas Chinese. Tourism played a major role. Non-PRC Chinese received special affordances, including permits for visa-free entry, priority acceptance to youth summer camps in China, and help with arranging "family visit" tours to Hong Kong and Macao while those territories were still under British and Portuguese rule. The PRC also encouraged outbound travel to countries with large overseas Chinese populations, including Thailand, Singapore, Malaysia, and the Philippines (Arlt 2006). All of these tourism policies strengthened ties between overseas Chinese and the PRC party-state. Inasmuch as they consolidated China's regional hegemony, they weakened the ROC's international reach, destabilizing Taiwan's political position even as it remained a powerful economic player.

The PRC's targeting of overseas Chinese was prefigured by its tourism industry's two-tiered structure, as well as by official state record-keeping practice. Two of the major state tourism companies, China Travel Service and China International Travel Service, had already been set up to serve different markets, overseas Chinese and foreigners, respectively. Given that these were state enterprises, their formal distinction between overseas Chinese and other tourists extended into state institutional record-keeping practices. Statistics for inbound tourism distinguished between foreigners (*waiguoren*), "compatriots" (*tongbao*, including Taiwanese), and overseas Chinese (*huaqiao*). Likewise, the ROC on Taiwan's statistics distinguished between foreigners and overseas Chinese (*huaqiao*, including mainland Chinese). They did not, however, include a compatriot category.

As Chinese citizens clamored for greater opportunity for outbound travel, China implemented the Approved Destination Status (ADS) scheme in 1995. Facing pressure from an increasingly mobile and wealthy population, the central government instituted this system both to keep outbound tourism under its control and to translate its growing economic clout into political gains. Three agencies with plural portfolios were tasked to conduct international negotiations and administer the program: the Ministry of Foreign Affairs, the Ministry of Public Security, and the China National Tourism Administration. The initial primary function of the ADS system was to prevent Chinese nationals from bringing too much hard currency abroad (Arlt 2006). At that time, Chinese travelers were already permitted to go to Thailand, Singapore, Malaysia, and the Philippines as part of a "visit friends and relatives" program. Those countries soon received ADS designation, followed by South Korea in 1998 and Australia and New Zealand in 1999. Since then, more than one hundred countries have signed ADS agreements with China.

If a country has an ADS designation, outbound group tourists may apply for visas through travel agencies, saving them a trip to the consulate. ADS also facilitates group tour marketing, making it a highly desirable designation for countries eager to boost inbound tourism revenue. ADS regulations stipulate that the receiving country should "have good political relationships with China," making it a useful negotiating lever for the PRC to pursue a variety of aims. Needless to say, only states maintaining official diplomatic relations with the PRC can be eligible for ADS. Those maintaining diplomatic ties with Taiwan must end them and instead recognize the PRC, as Costa Rica did in 2007 shortly before earning ADS. Simply having formal diplomatic relations with China is not a sufficient condition to earn ADS. For example, it took Canada over eighteen ministerial visits to China and a change to more pro-China rhetoric and policy positions before it earned ADS in 2009. This so-called gift was expected to bring over US$100 million in additional annual tourist revenues (Lo 2011).

Complementing international political and economic initiatives like ADS, the PRC exercises domestic cultural authority via the construction and management of tourism sites. Drawing on content analysis of tourism promotional brochures, historical review of Chinese literati travel discourse, and ethnographies of Chinese domestic tourism practices, the anthropologist Pál Nyíri demonstrated that the PRC "sponsors a discursive regime in which scenic spots and their state-endorsed hierarchy are tools of patriotic education and modernization, and in which the state has the ultimate authority to determine the meaning of the landscape" (2006, 75). This regime is enabled by deep institutional and personal overlaps between state regulatory agencies, tour operators, and site developers and management. Such a constellation of common interest allows scenic spots, many of which have an ancient history, to be recast as symbols of party-state authority over the nation. Such practices have been extended far beyond the claimed territorial bounds of China. For example, the Eiffel Tower was turned red during an official state visit of President Hu. Nyíri concludes, "One thing is certain: the Chinese state, as long as it exists in its current form, will attempt to assert its cultural authority over foreign landscapes" (108).

The case of Taiwan, where the foreign/domestic polarity is blurrier than that of, say, France, presents a complex and contentious interplay of state and market forces in the struggle over the operation and representation of tourist sites, particularly those weighted with symbolic significance. The case of the Chiang Kai-shek Cultural Park provides a striking example. Chiang is by no means beloved in China, but he remains an object of great historical interest. Even if he was an enemy of the CCP, he was at least a Chinese nationalist and thus vastly preferable to later Taiwanese leaders, including Lee Teng-hui and Chen Shui-bian, who ultimately championed a distinctively Taiwanese nationalism.

In 2005, in the midst of a national anti-Chiang campaign led by the then ruling Democratic Progressive Party (DPP), the KMT-led Taoyuan county government, anticipating a future influx of Chinese tourists, began planning a Chiang Kai-shek–themed park around a complex of Chiang-related buildings, including his mausoleum. The "generalissimo" was transmogrified from a stern dictator into a cool or even cute figure, his image appearing in a souvenir postcard literally drawn as "Mickey Chiang," complete with a Mickey Mouse hat. The then Taoyuan County magistrate (and 2016 KMT chair and failed presidential candidate) Eric Chu described Chiang as an "essence" of modern Chinese history, thereby placing Taoyuan into a Chinese "historical trajectory" (Woo 2011, 154). This attempted rehabilitation of Chiang for Chinese tourists demonstrates that a Taiwanese government agency attempted to construct a Chinese scenic site *in Taiwan*, without any apparent direct involvement from Chinese state agencies or industry actors.

Opening the Strait

Taiwan prohibited all travel to China during the martial law years from 1949 to 1987, although many Taiwanese traveled to China via a third country or territory (typically Hong Kong or Macao) and did not get their passports stamped. In 1987, Taiwan rescinded the ban and gave special travel permission to certain groups, particularly veterans or others who had been separated from their families in China due to the KMT's retreat to Taiwan. In 1988, 473,000 Taiwanese visited China. As restrictions on leisure and other forms of travel were gradually lifted, the number of annual tourist visits rose to 1.2 million by 1992 and 3.7 million in 2004 (Guo et al. 2006).

Starting in 1988, Taiwan's government permitted travelers from China to enter, but only to visit sick relatives or attend funerals. Gradually, visits for other purposes were permitted, including media projects, attendance at special cultural events, and business. The years from 1988 to 2004 saw a total of roughly 858,900 Chinese visitors to Taiwan, not an inconsiderable amount, but still a fraction of the flow from Taiwan to China (Guo et al. 2006). Without direct air or sea links, all such travel had to pass through Hong Kong, Macao, or another transit point.

In 1990, as military hostilities thawed and the potential for profits from cross-strait investment became increasingly evident, two "civil" agencies were set up in Taiwan and China to facilitate communication and negotiations: the Taipei-based Straits Exchange Foundation (SEF) and the Beijing-based Association for Relations Across the Taiwan Straits (ARATS) (C. Chao 2003). Such an unusual arrangement was necessitated by legal and political restraints shared by both sides. With the ROC constitution still claiming sovereignty over PRC territory and vice versa, neither state would recognize the legitimacy of an official agency of its counterpart. However "civil," these agencies are clearly tied to the state apparatus—the head of SEF is appointed by the ROC president, and the agency itself is funded and directed largely by the ROC's Mainland Affairs Council (MAC), which is under the jurisdiction of the Executive Yuan (executive branch). In the PRC, ARATS is managed by the TAO, which is directed by the State Council.

In 1999, when then ROC president Lee famously suggested that China and Taiwan had "special state-to-state relations," implying some kind of support for Taiwan independence, the PRC protested by suspending all talks between SEF and ARATS. A year later, Chen, of the more Taiwan-centric and historically pro-independence DPP, was elected president, marking the first time that the ROC in Taiwan had not been under KMT rule. China further hardened its stance and refused to negotiate with SEF or official ROC agencies while Chen remained in office.

Despite chilly public proclamations, low-key negotiations nonetheless continued. Charter flights to bring China-based Taiwanese businesspeople home for the Lunar New Year holidays began in 2003, but were canceled the following year amid Taiwanese election-year controversies. In 2006, an agreement was reached between China's General Administration of Civil Aviation and Taiwan's MAC to permit direct charter passenger flights during other major holidays, as well as cargo and humanitarian flights that could be individually approved throughout the year. Critics portrayed the agreement as a ploy by Chen, who was facing impeachment proceedings on corruption charges, to boost his sagging approval ratings (Bradsher 2006). With MAC polls showing 75 percent support for expanded charter flights, it was not an unpopular move. Yet an even higher percentage of respondents, 85 percent, supported maintenance of the de facto independent "status quo" of Taiwanese sovereignty, suggesting that the Taiwanese public wished to enhance cross-strait mobility at the same time they insisted on national autonomy and self-determination (J. Huang 2006).

Cut off from most formal means of cross-strait communication, the Chen administration attempted to reform mobility regulations through other channels. Cognizant of the economic opportunities offered by inbound tourism, the administration began planning to receive Chinese leisure tourists as early as 2001. Responding to the requests of China-based Taiwanese businesspeople for more convenient transportation, the Chen cabinet prepared a report advocating for direct regular flights in 2003, said the then MAC chairman Joseph Wu, according to a December 9, 2005, report (*Asia Times* 2005). Holding up tourism promotion was the sovereignty dispute and a matter of names—specifically China's unwillingness to list Taiwan as a foreign country and the Chen administration's unwillingness to refer to Taiwan as a province. In 2006, MAC vice-chairman David Huang said, "Taiwan is not listed as a travel destination. There is currently no legal basis for Chinese tourists to apply to visit Taiwan. . . . When we negotiate this . . . we will continue to express our stance that the Republic of China is a sovereign, independent country and that the People's Republic of China is a separate political entity" (Rickards 2006). In the meantime, limited sightseeing had in fact been permitted in some form by China, but diplomatic disagreements kept the numbers down.

The Chen administration wanted negotiations with China to proceed via "official government" channels without preconditions, but China's leadership was unwilling to speak with the Chen administration, which it repeatedly criticized as pro-independence. China instead insisted on holding the talks via "private" channels and organizations, so as not to lend legitimacy to the Chen administration or help it "earn any points," in the words of Johnson Tseng, the founding director general of the Travel Agent Association of the ROC and a participant in these talks.[1] One impasse was resolved in 2006 by the PRC's founding of the Cross-Strait Tourism Association and Taiwan's founding of the Taiwan Strait Tourism Association, which echoed the complementary structure of SEF and

ARATS. The names of the organizations had been a major point of contention, with China initially refusing to deal with any organization with the name "Republic of China." Even inclusion of the name "Taiwan" was initially rejected (T.-I. Tsai 2006). Although ostensibly private, the negotiations between these two entities were still dominated by state actors with industry ties.

While the DPP was shut out of negotiations, the KMT, anticipating a return to power, initiated direct contact with the CCP. The KMT-CCP Forum, a series of party-to-party meetings organized in Taiwan by former vice president and honorary KMT chairman Lien Chan's National Progress Foundation, proved at least as influential in formulating policy as domestic deliberations or the SEF-ARATS channels (Beckershoff 2014). Not only politicians but also leaders of industry, including tourism, participated in these meetings, and many of their agreements were passed into law quickly after President Ma's 2008 election. In interviews, Yao Ta-kuang, Tseng's successor at the Travel Agent Association of the ROC, confirmed that the legal substance of these agreements eventually implemented by the KMT differed little from earlier DPP administration–drafted versions but that these party-to-party channels were necessary to "build trust."[2] In July 2008, a few months after Ma's inauguration, Taiwan received its first Chinese tour group to enter on a direct flight. This was touted by the administration as a major breakthrough. Following yet more talks, regularly scheduled, commercial cross-strait flights finally began in August 2009, with departures from Beijing, Shanghai, Fuzhou, and Xiamen arriving at Taipei Songshan, Taoyuan, and Taichung. Chinese tourist numbers were initially kept down by China's rigorous screening process, at least according to the MAC. Prospective tourists were required by Chinese authorities to prove employment, pay a bond of 50,000 yuan (over US$6,000 in 2008), and submit to other paperwork and screening checks. All tourists were required to join group tours. Such rules and regulations were not much different for Taiwan than for many other approved destinations (Arlt 2006). Instead of the maximum of three thousand tourists per day permitted by Taiwan, the early daily average was only several hundred visitors.

Tourist numbers spiked sharply in 2010 and China soon pulled solidly ahead of Japan to become the number one market for Taiwan. Total numbers of Chinese arrivals in 2010 were over 1.6 million, with by then over 1.2 million listing "pleasure" as their primary purpose. Tourist numbers continued their rise in 2011, which saw a total of nearly 1.8 million Chinese arrivals, of whom nearly 1.3 million listed "pleasure" as their primary purpose. The overall numbers and stated purpose of visitor arrivals from "mainland China" are summarized in table 1, starting in 2008, the first year for which such statistics are available.[3]

Following the gradual opening to group tourism, the next major milestone was Taiwan's reception of independent tourists, who were first allowed to arrive

TABLE 2.1. Visitor arrivals by purpose from mainland China, 2008–15

YEAR	TOTAL	BUSINESS	PLEASURE	VISIT RELATIVES	CONFERENCE	STUDY	EXHIBITION	MEDICAL TREATMENT	UNSTATED OR OTHER
2008	329,204	36,621	94,765	57,047	13,358	1,216			126,197
2009	972,123	69,697	539,106	71,341	22,964	3,975			265,040
2010	1,630,735	89,544	1,228,086	104,038	32,843	8,259			167,965
2011	1,784,185	125,481	1,290,933	119,074	22,564	9,060			217,073
2012	2,586,428	49,185	2,019,757	58,052	3,707	3,366	3,392	55,740	393,229
2013	2,874,702	46,560	2,263,635	59,148	2,824	6,644	3,292	95,778	396,821
2014	3,987,152	20,470	3,393,346	63,636	797	11,906	135	55,534	441,328
2015	4,184,102	16,953	3,437,425	69,326	995	19,064	102	60,504	579,733

Source: Taiwan Tourism Bureau website. https://admin.taiwan.net.tw/English/infoEN/TouristStatisticsEN.

from Shanghai in June 2011. An initial total of five hundred per day was permitted from Beijing, Shanghai, and Xiamen. The quota was doubled to one thousand less than a year later, in April 2012, and several more sending cities were soon added.

The arrival of Chinese tourists, both group and independent, met with immediate controversy in Taiwan. Some politicians, including former Chen administration officials, portrayed them as security threats. Meanwhile, surveys and blog posts indicated an incipient public backlash against their behavior, which was often depicted as boorish and unsanitary. A May 2009 government poll recorded that only 24.9 percent of respondents had a "good impression" of Chinese tourists, with 33 percent holding a "bad impression" and the rest neutral or having no opinion (Research Development and Evaluation Commission 2009). Bloggers posted critical reports with photos of Chinese tourists washing their feet in public restrooms, urinating in public, and otherwise behaving in ways deemed inappropriate by commenters.

Vivid reports of poor tourist behavior provided fodder for DPP politicians who accused President Ma and the KMT of pursuing a cross-strait policy that benefited China more than Taiwan (Hsu 2009; Lee and Lin 2009). This criticism occurred despite the fact that much of the tourism policy had been prepared by the DPP itself.

With public opinion polls in Taiwan reflecting uneven support for receiving yet more Chinese tourist arrivals, even the Taiwanese travel industry started having misgivings. In early 2009, when lower numbers arrived than expected, Taiwanese tourist outflow to China rose, contributing to a trade imbalance. Nevertheless, numbers rose to an average of three thousand tourists a day in April 2009, only to plummet again a few months later, reportedly due to Chinese tourist concerns about the H1N1 influenza outbreak in Taiwan, which produced a "sense of shock" in the previously optimistic Taiwanese travel industry, according to a June 24, 2009, report (*United Daily News* 2009). Even after tourist numbers soared in 2010 and 2011, buttressing the Ma administration's claims of economic benefits, many tour operators in Taiwan said that they were losing money. Businesspeople complained publicly and privately about late payments from Chinese industry partners; the total delinquent amount was claimed to be as high as US$169.5 million, which led to late payments for local tour guides and other industry employees. Of the three hundred operators licensed by the Taiwan government to receive Chinese tourists, thirteen Hong Kong–based operators took 50 percent of the revenues. Taiwanese operators said they were forced to cut costs by their partners in China, who paid as low as US$20 a day per tourist, by offering substandard accommodations and service and to gouge customers with mandatory shopping excursions to stores with high commissions and markups. "Chinese tourists are getting up earlier than roosters, eating worse than pigs, and are totally exhausted from spending most of their days on inter-city buses," said an official at the Taiwan International Tour Manager Development Association (Wu 2011).

Such reports cast doubt on the Ma administration's claim that Chinese tourists spent US$2 billion annually on the island, a figure that was based on airport surveys of 1,896 self-reporting tourists, rather than on aggregate data received from hotels, shopping malls, or other industry actors. Indeed, the government's number may have been exaggerated by as much as US$700 million (Wu 2011). The Taiwan Tourism Bureau claimed that Chinese tourists spent US$224 per day, per person. This was likewise based on results from a contracted research team that used a collection of self-reported data from departing tourists at the Taoyuan International, Taipei Songshan, and Kaohsiung International Airports (Lee 2014).[4] These figures were not independently audited or cross-checked against tax or other revenues, and there is no other publicly available data to support Tourism Bureau claims or to compute a more reliable estimate.[5]

Widespread suspicion about inflated claims of tourism revenues, as well as the severe financial distress of many travel agents, was substantiated in my interviews with several travel agency owners as well as by Tseng, the former head of the Travel Agent Association of the ROC. A further problem faced by Taiwanese travel agents and tour operators was the impossibility of debt collection from Chinese agents, who were not legally required to pay in advance for the services of Taiwanese ground handlers. This forced the bankruptcy of several travel agents in Taiwan, particularly those without stronger informal and personal ties to Chinese partners.[6] Several surviving Taiwanese companies continued growing due to diminished competition and widely rumored but unverifiable inflows of investment capital from Chinese and Hong Kong businesses, possibly with state backing. This asymmetry and the tendency toward cartelization were described by many agents as some of the biggest failings of cross-strait tourism policy and ones that they claimed to have tried and failed to warn the Ma administration about.[7] Closeness between the tourism industry and the ruling party was partly determined by ethnocultural and partisan affinity. Interviews with tourism industry insiders confirmed a general alignment between the industry and the KMT and KMT-affiliated political forces. Given that the industry's leadership tended to be dominated by self-identified mainlanders, this alliance was congruent with Taiwan's ethnopolitical fault lines, in which a large number of the descendants of the mainlanders who arrived with the KMT in the 1940s continued to vote for KMT or KMT spin-off parties. Tseng, the past leader of a major tourism industry trade association, identifies as a mainlander and was a member of the People's First Party (PFP), a mainlander-dominated

KMT splinter party, and he claimed that most of his fellow industry leaders were either KMT or PFP supporters. In 2014, he organized and hosted a large, 150-table fund-raiser for failed Taipei KMT mayoral candidate Sean Lien, the son of Lien Chan. Several other industry leaders available for interview, including Tseng's successor, Yao Ta-kuang; Wu Hung-yi and Michael Chao of the Tourist Guide Association of the ROC; and four major agency CEOs also identified as mainlander and as being pro-KMT or PFP.

Likewise, those Ma cabinet officials who had major oversight over tourism, including premiers Jiang Yi-huah and Mao Chi-kuo and former minister of transportation and communication (which oversees the Tourism Bureau) Yeh Kuang-shih (who was preceded in office by Mao Chi-kuo), also came from mainlander backgrounds. This is not a sufficiently large sample to prove that business-political cartels form exclusively along ethnic lines, but it is not insignificant. As put by Chao, a tour guide, "Being mainlanders probably helps us business-wise. . . . We know more about their [mainland Chinese] culture and business practices."[8]

Mobility Devices and Mechanisms

Cross-strait tourism proliferated through complex institutional and interpersonal circuits that ambiguously performed and effectively transformed the practices of border control within Taiwan. In so doing, tourism reconfigured relations between state and industry. A case in point is that during the early years of the Ma administration, the verification of Chinese tourists' personal identification documents, which was legally mandated by Taiwan's National Immigration Agency as a necessary step before travel permits could be granted, was conducted not by the agency itself but by a trade group, the Travel Agent Association of the ROC.[9] In other words, a basic function of state administration was outsourced to an industry actor with complicated ties to both Chinese and Taiwanese state and industry actors.

Those travel documents likewise reflect the representational contortions of cross-strait tourism. To enter Taiwan, Chinese tourists apply not for a passport and visa, which would perform Taiwan as a separate country, but rather for a PRC-issued "Mainland Resident Taiwan Travel Permit" and an ROC-issued "Exit and Entry Permit for the Taiwan Region, Republic of China." Reciprocally, ROC (Taiwan) nationals are not able to use their ROC passport to enter China and must apply for a PRC "Taiwan Compatriot Permit." Such devices "explicitly enfold Taiwan into its [China's] domestic space," as Sara L. Friedman observed in her study of cross-strait marriage migration (2015, 32). In 2015, the PRC intensified this practice by no longer requiring "Taiwan Compatriot Permits" and instead adopting standardized cards that include an eighteen-digit identification number, the same length as those of PRC citizens. This unified the format of Chinese IDs issued to Taiwanese applicants with those issued to Hong Kong and Macao residents, suggesting a territorial isomorphism between the three regions (Chung 2015).

This chapter's history of quasi-official agencies, political party negotiations, and state and business networks has traced the complex institutional and interpersonal relationships that facilitated and were themselves transformed by tourist flows. To situate the remainder of the book, I would like to reiterate several observations:

1. There is a fundamental contradiction between the territorial claims of both China and Taiwan.
2. Taiwan itself harbors multiple, ambiguous, contradictory, and competing state territorialization programs.
3. Despite the above points, outbound tourism from China to Taiwan grew rapidly during Ma's 2008–16 presidency.
4. Tourism remained contentious between Taiwan and China and within Taiwan itself.
5. Tourism was put to work as a platform for the development of other forms of cross-strait interaction.

The following chapters will show, with ethnographic detail, how these fissures and ambiguities stoked social, economic, and ethnonational difference within Taiwan and between Taiwan and China, even or especially as they were conducted under the sign of "One China."

3

TAIWAN AS TOURIST HETEROTOPIA

Taiwan's national iconography presents a field of paradoxes to both residents and visitors. When Chinese tourists arrive, whatever their feelings and education about Taiwan's sovereignty, they are immediately confronted with the official regalia of the "Republic of China" (ROC), the name still used in official documents of Taiwan's state administration, such as its flag, national anthem, public holidays, and other symbols of a state the Chinese government holds to be illegitimate. As they travel the island, they thus encounter emanations not only of the ROC but also of manifest differences in political and cultural expression between Taiwan and China. This produces a sense of exceptional and even multiple and overlapping sovereignties, which is compounded further when Taiwanese independence activists dispute the legitimacy of both China's *and* the ROC's claims to Taiwan.

Yet, even while immersed in the distinctive ROC or Taiwanese symbolism that dots the landscape, many Chinese visitors are able to overlook markers of national-territorial difference and insist in interviews that Taiwan is still obviously a part of China. This effect is possible in part due to direct and conscious performances by industry actors. Incentivized by profits and sometimes by political favors, a sufficient subset of the Taiwanese public and private sector mobilized to produce a sufficiently consistent sense of being in "China" for tourists traveling within the liminal spaces of Taiwan. The production proved especially effective for group tourists, who usually said that they felt as if they were still in their home country—not just because of the official territorial claims, but because state and industry actors in Taiwan shaped, narrated, and translated their experiences in ways that made it seem more familiar than it might be otherwise.

The simultaneous overlap and disjuncture between the Taiwan of its residents and the Taiwan of its Chinese tourists finds an evocative analogy in the novelist China Miéville's work of speculative fiction, "The City and the City" (2009). This book tells a tale of two city-states, Besźel and Ul Qoma, that belong to different nations and juridical realms but in fact interlace throughout the same physical space. This space is divided into "total-alter" (either totally Besź or totally Ul Qoman) or "crosshatch" areas where the cities converge to share roads, train lines, and buildings.[1] On the edges in between the cities, and even on different floors of the same vertical buildings, the citizens of each city have trained themselves to "see" and "sense" what is domestic and "unsee" and "unsense" what is foreign. Protuberances from the other city are studiously ignored; color codes, signifying one or the other city, apply to buildings and cars and clothing. The mistakes of naive children and casual tourists notwithstanding, a "breach" of this division is taboo, heavily policed, and punished as a capital crime, yet car crashes, gas explosions, mentally ill attackers, and other "border-perforating catastrophes" can throw the "careful unseeing" into sudden disarray (66), provoking confusion or worse when citizens of either side are forced to see something unexpected or taboo about the other.

Like the fantastical realms of Besź and Ul Qoma, the Taiwan lived in by its residents and the Taiwan fabricated for Chinese tourists are performed as two different nations that intersect and interlace within the same physical coordinates. The first Taiwan is simply Taiwan as a lived space, socially distinct and politically de facto independent but, largely due to Chinese pressure, diplomatically unrecognized by most of the world. The second Taiwan is an indivisible part of China, an irredentist fantasy land sketched by official People's Republic of China (PRC) rhetoric, perceived by a dwindling number of dyed-in-the-wool ROC partisans, and performed by complicit parts of the Taiwanese tourist industry.

That these two Taiwans are the same Taiwan is a social (sur)reality that its residents are remarkably adept at living with. Breaching notions of national space has long been a fact of life, if not a daily requirement, for Taiwanese who are used to simultaneously asserting and denying both the overlap and the distinction between "China" and "Taiwan" and between the PRC and the ROC. Long before the influx of Chinese tourists, Taiwanese had accustomed themselves, with various degrees of assent, unease, or violence (epistemic or physical), to the ROC's performance of Taiwan as a part of China. While the affective salience of the ROC state apparatus has retreated in the face of a rising Taiwanese nationalism, the social and spatial transformations of tourism have simultaneously re- and de-Sinicized particular travel routes.

Even some Chinese tourists, particularly those who have crossed beyond the prescribed circuits of the group tour, understand the vagaries and ironies of what could be called, following Miéville, "total-alter" (exclusively Taiwanese or Chinese) and "crosshatch" (both Taiwanese and Chinese) spaces. Indeed, some tourist circuits overlap with residential spaces, and others do not. Some sites, such as the National Palace Museum or Kenting, are so crowded as to provoke resentment from locals and dissuade them from visiting. Others, including stores operated by the Chinese Nationalist Party (KMT) and seedy commission-shopping "museums," are out of the way and easy enough for most Taiwanese to ignore.

As Chinese tour directors with experience in Europe and elsewhere can attest, the Chinese language seen and heard in tourist sites produces a sense of cultural familiarity for tourists, as do many other changes made by the tourism industry. Many of these phenomena are not unique to Taiwan and can be found anywhere that Chinese tourists go in sufficient numbers. These changes include the adoption of simplified Chinese script, mainland Chinese accents, and Chinese tourist–oriented souvenir shops, which in some cases have spread to even less frequently touristed parts of Taiwan. In this way, Taiwan fits into a larger pattern of outbound Chinese tourist destinations that have found themselves adjusting their visual and cultural landscapes to meet the desires of the world's largest national market. While Taiwan's contested relationship with China makes the process especially fraught, for Chinese tourists who have been taught the hegemonic territorial interpretation of Taiwan as a part of China, such familiar features simply prove a point that most rarely question.

However, these effects manifest unevenly and often in contradictory ways, propelled by inconsistently applied linguistic and spatial strategies. This complication leads me to borrow from Foucault's concept of "heterotopia," a term for a kind of space that is "in relation with all other sites, but in such a way as to suspect, neutralize, or invert the set of relations that they happen to designate, mirror, or reflect" (1986, 24).

Taiwan itself can be read as a political heterotopia that subverts the Westphalian interstate system (Mengin 2008). As the nominal "Republic of China" with a distinct Taiwanese subjectivity, Taiwan juxtaposes Chinese cultural and political elements in idiosyncratic ways, calling ideas of China and Chineseness into question (Callahan 2004a). It is a sovereign state denied recognition by most other sovereign states, a putative province that rejects its provinciality, a nation whose nationalists take as their goal Taiwan one day becoming a "normal country," as seen in the name of just one of many such advocacy groups, the Taiwan Normal Country Promotion Association. It is thus "capable of juxtaposing in a single real place several places, several sites that are in themselves incompatible" (Foucault 1986, 25).

Foucault's "heterotopia," introduced in lectures and radio addresses that were not published in print until after his death, was very much a preliminary concept.

I use it here in a qualified and limited way to explore how Chinese tours of Taiwan suspect, neutralize, and invert both particular and universal concepts—those of "China" and "Taiwan" and that of the modern, bounded territorial nation-state system. In other words, drawing as much inspiration from Miéville as from Foucault, I use heterotopia less as a descriptor of what Taiwan really *is*, but more as an analytical *method* to highlight together the familiar and the uncanny in the spaces of Taiwan produced for and traversed by the Chinese tourist. This method attends to aesthetic and linguistic juxtapositions, as does Stephanie Malia Hom's (2015) vivid study of the (hyper)reality of Italy as a (post) modern tourist destination and imaginary, which was inspired by the montages of Walter Benjamin's Arcades Project. However, instead of focusing on tourism's rupture of temporality, my ethnographic attention privileges spatiality. Its tighter time span is consonant with work on the "border as method," which aims at "an acute critical analysis not only of how relations of domination, dispossession, and exploitation are being redefined presently but also of the struggles that take shape around these changing relations" (Mezzadra and Neilson 2013, 18). Taiwan's contemporary tourist heterotopias remain politically potent inasmuch as they perform and transform such struggles.

Translating Taiwan as a Chinese Tourist Site

As inbound Chinese tourism exploded in the early 2010s, Taiwanese locals often spoke of a growing sense of similarity between Taiwanese and Chinese tourist spaces, to the point that some even expressed an ironic sense of being within "China," as they lamented the influx of PRC tourists to popular destinations like Sun Moon Lake. "It's pretty but I don't go there anymore. If I wanted to feel like I'm in China, I'd just go to China," said a Taipei colleague during a mealtime chat. His friends nodded in agreement.

Sun Moon Lake, like most of the places depicted in this chapter, has been promoted within China as a must-see destination. Like many of the other sites I present below, it was given a facelift or even reconfigured entirely to appeal to Chinese tourists, with spectacularly mixed results. Attention to the specificities of these sites is crucial, but it is important to note that a tour of Taiwan is more than an accretion of moments. Rather, it is a gestalt composed of the projection of discrete experiences onto a reimagined whole. In other words, Taiwan is experienced not as a sum of individual places but as a complex territorial assemblage. Together, the assemblage often produces perceptual effects of Chineseness for many Chinese tourists and sometimes even for the Taiwanese locals who engage with them.

The perception of Sun Moon Lake and other Taiwanese places as being "in China" not only owed to the large number of proximate PRC tourists but also was produced by the political-economic structure of the tourism industry, the spatio-temporal structure of group tours, and the territorializing language of tours and destinations. Essentially, the collaboration of Taiwanese and Chinese tourism industry actors produced an experience so similar to that of Chinese domestic tourism that Taiwanese interlocutors expressed alienation while Chinese tourists were able to overlook markers of national difference. This effect was primed by the Chinese state's often-repeated territorial claims to Taiwan and their reinforcement through educational institutions and media organs.

Even in the southern city of Tainan, the oldest and perhaps most quintessentially "Taiwanese" of Taiwan's cities, a tourist from Anhui put it to me this way during a short conversation we had near the Confucius Temple: "I feel like this is more or less the same as touring in the 'interior' [neidi]. We get on the bus, get off the bus, take some photos, eat, shop, jump back on the bus, and go back to the hotel. It's all the same. We all know that Taiwan is a part of China, anyway." A Shanghai-based construction worker from Jiangsu—and my roommate for a full eight-day group tour of Taiwan (treated in greater detail in chapter 4)—said much the same to me in the far southern town of Hengchun: "Yes, it still feels like I haven't really left China. And especially here in the south in this poorer, more rural place. It feels even more like the countryside where I'm from. I don't see much of a difference." I heard similar remarks from nearly every other Chinese group tourist I spoke with in Taiwan, both in formal interviews and as passing remarks. It was remarkable that the further we traveled into the largely pro-independence, Taiwanese-identified south, the more he perceived the environment to be "Chinese."

Sometimes such comments were bookended with stock phrases drawn from Chinese nationalist discourse, for example, "same culture/language, same race [tongwen, tongzhong]," an expression first used among proto pan-Asianists in the late nineteenth century to posit commonalities between Chinese and other Asians as opposed to imperialistic Europeans and Americans (Karl 1998). This phrase has a complicated and ironic heritage. It was used in its Japanese form (dobun doshu) in the 1930s to justify Japanese colonialism in China and elsewhere. Several Taiwanese entrepreneurs have told me that while conducting business in China during the 1980s, they also used the phrase to portray their relative cultural advantage when competing for opportunities with non-Chinese investors. Later in the 1990s, Chinese leader Jiang Zemin used a similar formulation to argue that Taiwan is a part of China (Sautman 1997). It therefore comes as little surprise to hear Chinese tourists cite this same script.

The territorializing effects of Chinese tourism are perceived not just by first-time visitors but also by Chinese tour directors who have been to Taiwan many times. In an interview in Taipei at the Sun Yat-sen Memorial Hall, a shrine to the founder of the ROC, Cai, a young tour director from Hubei Province, told me, in between taking photos with her smartphone, that she felt as if she "hadn't really left 'the interior' [of China]." She explained that this is because the people look similar, the language is similar, and after directing several tour groups, she was already familiar with Taiwan.[2] More importantly, the commercially mediated experience of space and time was nearly identical. "I might as well be touring in the mainland. The tour sequence is almost the same . . . except for having to get a permit and pass immigration lines."

As a comparison, I asked her to contrast this with her experiences leading tours in Europe. "Yes, itineraries are also rushed there, and we do lots of shopping, but mostly for international brand name products. Everything there looks and feels so different from China. The language is totally different, the people don't look like us. We don't have a common history, or common race or nation." Again, the "same culture, same race" phrase emerged, showing how effective the territorial socialization engendered by PRC education has been for producing effects of PRC stateness for Chinese visitors in Taiwan.[3]

Familiarity and Friction

Throughout their journeys, Chinese tourists in Taiwan travel in and manifest heterotopic spaces that exhibit a sense of *superimposed* or *ambiguous* state territoriality. Tour guides, engaging in a process that I call *territorial translation*, mediate between these spaces and senses. Positioning themselves somewhere in the middle of the spectrum between guests and hosts, they serve as culture brokers, mediators, or entrepreneurs who bridge distinct ways of perceiving and being in the world (Salazar 2006; Satsuka 2015). In Taiwan, guides navigate between presenting themselves as both Taiwanese and Chinese. Subtly attending to the ways that their words signify regional, cultural, and national difference and identity, they variously conjure guests, hosts, and the spaces they share as Chinese or Taiwanese, or both.

However, the tactical use of territorially coded language—what I am terming here as territorial translation—is not the exclusive domain of the professional guide. On numerous occasions, I also observed retail salespeople using expressions like "the interior" and "we Chinese people [*zanmen Huaren*]," which are almost never heard otherwise in Taiwan, when conversing with Chinese tourists. A salesperson at an Apple electronics reseller at the Taipei 101 mall told me, "Yes, we adjust our speech to make them more comfortable. We're not really trained to do it, but we just learn what makes them comfortable. Look, we even list the renminbi [Chinese currency] price on all the items" (figure 3.1). Another

FIGURE 3.1.   Indigenous-themed clothing priced in Chinese currency, Kenting.

Taiwanese tour guide at Taipei 101 explained that he consciously modifies his speech to avoid language that suggests that Taiwan is politically independent, even when tourists asked about political differences. He did this, he said, in order to keep his workday smooth and enhance guest satisfaction.[4]

Other tourism professionals confirmed that they alter their language largely to reduce the potential for friction. One tour guide, Frank, told me how he and his colleagues often use PRC euphemisms to refer to Taiwanese political institutions. For example, he sometimes refers to the "Presidential Office [Zongtongfu]" as the "Taiwanese Leader's Office [Taiwan Lingdaoren Bangongshi]," which is the expression used in Chinese state media.[5] However, while accompanying Frank and a small group from Shanghai on a two-day tour of Taipei in July 2012, I found that Frank was very inconsistent with his language. Sometimes, Frank would compare Taiwan with "the interior," *neidi*, which is a politically acceptable term in China. Sometimes, however, he would compare Taiwan with "China" (Zhongguo), a common turn of phrase for many Taiwanese, but likely to get one in trouble with a Chinese visitor who believes that Taiwan belongs to China. In the recreational context of the tour and the rapport that Frank had already developed with his guests, this slip was not called out.

It is important to note that all the working Taiwanese tour guides I interviewed, as well as the heads of their trade industry association, confirmed that they *did not* receive any written instructions or explicit training to use "politically correct" language or historical narration specifically on behalf of Chinese tourists. All of these adjustments were informal, inconsistent, and partial. I frequently heard other Taiwanese guides and vendors slipping and using expressions that predate the arrival of Chinese tourists and may potentially be provocative for them. For example, an indigenous-attired salesperson at Sun Moon Lake, discussed in the section on Sun Moon Lake below, referred to her health-enhancing fungal products as "national treasures of Taiwan." Her language, which implied that Taiwan was a nation or country, could have triggered a heated dispute in less regulated circumstances.

To me, as a Western interlocutor, Chinese tourists often referred to Taiwan as "Taiwan region" (*Taiwan diqu*) or "Taiwan Island," as it is often named in Chinese public discourse, to underscore their stance. Indeed, the same woman from Anhui who had said, "We all know that Taiwan is a part of China, anyway" had earlier used the expression "Taiwan region" and later waved her finger while announcing to me in front of her companions, "Anyway, this [Taiwan] is our national territory [*guotu*]!" When I asked for elaboration on her opinion about national sovereignty, she said, "We are just commoners [*laobaixing*] and don't want to talk politics," despite having initiated the issue.

Although the very precariousness of Taiwan's (non)status as a Chinese province may compel some Chinese tourists to insist on its inclusion, the ambiguity of official representations within Taiwan itself further conditioned such expressions. It should come as little surprise to the reader that within China, Taiwan is represented as a province (*sheng*) on every domestic map and represented as such on the Chinese passport. Such representations conveniently converge with anachronistic ROC designations: one highly visible example is the appearance of "Taiwan Province" on vehicle license plates that were issued before 2012. The word "province" continues circulating in the distinction between native "Taiwanese" (*benshengren*, or "people of this province") and the "mainlanders" who arrived with the KMT (*waishengren*, or "people from outside this province"), however decreasingly salient this distinction has become for younger generations who simply identify as Taiwanese, not Chinese.

Difference and Disruption

The experience of cross-Strait territorial consistency was often undermined not only by variance in political terminology and bounds of acceptable public speech but also by other sensory differences. Some of the keywords used by most tourists in describing Taiwanese people and places include "quiet," "civilized" (*wen-ming*), "hygienic" (*weisheng*), and "warm" (*reqing*), especially in contrast to mainland China. While these key words will receive more detailed treatment in chapter 5's account of independent tourism, I here briefly introduce certain sensory qualities of both embodied and virtual spaces that produce senses of difference and unnerve the tourist experience of Taiwan as a part of China.

Taiwan's relatively quiet, relaxed environment can produce a sensual experience distinct from most Chinese cities. People speak at a lower volume. The accent is distinctive, "soft" (*rou*) or even "cute" (*ke'ai*), in the words of many tourists. Drivers do not honk their horns as frequently. People step outside of shared spaces when they want to speak on mobile phones. Visually, there are no hanging red banners or walls stenciled with Chinese Communist slogans. There are no mass campaigns advocating for "harmony" (*hexie*) or "civilized" behavior, apart from occasional reminders for subway riders to give up their seat to the elderly, pregnant, or disabled.

Taiwan's online and mass media spaces also afford openings for ideological disruption. With a plethora of political-themed talk shows, paparazzi-style reporting, and access to uncensored international news networks, Taiwan's cable TV offerings stimulated a sense of possibility and excitement for many Chinese tourists. They themselves often mentioned this in interviews, and many tour guides and Taiwanese hosts of visiting friends or colleagues reported that Chinese tourists found that watching Taiwan's talk and news shows and their satirical takedowns of political figures and celebrities felt at least as enticing as a night on the town. When tourists tired of Taiwanese domestic TV, they could freely tune in to more familiar news from China Central Television or Hong Kong's Phoenix TV. Such access is not reciprocated across the strait, where Taiwanese television news and even Hong Kong radio is blocked.

Taiwan's Internet is uncensored and unfiltered, and even if they do not often make use of such freedoms, tourists can easily search for keywords that are forbidden or blocked in China, including "Falun Gong" and "Dalai Lama." Further disrupting the mediascape in a more tangible way, Taiwan's bookstores contain a plethora of publications banned or unavailable in the mainland. These include books that are critical of the Chinese Communist Party (CCP), offer alternative histories of China, and advocate for Taiwan independence. These bookstores also feature live speakers on topics that may be forbidden at home, including dissident political opinions, radical art, and social movements. One young tourist from Shanghai, who is discussed in depth in chapter 5, had a self-described "transformative experience" while listening to such a talk about the dissident artist Ai Weiwei by a visiting Hong Kong professor held at the landmark 24-hour Eslite bookstore.[6]

Of all the places mentioned in this chapter's tour, the indigenous town of Dulan stands out as the most heterogeneous and indifferent to Chinese tourists. It should therefore come as no surprise that it was often identified by independent tourists as being distinctively Taiwanese. Reasons for this included ethnocultural and political visual cues, such as the indigenous motifs that cover the town's bohemian cafés and arts studios, which often also display campaign paraphernalia from Taiwan's long-running, grassroots No Nukes movement. Apart from the Water Running Up attraction, there are no areas with large tour groups or buses and few other Chinese tourists. People who spent more than a few hours in town usually departed with a more textured sense of Taiwan.

Touring Taiwan's Heterotopia

To illustrate the foregoing arguments, allow me to serve now as a guide of sorts and narrate a series of Taiwan's heterotopic spaces. As with most tours, we will begin at the airport.

Taiwan's Airports as Heterotopia within Heterotopia

Airports present a peculiar nexus of borders and bordering practices. Sites of bordering within bordered nation-states, they both enforce and problematize divisions between domestic and international space (Salter 2007). Inasmuch as airports themselves can exemplify the figure of heterotopia, an airport in a contested state such as Taiwan can be treated as a kind of nested, second-order heterotopia.

Taipei is served by two airports: Songshan Airport, located in Taipei City, and the larger Taoyuan International Airport (previously named for late dictator Chiang Kai-shek), which serves longer-haul flights. Other major points of entry elsewhere on Taiwan Island include the Taichung and Kaohsiung International Airports. In Chinese airports, Taiwan is consistently labeled as a not-quite-international destination, grouped together with the Hong Kong and Macau Special Administrative Regions in separate terminal and display areas: "International and Hong Kong/Macau/Taiwan Flights" (figure 3.2). In contrast, Taiwan's terminal layout and signage simply designates China-bound flights as "International" (figure 3.3).

Inside Taiwan's Immigration and Customs areas, Chinese nationals must line up with other international travelers in the "Non–Republic of China passport holder" queue, while ROC passport holders enter the area for local nationals,

FIGURE 3.2. Shanghai airport terminal display with "Int'l & Hongkong/Macau/Taiwan" signage.

航空公司 Airline	航班 Flight		目的地 TO	櫃台 Check In	表定離站 STD	預計離站 ETD	登機門 Gate	航班狀態 Status
全日空	NH 1188	羽 田	Haneda	3	16:45	16:45	08	已飛 Departed
長 榮	BR 2178	羽 田	Haneda	3	16:45	16:45	08	已飛 Departed
上 航	FM 5098	虹 橋	Hongqiao	4	17:15	17:15	04	已飛 Departed
東 航	MU 5098	虹 橋	Hongqiao	4	17:15	17:15	04	已飛 Departed
華 航	CI 8005	虹 橋	Hongqiao	4	17:15	17:15	04	已飛 Departed
川 航	3U 8978	成 都	Chengdu	5	17:45	17:45	05	登機 Boarding
日 航	JL 5044	羽 田	Haneda	6	18:15	18:15	07	報到 Check In
華 航	CI 222	羽 田	Haneda	6	18:15	18:15	07	報到 Check In
廈 航	MF 884	福 州	Fuzhou	5	19:45	19:45	08	準時 On Time
復 興	GE 9884	福 州	Fuzhou	5	19:45	19:45	08	準時 On Time

國際出境 International Departures

歡迎莅臨 臺北國際航空站 現在時刻 17:40

FIGURE 3.3. Taipei Songshan Airport, international departures board.

which is designated not by "Taiwan" but rather by "Passport holders of the Republic of China." This contrasts with transit practice in Chinese airports, where Taiwanese travelers must enter the same line as PRC travelers and use "Taiwan Compatriot" travel permits or ID cards, which have become essential not only for this border crossing but also for domestic train ticket bookings within China.

The "International and Hong Kong/Macau/Taiwan" signage in China's airports is distinct in both Chinese and English languages from the simpler "International" signage found in Taiwan's airports. This means that at the very point of entry for Chinese tourists in Taiwan, there is already the hint of political difference. Compounding this visual difference is the use of traditional Chinese characters, as opposed to the simplified Chinese used in China, further troubling the "same culture/language, same race" creed, especially given the difficulty many mainland visitors experience while parsing unfamiliar script.

Yet these linguistic and spatial arrangements resemble those of Hong Kong, which also uses traditional characters and where mainland Chinese travelers must also use special travel permits and line up separately for entry. Furthermore, Taiwan's national flag carrier is still named China (Zhonghua) Airlines, while China's similarly named flag carrier is Air China (Zhongguo). Many of Taiwan's largest companies, their brands on parade in airport advertisements, also include Chinese-sounding names, such as China Telecom (Zhonghua Dianxin) and Chunghwa Post (Zhonghua Youzheng), which briefly changed its name to Taiwan Post in 2007 under Chen Shui-bian, before being reverted back under Ma Ying-jeou the following year. This territorial-linguistic legacy of KMT party-state development, in which the management of such state-owned companies was staffed by party loyalists, is not entirely dissimilar to that of the PRC, but the use of Zhonghua versus Zhongguo implies a slightly more ethnocultural than national-territorial flavor.

Right away, then, travelers from China to Taiwan are presented on arrival with an unsettlingly similar yet oddly displaced visual field that simultaneously recapitulates and subverts the usual circuits of mobility and contours of territorial language. For example, after I landed at the Taoyuan airport with a tour group from Shanghai in August 2014, and my group entered the general non-ROC citizen immigration line with several hundred other Chinese tourists, the tour director reminded group members to take good care of their Taiwan entry permits, which he referred to as a "visa" (qianzheng). One of the group noted the image of the flag of the ROC on the top of the permit and asked, "Is that Taiwan's national flag [guoqi]?" His colleague replied, "What national flag?," in a tone that suggested he disapproved of the use of the term "national flag." One of the children in the group asked his mother, "Mom, why do we need this for

Taiwan?" He received no answer. For this group and many others, the airport served as the physical entry point to a long-forbidden island as well as the prelude to a journey that troubled the territorial ideologies with which they interpreted and transformed the island.

Sun Moon Lake, Scenic Spot and National Treasure

Sun Moon Lake, in Nantou County, has long been one of Taiwan's most visited tourist sites. Popular with Taiwanese families and honeymooners, Sun Moon Lake became a near mandatory stop for all Chinese group tours. Reliable statistics on visitor identity remain sparse, but as early as 2011, three years after the opening of group leisure tourism from China, Chinese tourists already vastly outnumbered domestic visitors, according to interviews with area vendors.

Sun Moon Lake is, along with the forested mountain range of Alishan, one of the two tourist sites in Taiwan that all Chinese tourists reported learning about in their high school textbooks. As one Shanghainese tour director told me, "If we don't go to both places, it's like we've never been to Taiwan." These sites combine several tropes that are familiar to Chinese tourists: the "scenic spot," with mountains and water, which has been inscribed with meaning and relevance by state-sponsored literati (Nyíri 2006), and the cultural attractions of indigenous people and customs. Sun Moon Lake's major draws are its alpine lake views and indigenous Thao ethnic culture. Indeed, one visitor from Anhui remarked, "This is just like back home in China proper [neidi]. We also have minorities too, and song and dance shows."

The influx of Chinese tourists dampened the Taiwanese desire to visit Sun Moon Lake. Recall the respondent from Taipei who said, "If I wanted to feel like I'm in China, I'd just go to China." But Sun Moon Lake is not viewed just by Taiwanese as a "Chinese" space—Chinese tourists themselves reported feeling as if they were still in China. Although this effect is not limited to Sun Moon Lake, I explore it first at this particular site before extending the observation to the entire island. I argue that this perception is not owed simply to the large number of Chinese tourists in the area, but is produced by the structure of the tourism industry itself. Essentially, the Taiwanese tourism industry, in concert with sales agents and tour directors based in Hong Kong and China, has produced an experience so similar to that of Chinese domestic tourism that tourists find themselves able to ignore other markers of national-territorial difference. This effect is primed and multiplied by China's territorial claims to Taiwan, and the maps and related imagery that have suffused China's education system, mediascape, and devices of mobility. Chinese tourists did not learn about Sun Moon Lake only from their high school textbooks and TV shows—they also could see it printed in their passports as an image that represents and performatively claims Taiwan as a province of China (figure 3.4).

Sun Moon Lake's leisure travel itinerary is straightforward. Most Chinese tourists arrive in large buses driven from Taipei or Taoyuan. The vast majority of these tourists stay in hotels in Shuishe, a lakefront tourist town, and eat pre-ordered group meals of so-called local specialty dishes like "President Fish," so named for being a favorite of Chiang Kai-shek. Either the same or the following day, they charter a boat from the Shuishe port and circle the lake to look at area temples and Lalu Island, the legendary origin of the Thao tribe, which is now off-limits to outsiders. The boats stop at Itashao, the home of the several hundred remaining Thao people, on the opposite side of the lake from Shuishe. Nearly all of Itashao's Thao live in prefabricated temporary housing, provided by state authorities after a calamitous 1999 earthquake destroyed many structures in town and caused widespread damage throughout central Taiwan.

Itashao is also home to the Formosan Aboriginal Culture Village, an ethnic theme park with replica villages of nine different indigenous groups in Taiwan. The theme park is connected to the boat dock via a cable car. Popular with Taiwanese tourists, it is rarely visited by Chinese group tourists. During a casual conversation outside a restaurant, one tour director from Hangzhou explained, "Mainland Chinese tourists aren't really interested in indigenous Taiwanese. We have our own minorities. Our tourists are more interested in seeing scenery and maybe some Nationalist history." However, according to three area vendors, shopping-focused itineraries and the high entrance price of the park (over US$20, even with a group discount) are likelier explanations for the park's dearth of PRC tourists. Indigenous heritage is certainly for sale throughout Itashao and serves as the theme for large restaurants and souvenir shops that cater almost exclusively to Chinese group tours.

By 2011, the structure of tourism in the area had become so commercially and spatially regimented that I encountered difficulty even entering the shops as an individual visitor. After being rejected at five shops by staff who explained that they host only prearranged tour groups, I found two shops where I was able to browse products while observing as groups entered and exited. The basic group sale sequence proceeded as follows: A large group of tourists entered the store and sat on chairs in front of a counter filled with goods for sale. These products included royal bee jelly, medicinal mushrooms, and other high-value items marketed as health supplements. After the tourists took their seats, a female store employee dressed in indigenous regalia, including feathers, animal skins, and a headdress, emerged to welcome the group with a Mandarin Chinese-language song about local indigenous culture. Several male tourists lit cigarettes in eye-

FIGURE 3.4. Images of Taiwan and Sun Moon Lake inside the PRC passport.

shot of the store's antismoking signs but were not admonished by store staff. After finishing her song, the store hostess offered a few more words about the local Thao people and then explained that the shop's products were "national treasures of Taiwan [*Taiwan guobao*]," a potentially provocative phrase that, intentionally or not, indexed Taiwan as a nation. Staff behind the counters poured copious amounts of tea and aggressively hawked their products to the tourists, most of whom expressed little interest in buying anything.

The above description of ethnicized marketing should be familiar to anyone who has gone on tour in China, especially in indigenous or minority areas. The anthropologist Louisa Schein has memorably written about similar scenes of women in colorful garb on display in Guizhou and uses such vignettes to theorize how the "fascination of more cosmopolitan Chinese with 'exotic' minority cultures in an array of polychromatic and titillating forms" gives rise to a kind of "internal Orientalism" (1997, 70). Such a dynamic may also be at work in Sun Moon Lake. Still, there is something novel and distinctive going on in Taiwan: the rapid domination of commission-based compulsory group shopping as an industrial mode and genre of tourist experience became crucial for ratifying the territorial ideology of "One China" and of producing a spectral sense of Chinese stateness for tourists and, sometimes, other people, too.

Taipei 101, Skyscraper and Geopolitical Stage

Although much of the Taiwanese travel industry has collaborated in a more or less persuasive performance of Taiwan as a part of China, Chinese tourists themselves, as well as Taiwanese passersby, have become unwitting audiences for the performance of different and often clashing geopolitical imperatives. There is no better place to witness such a spectacle than the Taipei 101 mall and skyscraper, which between 2004 and 2010 stood as the world's tallest building.

A mandatory stop on the Taiwan tourist trail, with a ground-level luxury mall and an observation deck on the eighty-ninth floor, Taipei 101 received at least ten thousand visitors a day. At the peak of inbound cross-strait travel in 2014, an estimated 55–60 percent of these visitors came from China.[7] This traffic made the public entrance of Taipei 101 a flashpoint for groups and individuals competing for tourists' attention, including demonstrators from Falun Gong, a religious group banned in China, as well as pro-unification and Taiwan independence activists. While these groups have a long record of demonstrations in Taiwan, it took the emergence of a regular Chinese tourist circuit for all of them to attempt to regularly occupy the same small public square. The resulting space is seen as unusual not only by tourists but by locals as well.

Falun Gong started demonstrating in front of Taipei 101 in 2009, shortly after the arrival of Chinese leisure tour groups. They quickly became a daily presence there and at other popular tourist sites such as the National Palace Museum. Their billboards soon dotted much of the Taiwanese countryside alongside the tour bus–filled highways. As with other international destinations popular with Chinese tourists, including Bali and Thailand, their appearance signaled that a tour bus might arrive at any moment.

In line with the PRC's policy, the Taiwan-based, pro-unification group, the Concentric Patriotism Association of the ROC (Zhonghua Aiguo Tongxinhui; hereafter referred to as the Patriotism Association) has decried Falun Gong as an "evil cult" (*xiejiao*). Unlike Chinese authorities, the Patriotism Association is unable to ban the group outright. Since 2013, in response, the Patriotism Association instead staged something that would be impossible in China—regular counterprotests at volumes so high that they sonically overwhelm the solemn Falun Gong demonstrators, even if the latter are present in larger numbers. Such events earned the Patriotism Association notice from police for disturbing public order, but few actual citations were issued. Members of the group had already been caught on video kicking police, who did not make any arrests until early 2015, when the pro-unification KMT mayor Hau Lung-bin was succeeded by Ko Wen-je, who had criticized the Patriotism Association before taking office (Wu and Chen 2015).

Patriotism Association members, typically dressed in military fatigues, regularly staged their performances in front of the entrance to Taipei 101. Unloading their van directly next to the Falun Gong demonstrators, they unfurled both ROC and PRC flags and loudly projected Chinese Communist anthems through loudspeakers. Chanting through megaphones, they declared, "Without the Communist Party, there'd be no new China!" and hailed, "Unity of the Chinese ethnicities" (*Zhonghua minzu tuanjie*). Banners calling for "Unity of Greater China" (*da Zhonghua tuanjie*) featured the ROC flag on the left, the PRC flag on the right, and a stylized dragon in the middle. At every demonstration a man in a military jumpsuit stood holding the PRC flag and saluting passing Chinese tourists.

In interviews, Taiwanese tourists and passersby expressed mild to extreme disapproval of the Patriotism Association. A twenty-three-year-old design student quipped, "This is so ridiculous. I wish I had a little bomb to toss in there." Another Taiwanese shopper, a thirty-five-year-old lawyer, asked, "Patriots? This is a patriotic group? For which country? Taiwan or China?" No Chinese tourists raised such questions. Instead, many expressed support for the Patriotism Association with both their cameras and their cash. Numerous tour groups took photos with the demonstrators. Some even posed for shots while waving not only the China flag but also the ROC flag next to it, a national symbol strictly taboo in most of China.

This heterotopic space, a political stage and battleground to influence the hearts and minds of the Chinese tourist in Taiwan, was laden with irony. The higher the Chinese flag was flown, the more obvious it was to some tourists that they were somewhere very different from China. As Peihan, a twenty-something secretary from Shenzhen who had just arrived to begin her eight-day Taiwan tour, told me during an impromptu in situ interview, "Wow, speech here is so free. Taiwan is definitely different than the mainland. See this? [*pointing to demonstrators*] We don't have this. Taiwan is a bit intense. It's kind of weird." A few minutes later, Peipei, a twenty-eight-year-old bank clerk from Hunan, provided a qualified endorsement of the demonstration: "We want both sides of the strait to be closer, so we're happy to see this, even if the commotion is unusual for us. At least someone is talking back to these Falun Gong types."[8]

The irony of protesters using tactics that would be illegal in China to assert Chinese sovereignty in Taiwan was clear to building management, which has expressed frustration about the difficulty of balancing citizens' speech rights with the mall's commercial bottom line. A Taipei 101 spokesperson told me in an interview, "All this [protest activity] only demonstrates that Taiwan is so free, unlike where they're coming from."[9]

In May 2014, another group of demonstrators, the Taiwan Independence Revolutionary Army (TIRA), joined the fray in front of Taipei 101. According to its convener, Lai Fang-cheng, the TIRA entered "to defend Falun Gong from intimidation . . . to show how sane and dignified independence activists are as opposed to groups like the Patriotism Association . . . and to let Chinese tourists know that Taiwan is an independent, democratic country."[10] As they had done elsewhere in Taipei, several dozen TIRA members lined up on the sidewalk in front of the bus zone, raising flags with slogans such as "I am Taiwanese, not Chinese," "Taiwan is not the territory of the Republic of China," and "The voice of Taiwan independence and nation building must not disappear without a trace." Many flags were signed with tags like "Taiwan Nationalist Force" and "Militiamen for Taiwan Independence" and were raised while a loudspeaker repeated Taiwanese-language marching songs. A woman wore a shirt with the phrase "Independence will solve everything," a sentiment I return to in the epilogue.

On the first day of the TIRA's outing, the Patriotism Association was nowhere to be seen. But one week later, on Saturday, May 25, all three groups protested for the first time in the same place, at the same time, allowing a remarkable photograph. In this image, we see a TIRA "militiaman" waving his independence flag directly between the Patriotism Association activists' Chinese and ROC flags (figure 3.5). While Taipei 101 may have lost its exceptional status as the world's

FIGURE 3.5.   Taiwan independence and pro-China groups demonstrating at the Taipei 101 building entrance.

tallest building, Taiwan's exceptional territoriality and ambiguous nationalism are on full display here.

   As remarkable as such a photo is, what it cannot convey is the sheer sensory chaos and semiotic overload of the scene. The TIRA's Taiwanese marching music clashed with the Patriotism Association's communist anthems. Confounded tourists were unable to tell who was who. Several asked each other if the TIRA and the ROC flag-bearers were from the same group. Unsurprisingly, while Taiwanese expressed amusement and several foreign tourists took photos with the independence flags, Chinese tourists responded more tepidly to the pro-Taiwan activists. A few took photos, but all attempted to avoid standing too close to them while waiting for their buses. Of the eighteen tourists interviewed over one month of weekend protests, all but one assumed that the TIRA and Falun Gong were the same group, when in fact members of both groups claimed and evidenced no membership overlap. Even Taiwanese passersby, more familiar with street demonstrations and symbolic implications than the Chinese tourists, could be confused by the iconographic oversaturation.

A microcosm of Taiwan's contested territoriality, this tourist site staged a protest dance of superimposed sovereignties, with each side spontaneously separating only to merge back to reoccupy the others' visual and sonic space. This space was not quite Chinese, not quite Taiwanese, neither both nor neither. A menagerie of contradictory national atmospheres, it was nothing if not heterotopic.

The National Palace Museum: "Umbilical Cord" of Chinese Culture

Holding as many imperial treasures as the KMT could carry to Taiwan during its wartime retreat, the National Palace Museum, in a green, suburban part of Taipei City, is widely regarded as the world's greatest museum of Chinese antiquities. Administered directly by the Presidential Office, it has long been crucial to the KMT's depiction of Taiwan as the "standard-bearer" or "bastion" of Chinese culture (Makeham and Hsiau 2005), and it has served as "a kind of cultural umbilical cord linking Taiwan to China's grand tradition" and cementing the KMT's role as its rightful guardian (Hughes 2011, 53). Featuring the "national treasures" of *China*, its display pieces differ significantly in provenance, function, and aesthetics from the so-called national treasures (of Taiwan) sold in the Sun Moon Lake souvenir shops. Like the cross-strait tourism trade, the museum is also itself a platform for broader quasi-official collaborations between China and Taiwan, including the limited exchange of artifacts for exhibition.

For most of the museum's existence, a visit was a subdued and quiet experience geared primarily at scholars and domestic and (non-Chinese) international guests. But its potential appeal for Chinese tourists had been noted long before 2008, and after the floodgates opened, large groups of Chinese tourists radically transformed the museum-going experience. Instead of the notably hushed ambience of years past, the museum soon became at least as notorious for flag-waving tour guides and sprawling lines for star attractions, particularly the famed

FIGURE 3.6. Falun Gong demonstrators outside the National Palace Museum, Taipei.

jade carvings that resemble a head of bok choy cabbage and a slab of fatty meat. Taiwanese commentators complained of overcrowding, and, in response, the museum experimented with piecemeal mitigation measures, including reserving Friday evenings for independent visitors. Museum staff were dispatched to patrol the halls, waving signs that requested visitors to keep their voices down. Still, an atmosphere of chaos, mismanagement, and poor planning was observed even by KMT-aligned scholars, one of whom suggested that the owners of the popular dumpling restaurant Din Tai Fung would do a better job of managing it than its current administrators.[11]

Like Taipei 101, the National Palace Museum also became home to a regular display by Falun Gong demonstrators and meditators. The opportunity both to target Chinese tourists and to superimpose their brand over the museum's cultural authority matched Falun Gong's claims to be the true heirs to "5,000 years of Chinese culture," as opposed to their CCP antagonists (Ownby 2003; Zheng 2011) (figure 3.6). For their part, the Patriotism Association and the TIRA rarely staged counterdemonstrations at the museum.

For Chinese tourists, the National Palace Museum serves much the same function the KMT had lent it: an invaluable repository of Chinese material culture and performance of the political authority it underpins, as well as a reminder of the CCP-KMT split and the Cold War–era military tensions that followed. It is a key site in the performance of Taiwan as a *Chinese* territory and therefore both an essential stop on the tourist trail and a site of ambivalence for Taiwanese nationalists.

Shilin Night Market

For many visitors, the inexpensive delicacies of Taiwan's night markets are at least as enticing as any prized museum pieces. Indeed, many tourist itineraries, whether listed on online booking engines for independent tourists or designed for group tours, highlight food above all else. The Shilin Night Market, in the north of Taipei, remains the island's biggest and most famous. As the most emblematic of food destinations and the greatest recipient of tour groups, the Shilin market found its popularity to be a double-edged sword.

When I first lived in Taiwan, in 2001, Shilin was a place where local friends were eager to take me to taste the best of Taiwanese street food and enjoy the "hot and noisy" (*renao*) atmosphere, seen by many people as an attraction in its own right (S.-D. Yu 2004). After 2008, those same friends scoffed at the market, decrying it as poor value for money and a generally miserable experience. Market traffic patterns and access points changed, with pickup and drop-off points separately designated for large tour buses. Like the southern beach town of Kenting, it turned "entirely for mainland tourists," in the slightly hyperbolic words of a twenty-six-year-old female schoolteacher, a thirty-eight-year-old male tour bus driver, and several other Taiwanese informants.

To be sure, Shilin still attracts Taiwan residents and non-Chinese tourists, but the timing changed. According to Shilin vendors and confirmed by firsthand observation, these other visitors started to arrive later at night, after the Chinese tourists returned to their hotels. As Shilin "fell to the Chinese," other smaller night markets in Taipei gained in the esteem of local foodies, including the Raohe and Liaoning markets. Inevitably, they also became destinations for more adventurous Chinese culinary tourists looking for less obvious destinations. Meanwhile, Shilin took on a minor ironic appeal as a place where Taiwanese could go to watch tourists, like Bangkok's Khao San Road for Thai locals, only with oyster omelets and luridly colored fidget spinners instead of banana pancakes and tie-dyed sarongs.

Dulan, a Cosmopolitan Aboriginal Outlier

On the southeast coast, Dulan is about as far as one can get from Taipei and still stay on the Taiwanese mainland. Founded as an indigenous Amis village, Dulan takes its name from the Chinese transliteration of an Amis word, A'tolan, which means "pile of rocks." Nestled between high mountains and one of the island's most well-regarded surfing spots, it is home to only one free, minor tourist site, Water Running Up, a landscaped hillside built around an optical illusion that gives viewers the sense that its man-made rivulet is flowing upward against the force of gravity. Built along the highway between Kenting and the entrance to Taroko National Park, the site offers a convenient rest stop for tour buses.

Apart from Water Running Up, Dulan is largely unknown and illegible to Chinese tour groups—not much more than a roadside attraction—but it looms increasingly large as an offbeat destination for independent Taiwanese and Chinese tourists. More than anywhere else in Taiwan, it appears to be following a classic pattern seen in Southeast Asia and other international tourist destinations in which it is first "discovered" by foreign backpackers and avant-garde local nationals as an "off the beaten path" site of small guesthouses and homestays before being redeveloped for more mass-market tourism. In the process, real estate prices rise and many local residents complain of being squeezed out, while others delight in dreams of profit.

Dulan's charms include its dramatic mountains and coastline, lively community of Amis woodcarving artists and musicians, and international surf and culinary culture. A hot spot in Taiwan's burgeoning bed-and-breakfast scene, it is also home to several Italian restaurants, indigenous-themed (if not owned and operated) cafés, and live music houses that feature folk or aboriginal music. A typical stroll down the main street of Dulan includes sights of Amis grandmothers rolling and chewing betel nut (a traditional stimulant), a European expatriate slinging a surfboard onto a motorbike, a young Chinese tourist couple taking cell phone photos, and a newly arrived vendor from central Taiwan selling homemade "stinky tofu" to tourists and locals alike.

The construction of the now derelict beachfront Miramar Hotel, likely aimed at the Chinese market, by a company that pioneered all-in package tourism has been a major point of contention. Local activists took the issue to court, contending that the massive project was approved by a corrupt city administration without first conducting the required environmental impact assessments and consultations with indigenous communities. In 2016, after years of legal battles and mass demonstrations that drew participants from across Taiwan, the Administrative Supreme Court barred the hotel from opening. It has since sat silent and empty, an eyesore with an uncertain fate.

While tourism plays an increasingly large role in the day-to-day life and economic base of the town, Dulan, more than anywhere else described in this chapter, presents as a heterogeneous space. It spans, attracts, and mixes multiple generations, ethnicities, languages, and landscapes, affording the Chinese independent tourist the opportunity to interact with a wider variety of Taiwanese people in a less controlled space and time frame than a curated enclave like the National Palace Museum.

Such an encounter took place at a musical performance in April 2015 at Hao De Wo, a café and event venue run by Homi Ma, a second-generation mainlander and small business woman married to Dakanow, an indigenous vocalist well known for protesting against the Miramar Hotel. As I sat in the back of the café, an indigenous Amis singer asked the audience to clap to welcome "our friends from the interior [*neidi*]." Homi then took the microphone to welcome them, but as "Chinese guests visiting our Taiwan" (*Zhongguo de keren lai dao women Taiwan*). During the next break in the set, I engaged the tourists and requested an interview, during which one of them, Mingqi, a twenty-two-year-old female college student from Chengdu, Sichuan, described Taiwan as "an island in the Pacific."[12] This rhetorical move, popular with Taiwanese nationalists and extremely rare among Chinese tourists, decenters China in Taiwan's territorial imaginary. However brief, this episode in an otherwise casual performance space in an "off the beaten path" village shows the profound complexity of the cross-strait situation. Likewise evident, at least for a certain kind of tourist, was the potential of a place like Dulan to rupture hegemonic territorial narratives of Taiwan as a part of China.

Scenic Spots and Tangled Territories

Taiwan's tourist sites simultaneously trumpet, question, critique, and reinterpret their colonial and indigenous histories. Variations in site design and management, as well as the different genres of experience accessible to groups and independent visitors, make Taiwan a kind of territorial Rorschach test for tourists that travel through its heterotopic spaces. Taiwan's own ambiguous national performances, overcoded by the PRC's insistent claims, instantiate a multiplicity of territorial effects. For the most part, Chinese tourists' varied experiences of Taiwan are compatible with a preexisting territorial ideology, papering over heterotopic realities that might otherwise undermine the consistency demanded by the singularity of state sovereignty. This allows the spaces of cross-strait tourism to remain flexible and labile enough to facilitate an uneasy commerce of bodies, souvenirs, and services.

Some sites, such as the National Palace Museum, performed Taiwan's place in the mainstream of Chinese civilization. Others, like Dulan, showcased a distinctive Taiwanese indigeneity for those independent tourists with the time and inclination to seek it out. In some cases, whether or not tourists wanted to encounter something unusual, they found it anyway. For example, when anti-CCP Falun Gong demonstrators, pro-China antagonists, and pro-Taiwan independence activists coalesced around a symbol of Taiwan's modernity such as Taipei 101, Chinese tourists and Taiwanese locals could not escape their roles as both performers and audience in the nascent nation-state theater of contemporary Taiwan.

As chapters 4 and 5 will demonstrate, some independent tourists, especially those who made time to visit less tightly managed spaces, reveled in moments of difference. For group tourists, however, the curation of places and timing of sightseeing, shopping, and eating in a cadence familiar to Chinese domestic tourists sutured together these variegations into a coherent experience of Taiwan as a Chinese destination. Such curation included the sequencing of not only public "scenic spots" but also its more private spaces. Invisible to most people outside the industry, the many hours spent inside the tour buses and at the tourist-only shops and restaurants proved as generative for the territorial imagination of Taiwan as visitation of its landmarks did, as I learned after joining a group tour.

CIRCLING TAIWAN, CHINESE TOUR-GROUP STYLE

"Get on the coach and sleep, get off the coach and pee, go home knowing nothing," sang the guide to me toward the end of our August 2014 group tour. A typical low-to-mid-budget package tour, priced at approximately US$900 and including round-trip airfare from Shanghai to Taiwan, hotel accommodation, most meals, and mandatory shopping trips, I had chosen to join this trip precisely for its banal, unexceptional, mass-market qualities. After eight days of touristic tedium, the guide's deprecating ditty rang true enough. But after getting on and off the bus countless times, I had learned that this trip's medium—and its tedium—was its message. The tour's design and conduct, even or especially at its most banal and repetitive, had a straightforward territorial effect—it was structured just like any group tour in China, but transposed to Taiwan. The genres of experience fabricated by the cross-strait travel industry, as well as the narrative strategies by which guides helped travelers make sense of them, were driven by convergent market logics and nationalist ideologies that consistently produced a sense of being in China for the tourists.

By walking into a brick-and-mortar travel agency office in Shanghai in mid-2014, I had inquired, booked, paid, received pre-trip documentation, and begun my tour in much the same manner as a Chinese national would. The only major difference was that my US passport allowed me to enter Taiwan without a visa, and I therefore had no need to apply, and was in any case ineligible, for the special travel permits used by other members of the group. Several Shanghai travel agencies rejected my initial inquiry, maintaining that they operated tours to Taiwan only for Chinese nationals or their spouses, while refusing to explain the legal or operational rationale for this exclusion. The front desk staff simply told me that my participation was against the rules, which they were unable to proffer in writing. The staff at the large state-owned agency where I was finally able to book my tour mentioned no such rule, and I was unable to confirm whether the other agencies had refused me for legal or other reasons.

Even after I surmounted my passport's foreignness and started the tour, my foreign appearance precluded any possibility of passing as a regular Chinese tourist. "You're the first foreigner I've ever spoken with," said my seatmate and eventual roommate, Sun, as we buckled our seatbelts on the departure flight from Shanghai Pudong to Taiwan Taoyuan Airport. This was true not only for Sun but also for everyone in my group, who stated that, as an American, I no doubt held particular opinions and biases about China, Taiwan, and global geopolitics, as well as distinct dietary and lifestyle preferences. While they all said that my presence made the tour a more interesting and unusual experience, it could not help but also slightly affect its conduct. Even the guide, after noticing my gaze, occasionally commented on or tempered his more bracing digressions, including expressions of extreme anti-Japanese sentiment. He also had to take the time at nearly every shop we visited to quickly mention that I spoke Chinese and that the staff "should treat the foreigner as if he were Chinese." This raised a few questions and comical responses because, augmenting my non-phenotypically Chinese appearance, my spoken Mandarin sounds somewhat Taiwanese.

Making myself invisible was of course impossible, and I did have to answer a battery of typical questions in which I was assumed to represent and speak for all of "America." Still, attempting not to draw additional attention to my "foreignness," I asked few questions throughout the tour. Instead, I aimed to observe guide, tourist, and local interactions at distances that spanned the liminal spaces between insider/outsider and Chinese/Taiwanese/foreigner, while taking notes on my mobile phone or tablet in unobtrusive, unobvious ways. Especially given the high frequency of phone use and photo-taking among tourists, my note-taking was largely ignored by my fellow travelers.

Like any ethnographic recounting, this tale is certainly a partial account. The bulk of communication occurred in Mandarin, a language in which I am comfortable. However, not all conversation was legible. Like the tour guide and driver, I do not speak Subei dialect, the primary language of one segment of our group, and was unable to understand or participate in their private conversations. I understand more Hoklo Taiwanese than the tourists did, but I was still only able to guess at much of the content of the conversations between the guide, the driver, and some other Taiwanese interlocutors.

Joining this tour as a fellow participant afforded insight into the territorial socialization of guests and hosts. Having worked as a tour guide in China in

2006, I was also attentive to the complex negotiations, routings, and improvisations of industry practice, including the complicated business and personal relationships between guides, drivers, agencies, and vendors, and the commissions, sideline sales schemes, and other gray market practices that bind them together. Still, as a paying customer on this tour, I could only ask a limited number of questions in an attempt to sketch the contours of these murky and submerged business circuits without provoking suspicion or resentment from my interlocutors. Even then, the transposition of these forms into Taiwan allowed for extraordinary and unexpected discoveries.

Itinerary

I hardly discuss the printed tour itinerary in the following ethnography, because it was hardly noticed by our group. We did not receive a second copy on arrival in Taiwan. Although I carried the printed tour itinerary that the agency provided for my review prior to the trip and reprinted on receipt of payment, at no point during the trip did I observe any other tourists reviewing their own copies. Not checking the itinerary's terse lists of sites and meals and terms and conditions against what was actually provided on the tour, this group's members were largely content to follow directions from the guide without reference to our contract with his company. This approach corresponded with the general emphasis on the "convenience" of the group tour. As my roommate, Sun, observed, "I'd still rather go with a group. There's no need to think about where to stay or eat. It's easier."

Yet despite our itinerary's apparent unimportance, it had already served many functions—it was an advertisement, designed to sell a tour. It was an informational document, designed to provide background on a destination to a prospective or current tourist. It was a quasi-legal contract, designed to clarify the rights, responsibilities, and obligations of the tourist and the travel agency. Most importantly, it was the key to the guide's tool kit, designed to structure and shape daily operations and tourist experience. The itinerary was also the script that allowed the guide to perform a destination within certain spatial and temporal constraints, yet was flexible enough to allow for improvisation and variation depending on environmental and other unpredictable conditions. It was, in the words of the sociologist Ning Wang, a "temporal-spatial carrier of tourist experience" (2006, 66) and a product of and for negotiation between a variety of actors—a travel agency, a local tour operator or ground handler, and the immigration, tourism, and other relevant agencies of a sending and receiving region.

The format of our particular printed itinerary, stamped with the imprimatur of a major Shanghai travel agency, differed little from those of domestic Chinese destinations, apart from its carefully worded mention of Taiwan's different travel permit regulations and its explicit warning against participating in political activities or appearing on local TV news. Besides this, it also differed little from domestic itineraries used within Taiwan, except for its use of simplified characters and its use of territorial designations considered politically correct in China. In particular, it did not refer to Taiwan as the Republic of China (ROC).

Our itinerary divided the trip into eight days and specified the names of the sites to be seen in a mostly fulfilled temporal sequence connected via hyphens. In accordance with China's first-ever comprehensive tourism law, passed in 2013, it explicitly labeled six shopping trips, the permitted limit, without providing the actual names of the stores. The less obvious shopping stops, such as a tea shop in Alishan and the so-called Teresa Teng Memorial Museum, were labeled as "lunch" and "museum" sites. Importantly, the itinerary did not specify the names of hotels and only loosely specified their locations (counties, towns, or regions), allowing the ground handler maximum flexibility in choice of hotels.

More than in its ability to name sites and territories, a performative capacity little noticed by this group, our itinerary—both the printed document and the spatiotemporal form it simultaneously reflected and constructed—accrued its power from its formatting of Taiwan into a space of discrete, consumable sites and shops, connected to one another via a transportation infrastructure of rest stops, highways, and our own private coach. The printed itinerary, as both a product and a determinant of our destination, flattened Taiwan's sensuous spaces into a physical document and translated Taiwan's polysemic multiplicity into a tightly bounded series of "scenic spots" connected via a spatial topology and temporal sequence all too familiar to Chinese tourists.

Augmented by the tour guide's narration and the tour operator's choice of sites, the agency's itinerary outlined a script with which Taiwan could be performed as a touristed, if divided, part of China. But as much as the structure of the itinerary determined the operation of the tour, its gaps and vagaries allowed guide and ground handler to select and omit sites to suit this particular eight-day performance. It also enabled the ground handler to direct tourists' economic power into very partial circuits of Taiwan's political economy in which the Chinese Nationalist Party (KMT) and affiliated private business groups combined profit and political motives, enriching each other while collaborating in the Chinese national-territorial project.

The Group

This tour group, marketed and sold by a major Chinese state-owned travel agency and operated by a Taiwanese company incorporated in Kaohsiung, was composed of two contingents: a family of four from a Shanghai suburb and a group of five construction workers originally from northern Jiangsu Province. The family of four consisted of a thirty-two-year-old woman, Yiqing, with a nine-year-old daughter and a six-year-old son, and her mother-in-law, who preferred to speak in Shanghainese and interacted little with anyone outside her family.[1] The construction workers spoke in Subei language with one another and Mandarin with everyone else. They worked for a Taiwanese-owned company in Shanghai, and Sun explained that their boss was sending them on this trip as an incentive for good job performance and also to give them some more local context about their company's background. Apart from basic vocational and technical training, no one in the group had a postsecondary school education.

The tour director was Shanghainese and forty years old and said he had been to Taiwan about fifty times. An English speaker, he also frequently led tours to Europe and North America. The local tour guide, Jerry, was a fifty-year-old ex-military officer who hailed from Tainan. He usually spoke Hoklo Taiwanese with the driver and older locals and Mandarin with me and the other guests. He had worked as a tour guide for three years, exclusively for Chinese guests. The driver came from Keelung, an industrial port town on the northern tip of Taiwan, and had driven commercial trucks prior to joining the rapidly expanding China-oriented tourism industry in 2009.

Travelogue
Day One

Our tour began inauspiciously at the Shanghai Pudong airport when the tour director showed up over half an hour late. As he strode into the meeting place, he said that he had been delayed by a traffic accident. After ensuring that all our documents were in order, he showed little interest in socializing with the guests. Instead, he sat, read, and talked on his mobile phone as we waited to board. During the lull before the flight, I asked Yiqing what she most looked forward to. "The food, the night markets, and the bok choy jade piece at the National Palace Museum. But I guess I'm really just out to take the kids somewhere."

On the plane, I sat next to Sun, who was taking his first trip outside of mainland China. Sun and I ended up being roommates for the next seven nights. He told me that I was the first foreigner he had ever been in such close proximity with as we buckled our seat belts and began to small talk about life in the United States and China. He then explained to me, "I think Taiwan is more democratic and civilized. . . . I work for a Taiwanese-owned company. This is sort of a reward for us, from our manager, who wanted us to see Taiwan. At first he'd wanted us to just come here independently, but that wasn't allowed because of where we're from [Subei], so we had to join a group."

After we landed and entered the general immigration line with several hundred other Chinese tourists, the tour director reminded the group to take good care of the Taiwan entry permit, which he referred to as a "visa." Mingwei, one of Sun's colleagues, noted the image of the flag of the ROC at the top of the permit. It was then that, as recounted in chapter 3, someone asked, "Is that Taiwan's national flag?" Chao, another of the construction workers, muttered, "What national flag?" in a dismissive tone. Yiqing's son asked her why the permit was needed for Taiwan, but received no answer.

We cleared customs and were met by our guide, Jerry. He led us to the coach and distributed maps of Taiwan produced by the Tourism Bureau and labeled in simplified Chinese. "Take it. You can keep these as your first souvenir!" Jerry said. Sun observed, "Wow, these maps were made especially for us." Jerry took the bus's built-in microphone and formally began his performance with a personal delivery: "How should I address you? Some are from Shanghai, some from Jiangsu?" He glanced briefly at me with raised eyebrows and then continued, "I guess I'll call you our Southern Jiangsu VIPs! Welcome to Taiwan, the treasured island [*baodao*]!" He bowed and said "thank you" in Taiwanese-accented Shanghainese. I politely clapped along with the other Southern Jiangsu VIPs.

Jerry revealed his strategy for handling the question of Taiwan's sovereignty when he introduced the first site we would visit the next day, the Chung Tai Chan Monastery, a massive Buddhist complex that also receives Chinese tourists for paid meditation and spiritual-themed retreats. "Our former premier, Wen Jiabao, had said he wanted to go to Chung Tai and Alishan. But Taiwan and the mainland haven't unified yet, so how could he come here? Well, he couldn't, so you come earlier for him instead." Such a statement quickly established two things: for one, he declared support for the political unification of Taiwan and mainland China; for another, despite being a retired ROC soldier, he had no compunction about depicting former People's Republic of China (PRC) premier Wen as "our" premier, at least when speaking with Chinese tourists.

As we settled into the drive to the hotel, he played an orientation video produced by the Taiwan Tourism Bureau expressly for Chinese tourists. It featured a lively young woman with a prominent Taiwanese accent instructing a man in a blue bear suit on how to behave in Taiwan, punctuated with iconic images of the National Palace Museum and Sun Moon Lake. These were the key takeaways: *Don't litter, don't spit, don't talk loudly, don't smoke indoors. Your tour guide shouldn't force you to shop. Pay attention to food product ingredients and price labels. Taiwan uses New Taiwan dollars, not renminbi. Chinese Union Pay credit cards are increasingly accepted. Buy certified goods.* The blue bear, it turned out, was a quick learner and went on to correct other tourists who were doing unacceptable things. This bear-man had a precedent: A similar sort of cosplaying panda appeared in a tourist educational video produced by China Central Television in 2014, which proved controversial within China for its overt discussion of tourist misbehavior ("besmirches the Chinese public," said a blogger) and even for "smearing pandas" by associating them with "low-class tourists" (Wong 2014).

The video ended as we approached our suburban mid-range hotel. Jerry took the remaining time to finish his general orientation: "Taiwan is a free democratic society, so people may express different opinions. You may see some protesters here and there. But me, I like the warmth of the people here and the food and the sites. As for the food, old Chiang [Kai-shek] brought two million mainlanders and lots of food styles with them, but they've since been adjusted to Taiwanese tastes. If the food is not to your liking, let me know. I'll talk a lot later about differences between the mainland and Taiwan. I've been there twice, to Shanghai and Guangdong."

On arriving at the hotel, the tour director and guide handed out room keys and reminded us not to smoke inside the building. As I had not paid extra to have a private room, a quick collective decision had to be made about which of the five construction workers would share a twin room with me. Having already built up a rapport while sitting next to me on the plane, Sun was the obvious choice to be my roommate for the duration of the trip.

Day Two

Sun's colleagues, Xiaoming and Mingwei, entered our room after the 7:00 a.m. wake-up call. They turned on the TV and channel flipped to a Taiwanese political talk show. Chiu Yi, a legislator from the pro-KMT "pan-blue" camp, was discussing the arrest of Chinese Politburo member Zhou Yongkang, who was the highest-profile target yet of Xi Jinping's anticorruption drive. Zhou's arrest had been reported in China, but the tourists expressed surprise and amazement at the personal details being discussed on Taiwanese TV, including his alleged three mistresses.

After our buffet breakfast, we boarded the coach to depart to Chung Tai, Wen's dream destination. Our guide continued his cultural/political introduction to Taiwan: "Taiwan is a democratic place, so we'll see different groups, like Falun Gong. Falun Gong practices are okay, but their leader, Li Hongzhi, told people that the Communist Party is evil. This is not so good. Don't take their stuff, because if you do, you'll have trouble when you return. Even their pens have their name and information printed on them. Be careful. They'll use newspapers, whatever, anything, to tell you to leave the Communist Party. Pay no attention."

He continued his discussion of Taiwan's differences with China by making his first pejorative reference to Japan, an apparition that would become central to his narrative of Taiwan: "Look out the window. We'll see more Japanese cars here. It's not because we like Japan, but because their cars have higher fuel efficiency."

Jerry then used the trope of separation from China to opine on unification with it: "There's been sixty-something years of separation between Taiwan and the mainland. I'll play you some videos that talk about Chiang Kai-shek and other things. These are of course from a Taiwanese perspective. As a kid, I learned that our mainland compatriots were poor and needed rescuing. We learned that we need to unite to be strong. We don't want to be like or ally with the Philippines or Japan or those places." The tourists nodded.

Jerry continued, "Now, 70 percent of people want to keep the status quo, not because they don't want to unite, but because they're worried about being controlled too strictly. But naturally, things will improve. We are ethnic brothers [*xiongdi minzu*]. Of course there are some people who disagree, and there are protests, like the Sunflower Movement against the services trade pact. Well, the first person to protest that was a National Taiwan University professor who is also a Falun Gong adherent. You know, Taiwan is just too democratic."

One of the construction workers, Chunkai, asked the guide about former president Lee Teng-hui's support for Japan's claims to the disputed Senkaku (Diaoyu) Islands, which are also claimed by the ROC and the PRC. Jerry replied, "People say he's Japanese inside. His grandfather was a policeman under the colonial regime. It's better not to say too much, but . . . Taiwan is too democratic."

Chunkai asked again, "Why does Lee care so much? He's so old and yet he's still on TV. I can't make any sense of it." The guide replied with enough feedback to indicate he had at least heard the question and then skillfully transitioned the topic of conversation to something more palatable: "He's got Japanese influence, yes, but he has an agricultural economics PhD. He still made a contribution to our country and its agriculture. You know, Taiwanese fruit is good. You should buy some while you're here, but not too much that it goes bad."

Jerry then introduced a video about Chiang Kai-shek, reminding us that it was made according to a "Taiwanese" perspective, so it might differ from the official narrative in mainland China. The documentary focused on Chiang's family background in China, the anti-Japanese war, and 1950s land reform and later industrialization in Taiwan. It mostly elided state violence under Chiang's rule, including the 228 Incident, the White Terror, and other well-documented episodes from the martial law era that continue to haunt Taiwan's collective memory and condition its contemporary politics.

After the video ended, we arrived for lunch in a cavernous, mostly empty Taiwan-themed restaurant in a nondescript roadside location on the way to Chung

Tai. The guide seated us at our tables before eating separately with the driver. At the table, the Southern Jiangsu VIPs wondered aloud how we should address the restaurant staff. Said one, "Should we call them servers [*fuwuyuan*] or 'miss' [*xiaojie*]?," the latter being a neutral and common form of address for women in Taiwan, but a term sometimes used in China to refer to sex workers. Consensus was not achieved.

We arrived at Chung Tai shortly after finishing lunch. With only one hour allotted to visit the temples, halls, and grounds, the guide focused particularly on one installation in the main plaza, the Tongyuan Bridge, made of bronze and designed to represent the unity of China and Taiwan. In Mandarin, *tong* is homophonous with the words for "sameness," "unity," and "bronze," while *yuan* means "origin." The guide explained, "Taiwan, mainland China: same race, same origin [*tongzhong, tongyuan*]." The plaque on the bridge, dedicated jointly in 2006 by Chung Tai and Lingyin Temple in Hangzhou, confirmed his interpretation: "The two temples have the same origin. The same dharma, the same origin and culture, both sides of the strait are integrated and can't be independent . . . true peace and blessings for people on both sides of the strait [Liang si tong yuan, tong fa tong yuan liang'an wenhua hurong bu du . . . chengwei liang an renmin heping qifu]."

Jerry then pointed to a nearby sculpture and said, "This marble is from Shanxi." Chunkai asked, "Oh, it's imported?" The guide replied, "Imported? No . . . this . . . well, it's all one China! Well, I guess you can still say it's imported for now because it has to go through customs." Jerry then made another comparison between Taiwan and China: "Our Buddhism is more legitimate. In the mainland, you have monks who wear Western clothes and drive BMWs to temple, before changing into robes for the day and taking them off to have a drink. Ours are for real. And they're vegetarian too."

After taking our forty minutes of free time to walk the manicured grounds and shop for temple goods, we boarded the coach and departed for the iconic Sun Moon Lake. Both the guide and the video he played, which was produced by the local tourism administration, recited quotations about the lake written by a Qing dynasty poet in 1821. The video also noted the presence of Taiwan's smallest registered indigenous tribe, the Thao people, who view Sun Moon Lake as a sacred place.

After arriving at the lake and passing through dense crowds to board our boat, Xiaoming said to Jerry, "This is like mainland China. I don't really feel like I've left." The guide replied, "Well, this is a tourist destination. If you go to more out-of-the-way places, you'll observe some differences." Mingwei continued the conversation: "Everything here is condensed. It's not as big or expansive as the mainland." I asked Mingwei what he had heard about Taiwan or Sun Moon Lake. He answered, "We read about this and Alishan growing up. Perhaps the political perspectives are different, but the place descriptions were pretty neutral."

After our boat docked at a nearby site, the guide gestured to several costumed performers on a stage nearby. "You can listen to High Mountain ethnic [*gaoshanzu*] music and buy their CDs [*guangpan*]." His use of the term *gaoshanzu*, an official PRC ethnic designation, otherwise unheard in Taiwan, collapses Taiwan's many indigenous groups into one "High Mountain" ethnicity (as Taiwan's now taboo term *shandiren* used to) and will be discussed in some detail in a section below. His use of *guangpan* for CD, common in China, instead of *guangdie*, used in Taiwan, was another skillful adjustment, even if this choice of diction was less ethnonationally charged than *gaoshanzu*.

As we walked to the "restaurant," which turned out to be an unmarked room in a basement by a parking lot, Jerry gestured toward some sugarcane drink vendors. "That's white sugarcane. It was used to produce sugar when the Japanese occupied Taiwan. They took our resources and treated us like a colony." The parking lot's bathroom had signs in simplified Chinese reminding guests not to litter in urinals. As we ate a soggy and mediocre meal, the guests remarked that neither the food nor the lake was as grand as they had expected.

On the way to our hotel in Changhua County, the guide explained the differences between Taiwanese usage of the words *fandian* and *jiudian*. In Taiwan, *fandian*, literally "rice shop," refers to hotels, while *jiudian*, commonly used for "hotel" in China, refers to hostess clubs. His descriptions of *jiudian* were graphic, pitched more in the presumed register of the construction worker guests and delivered without any apparent regard for the women and children on the coach. Belaboring the bawdiness, he gestured out the window to the neon-lit roadside stalls where lightly dressed and heavily made-up young women sold the botanical stimulant betel nut, which he described as a quintessentially Taiwanese health remedy. As we pulled over to a stall so he could demonstrate the purchasing process, he told the guests that they could take sneak photos of the women. He completed his purchase and then played a karaoke disc titled *Good Sounds of China*.

After we checked into the hotel, I asked the front desk staff about their business model. They explained that the hotel was owned by a Taiwanese designer with extensive business interests in China and that it received up to 90 percent of its bookings from Chinese tourists. Thus it came as no surprise to find that the interior signs were printed primarily in simplified Chinese.

Day Three

After the collective anticlimax of Sun Moon Lake, this was our day to visit the second-most well-known site in Taiwan, Alishan. We were woken up at 7:00 a.m.

to eat a quick breakfast and rode the coach up a winding mountain road, only to arrive at our lunch site at a suspiciously early 11:00 a.m. This entirely too-convenient arrangement gave us time to "learn" about highly priced "local" tea from costumed Tsou aboriginal people at a "cultural center" adjacent to the dining room. In response to my private query, the guide explained that this maneuver was technically legal because the site was attached to our dining establishment and therefore did not count toward the legal cap of six shopping stops per trip.

Beyond the subterfuge, this tea shop featured other exceptional attractions, including a live bear and the personal endorsement of President Ma Ying-jeou. The shop's owner claimed that the unfortunate animal, kept in a tiny cage in the parking lot, was a Formosan black bear, an iconic and endangered species that is illegal to keep in captivity without a special permit (I verified after the tour that it was in fact a Malaysian sun bear and therefore not subject to such strict regulation). The shop's custom-made tea boxes not only were high-priced, but they also featured the picture and signature of president and KMT chairman Ma, whose image loomed over the shop's interior in a photo of him shaking the hand of the owner of the company, who happened to be a KMT official.

Otherwise, this ethnic-themed tea experience could have taken place almost anywhere in China. Most of the group bought tea, bargaining the standard small box down from the list price of 2,800 New Taiwan dollars (NTD) (US$94) to 250 renminbi (RMB) (US$40). While the Tsou saleswomen focused on the Chinese tourists, the boss of the restaurant attempted to sell me on not only the tea but also the sex appeal of his staff: "I'll throw in an Alishan girl if you buy some tea." The rest of his sales pitch pushed the limits of taste and will not be recounted here, but it further clarified that gender is an important determinant and product of tourist experience and industry practice.

After lunch, we toured the forests and antique train tracks of Alishan, which were filled with other Chinese groups. Our guide narrated the colonial history of Japanese logging trains and other extractive and infrastructural projects while repeatedly slurring Japanese people as "little Japanese devils [xiao Riben guizi]." At one point, he caught my eye and asked me if I found such language acceptable. I feigned indifference.

After an hour of walking along a crowded path, we reboarded our coach and headed toward the major southern city of Kaohsiung. Our guide explained that we would be visiting the Teresa Teng Memorial Museum the following day and played us a video of the late, popular singer. "The mainland has old Deng [Xiaoping], Taiwan has young Teng," he said, reciting a cliché that relates two personalities with the same Chinese surname who achieved fame in both China and Taiwan.

This night offered our first opportunity to stroll through one of Taiwan's night markets, which, my companions declared, are as well known in China as Alishan or Sun Moon Lake. As the guide introduced the famous local foods of Liuhe Night Market, the driver yelled from the front to tell us that most of the goods for sale are made in mainland China. The guide confirmed the driver's claim and turned it around to praise China: "Yes, that's true, because the mainland is the world's industrial powerhouse."

For the first time since we landed, the group broke up into two separate contingents. The construction workers had made plans in advance to eat with colleagues from their Taiwanese parent company. This meant that they would forgo guide services for the night and were responsible for finding their own way back to the hotel. Meanwhile, the family explored the night market and ate on their own. I took the solo time to interview several food vendors and ask about the changing ecology of the market. Said one tofu vendor: "The mainlanders don't like our stinky tofu. It's not black or stinky enough. They go for these seafood places because seafood is expensive for them in China. But all the seafood here is from Thailand anyway. So, a lot of the more traditional Taiwanese stalls have been disappearing. They're getting replaced. And rent is going up for the rest of us." A roasted squid vendor said, "Fewer Taiwanese people come because the Chinese tourists are so noisy and they cut lines. Locals can't stand it." A nearby mullet roe vendor repeated similar claims, but added that locals have shifted their timing to arrive at the night market later in the evening, after the Chinese tourists return to their hotels. These are revealing statements because, as observed in chapter 3's narration of the Shilin Night Market, a "hot and noisy" atmosphere can indeed appeal to many Taiwanese, until the addition of Chinese tourists switches the valence of "noisy" from positive to negative. Like clockwork, the family and I indeed arrived at our hotel at a rather early 8:30 p.m., while the construction workers were still out with their colleagues.

When my roommate returned, he turned on the local TV news, which had been reporting for days on a deadly gas explosion in Kaohsiung. He said, "Taiwanese news should be broader. Why don't they give equal time to other places?" I asked him if mainland news gives broader coverage of events outside of China. He answered, "Well, no, not really."

Day Four

The day started with a visit to the seaside walkway at Xiziwan in Kaohsiung. It was a rare hour-long segment of unscripted time in extremely hot weather, and there were no suggested activities apart from taking photos of the ocean. Everyone complained that they were bored and wandered in tight circles inside the small 7-Eleven convenience store for twenty minutes, enjoying the free air-conditioning and testing the patience of the staff.

Our next stop was the Love River. We parked next to Kaohsiung's small 228 Memorial Park and walked through it on the way. Up until this point on the tour, the guide had not mentioned anything about the 228 Incident, the 1947 mass uprising that the KMT military brutally suppressed by killing thousands of Taiwanese. Although Jerry navigated us through the memorial, which was the most direct path to the river, he did not take this opportunity to mention such a pivotal historical episode. Walking in front of the rest of the group, I caught up to him to ask why. He answered, "I don't introduce things like 228 to guests from the interior [guonei keren] because it's political, and it's something their people did when they came here. I don't like to talk politics while on tour anyway."

The guide introduced the Love River once we reached the boardwalk. He started by criticizing the Democratic Progressive Party (DPP), which had held the Kaohsiung mayoral seat since 1998, and accused it of insufficiently cleaning up the waterway. He did not mention that the river was in far worse condition under earlier KMT rule. The problem, he said, was not just party politics but the entire system: "Taiwan is too democratic, so we're not united [tuanjie] enough. Sometimes too much democracy is not a good thing. . . . In the mainland, if the government wants to move a path by a meter, it can just do it, it doesn't need to get everyone to sign." As we prepared to depart from the boardwalk, a Toyota Prius pulled up. The driver turned out to be one of the construction workers' Taiwanese colleagues delivering a gift box of local pastries as a follow-up to their meeting the previous night.

We then headed toward a "museum" dedicated to Teresa Teng. Before we got off the coach, the guide claimed that the site was operated by Teng's family, funded with private donations and unsupported by the government, and so therefore might be a bit shabby. Falun Gong adherents demonstrated outside even this small site, which was all but unknown to tourism industry outsiders. After we got off the coach, site staff handed us necklaces with the number seven, to wear throughout our visit. Other tour groups wore different numbers, which made it easier to identify them and account for tour guide commissions. As it happened, there were no actual personal items or artifacts of Teng in the museum—the majority of the display items were photo reprints and text plaques.

The commercial function of the museum became clear when we exited from the display area and entered into the adjacent shop, which sold not only Teng's music but also the usual gamut of Taiwan-themed souvenirs, including tea and pineapple cake. We were not allowed to take photos in the store. The prices, listed in Chinese currency, were exorbitant. When I asked the staff about this, they said that the prices were calculated based on the exchange rate from three years prior, "because it is too difficult to update the computers," but that guests could pay in Taiwanese currency if they preferred. No one purchased anything, and we returned our numbered visitor cards before heading to lunch at a chicken-themed restaurant.

Back on the coach, Sun, my roommate, gestured toward a Taiwanese electronics retail chain outlet and said to the guide, "That electronics store is pretty small. I saw a car dealership under a corrugated iron roof. Mainlanders wouldn't trust a shop like that." Jerry replied, "We Taiwanese just want a cheaper price and get by more on trust."

After lunch, we headed to Fo Guang Shan, a major Buddhist monastery and monument led by Master Hsing Yun, originally from Nanjing, China, where his reflections are etched into the wall of a "national patriotic education" museum that commemorates World War II–era atrocities committed by the Japanese military. Fo Guang Shan has received many semiofficial visits by Chinese officials and was once even proposed by KMT-affiliated academic Charles Kao as a possible site for Taiwan's president to sign a speculative "peace treaty" with the PRC based on a "one China" principle. The guide introduced Fo Guang Shan by comparing it with its putative mainland counterparts: "Our China [*Women Zhongguo*] has some sacred mountains, E Mountain, Hua Mountain, and so on, and this was patterned after that." One of the construction workers, Chunkai, said, "This site is grand, indeed." As with Chung Tai Chan Monastery, food and souvenir shops festooned the temple grounds.

After admiring the grandeur of Fo Guang Shan, we headed to Hengchun Old Town, which like Xiziwan is a no-cost site with little tourist-specific infrastructure. As we watched local kids play baseball, the guide slipped up his territorial language for the first time, contrasting "China" (not "mainland China") with Taiwan: "China beat us in baseball. China's got a lot of people, more than we do in Taiwan. So they've got a lot to choose from." No one seemed to notice the difference in terminology. We watched the kids hit a few more balls before he continued a few moments later, "Taiwan's economy is going nowhere because of political infighting. We're too democratic. Also, labor is too expensive, so Taiwanese have gone to China to set up shop."

Back on the coach, Sun said to Jerry, "These tour routes are pretty similar to what we do in the mainland. It's just that here we circle an island." The guide nodded. After we checked in at the hotel in Checheng—listed in the itinerary as the far more famous and popular site Kenting, which was actually thirty minutes away—Sun said to me privately, "Yes, this still feels like I haven't really left mainland China. And especially here in the south in this poorer, more rural place. . . . It feels even more like the countryside where I'm from. I don't see much of a difference." He expressed concern when I wanted to go out alone for a walk: "I bet people here really aren't used to seeing foreigners. They will probably stare at you."

He continued analyzing the dynamics of the tour: "I could tell right away when we entered that lunch restaurant today that everyone was from the mainland. It's okay, though. I'd still rather go with a group. There's no need to think about where to stay or eat. It's easier. Our guide is good too. He doesn't force us to buy things. He even told us that fruit was overpriced at that rest stop."

At a pause in the conversation I asked him about politics. He said, "I don't really care that much about Taiwan independence one way or the other because we're all Chinese anyway. It's not like with the Japanese. Taiwanese should be free to choose. I mean, if your parent sends you to another person to raise you and then demands you back after you're grown up, is that fair? Well, I guess if pressed, I'd say I prefer unification. Why not? It would make everyone stronger. I think the US is getting in the way. They keep supporting these places, like . . . Vietnam . . . the Philippines . . . to weaken China." After showering, he turned on the TV and tuned in to Chinese news, saying that he was already bored of local shows.

Day Five

In the morning, we rounded the southern tip of Taiwan Island, marking the midpoint of the trip in both space and time, and headed toward Taitung County. On the coach, one of the construction workers, Mingwei, talked loudly on the phone with his business associates who were calling from China. Mingwei's colleagues on the bus spoke with one another about the prolific Falun Gong billboards hugging the roadside. They read the slogans out loud in Mandarin and then discussed them briefly in Subei dialect while shaking their heads.

We stopped at several small, free scenic spots along the way. Before we disembarked at one of them, a lighthouse in Kenting, guide Jerry told us that he liked to visit a small seafood shop run by a Chinese immigrant married to a Taiwanese man, who also kept a large domesticated pig. After visiting the lighthouse at our own pace, we convened at the shop, where the guests expressed delight to chat with another Chinese person. The conversation was brief, simple, and friendly, with the woman saying she enjoys her life in Taiwan. Her shop, like all the others at the site, listed its prices in Chinese currency.

Falun Gong demonstrators were as omnipresent as Chinese currency signs. At Maobitou, one of the stops, Chunkai accepted a free copy of *Epoch Times*, the Falun Gong newspaper. I also picked one up. Chunkai read his silently, and one of his colleagues later grabbed mine off of my coach seat and quickly thumbed through it.

After five days of traveling together, small tensions within the group started growing. Several of the construction workers expressed irritation with Mingwei's loud conversations on the phone. Adding to the cacophony were the two children from Shanghai. As one belted out yet another piercingly loud scream, two of the workers yelled in protest, "We've had enough!" The guide stepped in to mediate by telling a uniquely cross-strait bogeyman tale. With a winking smile, he said to the children, "When we get off the coach and Falun Gong sees you crying, they'll kidnap you!"

With the mood still tense, the guide continued to fill in the silence before again tranquilizing us with videos. He said, "On our last day, we'll go to the famous National Palace Museum, which holds the great treasures of five thousand years of Chinese history. Dress a little more formally then. After all, there are foreign travelers there. It's better to be dressed up a bit." He then played a documentary produced by a transnational Chinese-language channel, Phoenix TV, about the memories of old KMT soldiers exiled in Taiwan. Sun, having seen the video before, turned to tell me that it was worth watching.

Guide Jerry soon announced our arrival on the eastern, Pacific Ocean side of Taiwan.

"Is there an island over there?" Chunkai asked, pointing toward the sea.

"No. America is that way though, maybe," said Jerry.

Sun asked me, "Want to go home?" He then asked, "The US is on the Pacific, right?"

"Yes, the west coast is," I answered.

Sun asked, "There's another coast? What ocean is on that side? The Indian?"

After I used my mobile phone's mapping application to help Sun visualize the position of the Atlantic Ocean, he suddenly switched the topic to US electoral politics. He had heard that Hillary Clinton would run to succeed Barack Obama as president and expressed concern about her alleged anti-Chinese (*paihua*) views. He learned this, he said, by watching TV news and reading the newspapers in China.

At a petrol and fruit shopping stop, I asked the driver for his thoughts on this tour. He said, "These tourists just want to see the so-called Taiwan they've heard about. It was inaccessible for a while and now they can come. They don't really care about how they do it. At least not these ordinary ones."

After passing through Taitung City, we stopped at the free tourist attraction in Dulan, Water Running Up, with its small man-made stream that appears to flow upward against the direction of gravity. Two young Taiwanese women, independent tourists, used a mobile phone to take videos of each other while the Shanghainese kids, paying them no heed, ran in and out of the camera frame. One of the women said to the camera, "We're at Water Running Up. We rode an hour and a half just to get here, and now we have to go back the same way. Just for this." She pointed at the site and shook her head. "Whatever, I'm dumbfounded [*shayan*]. Oh, and yeah, there are a lot of Chinese tourists here." They rolled their eyes at each other and the camera, finished filming, and walked away.

As we got back on the coach to head north from Water Running Up, guide Jerry said, "The hotels in the city are not very nice, so we've arranged one just a bit out of town." The hotel turned out to be a mammoth, aging complex in the quiet fishing harbor town of Chenggong, forty kilometers north from Taitung City. Jerry set the next day's departure time at 8:00 a.m., requiring an early wake-up call and breakfast.

Day Six

In the morning in our guest room, Sun turned on the TV news and complained, "The news is all about Kaohsiung. There's nothing about our mainland."

"Should the news include the mainland?" I asked.

"News should be international, without borders," Sun replied.

"Is your news borderless?" I asked.

"Well, no. What a contradiction," Sun said.

We went downstairs to eat breakfast together. Sun observed other tourists asking our guide some questions at a nearby table. "Everywhere we go on this tour, it's all mainlanders [*dalu ren*] all the way. I think we've seen these people before," said Sun.

We boarded the coach and backtracked forty kilometers to the city to visit the so-called Red Coral Museum, which was listed as a shopping stop on our itinerary. Jerry explained, "The wife of Chiang Kai-shek, Soong Mei-ling, liked red coral. . . . Taiwan produces 80 percent of the world's red coral. Red coral wards off evil and represents longevity. . . . The emperors Qianlong and Kangxi also liked it. So did the empress dowager Cixi. . . . Soong Mei-ling lived to 106 years old, so you can see it has this function." He then played a promotional video about red coral. Chunkai noticed that we were going back the same way we came the day before. He complained quietly to his friends that this shopping trip was a waste of time and had caused us all to wake up too early.

We arrived at the "museum," a large and poorly maintained store featuring portraits of Madame Soong. The construction workers were uninterested in making any purchases. Yiqing, the Shanghainese mother, bought a necklace for 1,000 RMB. "It's not much money," she told me.

As I waited outside the store, nearby several Falun Gong demonstrators, the driver asked me, "Have you cursed at Falun Gong yet?"

"Should I? They haven't bothered me. Have they bothered you?" I asked.

"Yeah, they bother me every day," he said and then yelled at them in Taiwanese.

Sun soon emerged from the store. I stepped away from the driver to ask Sun what he thought about the shop and its products. "We've seen all this before in the mainland and Hong Kong. So, this kind of thing is familiar. Yes, Taiwan has scammers too," he said.

We boarded the coach, and Jerry talked about old soldiers while we passed by several veterans homes. "Chen Shui-bian cut all their benefits, so now they get by with money donated from KMT-run businesses." As he spoke about the Chen administration, he said the words for "that time" (*na ge shihou*) in a theatrically mainland Chinese-style pronunciation, instead of the *nei ge shihou* more common in Taiwan. Chunkai noticed the affectation and mockingly repeated it out loud to no one in particular, "*Na ge shihou.*" Jerry finished his narration and put on a violent slapstick Chinese boxing film called *Long's Story*.

We covered the distance between Taitung and Chenggong for the third time before continuing north to Hualien. After the movie finished, Jerry introduced the county by noting that "Hualien has many 'High Mountain aborigines' [*gaoshan yuanzhumin*]. Of the 500,000 total in Taiwan, the most numerous are the Amis, with 150,000 people. Some of them are pale and white [*baibai de*] and very beautiful. Of course others are darker [*heihei de*] too."

We took a brief stop at a plaque marking the Tropic of Cancer. Before we got off the coach, Jerry let us know that it was a good site for photos, that we may see an indigenous musical group with live performances and CDs (*guangpan*, again the Chinese term) for sale, and that we should keep our eyes out for an old mainland soldier collecting recycled goods in the area.

After we returned to the coach, Jerry said that although Taroko National Park, just north of Hualien City and famed for its scenic gorge, was on our itinerary, we might only be able to see the entrance of it due to a landslide within the park and the likelihood of an ensuing traffic jam. Indeed, as we pulled into the park entrance, a long line of coaches came into view on the highway above. Jerry announced that instead of joining the crush, we should content ourselves to take photos by the small tourist shops alongside the adjacent river.

As a consolation stop, we visited Qixingtan, a pebble-strewn beach near an air force base. The beach was full of other Chinese tourists watching military pilots practice their takeoffs and landings in old fighter jets purchased from US military vendors. Mingwei and Chunkai were familiar with these particular jet models and surprised by my ignorance of armaments. They, like the tourists from other groups, busied themselves taking photos.

We returned to the outskirts of Hualien City and stayed in a cavernous mid-range hotel that had opened three years prior, just in time for the tourist wave.

As with most of our previous hotels, all guests came from mainland China and all indoor signage was in simplified characters.

Day Seven

Our penultimate day started with a visit to a jade shop. On the coach, Jerry introduced jade's ancient Chinese cultural function as a protective token of health and longevity and symbol of wealth and purity. He also mentioned its special role in mediating cross-strait relations, pointing out that several pro-unification Taiwanese politicians had given jade pieces to their mainland counterparts. The specialness of this jade, we learned, owed not only to its scarcity but also its geopolitical and numerological properties. Jerry noted that in 2005, KMT honorary chairman Lien Chan gave a jade vase to then Chinese president Hu Jintao. "It was 192 centimeters, 100 for 'One China,' 92 for the 1992 Consensus. Now it's in the Great Hall of the People. James Soong, another Taiwanese politician and Lien's running mate in 2004, gave a rose stone to Hu Jintao on his visit, which followed Lien's trip. Since Soong has a Hunanese family background, Hu had it put in the Hunan museum." After finishing his short speech, he played a video about Taiwan jade, which featured captions in simplified characters and a quasi-indigenous techno-pop soundtrack.

After the video finished, he pointed out another group home for veterans and used it to promote not just jade but the particular store where we were to buy it. "The store we're going to is KMT run. Everyone likes to come here because 25 percent of the profit is used to support veterans. Chen Shui-bian cut all their benefits, so life is hard for them. We also hope that you can get something that represents Taiwan, a nice memory, a good souvenir."

We arrived at the entrance to the jade store, which, like the coral shop, billed itself as a museum. It was indeed proudly operated by a subsidiary of the KMT, and the entrance featured photos of Chiang Kai-shek, Chiang Ching-kuo, Lien Chan, and other KMT leaders, as well as images of Chinese leaders Deng Xiaoping and Hu Jintao. Jerry told us that we would spend an hour there before he handed us over to the "guides" of the museum.

Our microphone-wearing guide confirmed Jerry's story. "Everyone working here is KMT, and this business is used to support soldiers. Me, I have this background too. I'm the son of a soldier from Hunan," he said.

He pointed to sample items in a case in the entrance display area. "These are the styles that Lien Chan gave to Hu Jintao. You should consider taking a pair of vases [ping] to support peaceful unification [heping tongyi]," he said, emphasizing the homophonous wordplay of ping for both "peace" and "vase." He walked us upstairs to a private room and gave a presentation on the provenance and varieties of the shop's jade, using strobing lights and other special effects to perform its purity and quality.

After ten minutes of this tightly scripted sales show, we were turned loose to browse rings, bracelets, necklaces, and assorted decorative items. No one in my group bought anything. "This stuff is all fake. We're so used to this from China. Who knows if they even use the money to support the veterans, anyway?" Ming-wei said to me, after asking if I would buy anything. I asked and received affirmative replies from three different shop staff about their KMT affiliation. They all said that they were brought into the store through friends or family.

After exiting the shop, I shared a juice with Jerry. He suddenly recited a rhyming song while shaking his head: "Get on the coach and sleep, get off the coach and pee, go home knowing nothing [Shang che shuijiao, xia che niaoniao, hui jia shenme dou bu zhidao]." I asked him to elaborate, and he said, "Some tourists like to say this rhyme, and also this one too: 'I'd always regret not going to Taiwan, but having gone to Taiwan is something to regret always [Bu qu Taiwan shi yibeizi de yihan, qu Taiwan yihan yibeizi].'" This line, familiar among jaded Chinese tourists, can be adapted to nearly any destination and is a sentiment I will address in the epilogue.[2]

We returned to the coach and watched a music video of Taiwanese pop star Jay Chou. The guide then explained that the stretch of highway between Hualien and Su'ao, in adjacent Yilan County, is dangerous and difficult, so we would take the train and the driver would meet us later. As always, Falun Gong demonstrators flanked the entrances and exits of these otherwise minor train stations. The tourists seemed unimpressed by the appearance of the station and the train itself, which they said was slower and older than those in China.[3]

After returning to the coach, we took a brief trip to the Yehliu Geopark, a coastal site northeast of Taipei popular for its rock formations and inexpensive entrance ticket. We then embarked to Taipei City for our second official shopping stop of the day, Vigor Kobo, a pineapple cake and delicacy specialist that is 25 percent owned by China-based investors. Photos of President Ma and of former Taipei mayor and KMT stalwart Hau Lung-bin loomed large over the cash registers.

Along the way to the Everrich Duty-Free flagship store, our third and final shopping destination of the day, Jerry attempted to sell us a medicinal menthol cream that he had first introduced during our nauseatingly winding ride up Alishan. After Jerry passed a sample jar around for further inspection, he said that it could be delivered to our hotel. The guests helped themselves to more of the cream but did not place any orders.

We were given ninety minutes to shop in the six-story Everrich complex. A privately held group that holds a near monopoly on duty-free shopping outlets in Taiwan, Everrich notably claims not to offer commissions to tour companies and guides. Our group split into several parts, with the Shanghainese family browsing the cosmetics and handbags areas and the construction workers checking out the tobacco and liquor outlets. Mingwei bought an 850 RMB bottle of Chabot XO Armagnac. "I've never had this before, but I guess it must be good because it has XO in the title," he said.

Back on the coach, as we pulled away from the Everrich commercial traffic orbit, Sun exclaimed, "Wow, look at all these tourist buses! How can Taiwan still oppose the Services Trade Agreement?" We visited the Danshui boardwalk, a pedestrian area of food carts, inexpensive restaurants, and vendors, before checking into a hot springs hotel in the suburb of Beitou. Jerry did not mention that Beitou was first developed as a hot springs resort by Japanese colonial administrators.

Sun joined his colleagues to take a taxi to the Carrefour department store, their second and final unescorted outing. They bought local condiments and snacks as gifts for friends and family back home. In our shared room, Sun summed up his Taiwan experience:

> I used to think Taiwan was mysterious. Now I know what it's like. I'm no longer curious about it. It's not as developed as I thought. . . . You know, it was one of the four Asian Tigers, like Hong Kong, Korea, Japan. . . . But our city standard now is Shanghai, and now that I've seen Taipei and Kaohsiung, they just don't compare. But like I told you before, these smaller places, like around our hotel in these small towns, are nice and orderly. This is worth it for us to learn from. People's quality [suzhi], their etiquette [liyi] . . . these are good.

Day Eight

After a final breakfast together at the hot springs hotel, we boarded the coach for our last day, which would include several important stops. First up was the National Palace Museum, which, Jerry explained, "holds the treasures of five thousand years of Chinese nationalities [Zhonghua minzu]." Most of our two hours inside the museum involved waiting in lines, first at the entrance for audio receivers and then to glimpse the famous jade cabbage.

During some of the time in line, I asked Jerry for a little more background on his personal political beliefs. He explained to me that he had joined the New Tongmenghui, a far-right pro-unification group named for Sun Yat-sen's Tongmenghui association, the predecessor of the KMT. He explained that the Taiwanese membership is largely composed of ex-soldiers and members of pan-blue parties, including the KMT and its spin-offs. He had traveled to China in the past year as a group member and met minor officials, developed personal relationships, and learned more about Taiwan's "Chinese roots." He said that this trip had nothing to do with his post-military career as a tour guide, which he was doing for personal enjoyment and extra income.

For lunch, we ate at the Beiping Restaurant. Named for an anachronistic term for the Chinese capital, Beijing, this was a striking choice for a final meal in Taiwan. Like many of our Taipei group shopping outlets, this restaurant also displayed signed photos of KMT mayors Ma and Hau, but not of former DPP mayor Chen.

After lunch, we visited the Sun Yat-sen Memorial Hall, where not only Falun Gong demonstrators abounded but also an elderly man strode around wearing and vending ROC and KMT memorabilia, including flags, hats, and banners. He said he has been there daily at least since 2012, and, indeed, I had seen him there at nearly every visit since then. We were allowed only thirty minutes to pay our respects to the large statue of Sun Yat-sen and explore the attached museum, which included artifacts from Sun's trips to Taiwan while it was under Japanese rule. The exhibitions presented the KMT party-state administration of Taiwan as a glorious manifestation of Sun's Three Principles of the People and his commitment to democracy and freedom.

Finally, we visited the nearby Taipei 101 skyscraper. The tour package did not include entrance tickets (approximately 500 NTD, or US$16) for the viewing platform on top of the building, so the group instead split into several smaller groups and window-shopped around the luxury outlets in the adjacent mall. My roommate, Sun, and I walked together for most of the hour allotted to us, taking photos of ourselves and each other, reminiscing about the highs and lows of the week, and comparing this mall to similar ones in mainland China. "Yeah, this is a nice mall, but I can see this kind of thing in Shanghai too, and there are more impressive buildings there anyway. But the people here . . . I'll miss their courtesy and kindness."

We reassembled in the mall lobby at 3:00 p.m. and walked to the coach. Having already decided to continue my field work in Taiwan and forfeit my return flight to Shanghai, I removed my bag from the back of the bus and waved the group good-bye as they departed for the airport.

Analysis

From start to finish, the tour guide consistently performed Taiwan as a part of China and presented Taiwanese people as Chinese ethnic subjects. This was achieved via the tour guide's choice of territorial language and his selective narration of Taiwanese history. The effect was reinforced by the spatiotemporal contours of the tour operator's itinerary, which routed us not only to "scenic spots" presented in a culturally "Chinese" register but also to shopping destinations that, while offering "local specialties," were spun as threads of a greater Chinese tapestry. Augmenting this was the fact that our hotels, restaurants, sites, and shops were primarily if not exclusively oriented toward Chinese tourists—with simplified Chinese signage and cashiers accepting Chinese currency. After a few days on tour, it became easy to see why Chinese group tourists perceive Taiwan as a part of China.

This performance of Taiwan as China was informed by a hybrid of KMT and Chinese Communist Party (CCP) historical, territorial, and cultural claims. Japan's colonial legacy was either effaced or criticized and Taiwan's indigenous past and present were conflated with China's modern discourse of "minority nationalities" (*shaoshu minzu*), as opposed to the "ethnic group" (*zuqun*) terms increasingly used in contemporary Taiwan (Cheng and Fell 2014; Damm 2011).[4] It was also a performance with an imaginative inversion of the usual direction of cross-strait tourism's political and economic instrumentality: At jade shops and other stores, KMT-affiliated capitalists sold not only physical products but also the phantasmic promise of political unification via tourist spending. Meanwhile, Falun Gong was represented by the guide not just as a religious organization that is banned in China but as a veritable child-snatching bogeyman.

Guide as Territorial Translator

The guide's tactical use of language was key to his depiction of Taiwan as a part of China. Jerry frequently contrasted Taiwan with "the mainland" (*dalu*) or "mainland China" (*Zhongguo dalu*). He used "interior" (*neidi*) less frequently, but usually as a modifier, as in "guests from the interior." I observed only one instance in which he contrasted Taiwan with "China," while watching a local baseball game in Hengchun. As with guide Frank's slip, mentioned in chapter 3, this occurred later in the tour, after rapport between guide and guest had been established, and no one commented on it.

Selective use of territorial terms like "the mainland" is not unusual in Taiwanese political discourse, especially among Chinese nationalists and among Taiwanese who conduct business or other forms of exchange in China. However, our guide's frequent use of phrases like "our China" and "our former premier, Wen Jiabao," went beyond the usual bounds of mainstream speech in Taiwan's post–martial law era. While he frequently contrasted Taiwan and mainland China as *places* or *societies*, he rarely contrasted individual Taiwanese and mainland Chinese as *people* or as ethnonational subjects. His frequent use of "we

Chinese people" (*women Zhongguoren*), whether to claim the inevitability of political unification or to make more banal comments on food preferences, recapitulated the informal stance shared by both the KMT and the CCP that Taiwanese and Chinese are "fraternal nationalities" (*xiongdi minzu*).

Although the guide emphasized ethnocultural commonalities, he could not avoid mentioning institutional differences between Taiwan and China. In so doing, he usually valorized the supposed efficiency of China's one-party system and conversely lamented the inefficiency and contentiousness of Taiwan's multiparty system. His refrain "Taiwan is too democratic" was repeated at least five times during the trip, usually to nods of approval from the tourists, at least when they were paying attention. However, he did occasionally praise Taiwan's relatively high degree of "freedom" and religious tolerance, which enabled a more "humane" (*you renqingwei*) society, even as he advised guests to steer clear of Falun Gong demonstrators.

Citing overlapping KMT and CCP discourses of ethnic unity in opposition to a common enemy, and reflecting his own military background, the guide frequently criticized Japan's past and present role in Taiwan. He also deployed the specter of Japan, Japanese colonial education, and putative Japanese ethnic identification as a trope to criticize Lee Teng-hui, the DPP, and Taiwanese nationalism and independence activism more generally. This served to bond him intersubjectively with the tourists as fellow Chinese ethnonationals, to "cater" (*yinghe*, as he told me privately) to their assumed racial biases, to evoke reconstructed shared memories of war atrocities, and to appeal to their shared territorial imagination of "one China."

Another example of the guide's selective historical narration was his frequent invocation of the phrase "sixty-five years of separation between the mainland and Taiwan," referring to the post-1949 period of division between the PRC in mainland China and the ROC in Taiwan. This phrase elides the fifty years of Japanese colonial administration that he so frequently criticized, which would add half a century to the supposed sixty-five years of territorial division. A further problematic assertion here is the guide's claim that Taiwan was ever fully subject to "Chinese rule," which is questioned by historical analyses that suggest that Qing rule of Taiwan was hesitant and incomplete at best (Teng 2004; Shepherd 1993) and further complicated by the Qing's legacy as a Manchu-dominated, multiethnic conquest dynasty that issued from China's geographical periphery.

The explicitness of the guide's stances belied his private comments to me that he did not like discussing politics with guests. His ideological commitments were evident not only from his conduct of the tour but also from his membership in the pro-unification New Tongmenghui association. He did not mention this organization to the other tourists, as far as I observed, but he certainly engaged them in political conversation. Jerry's ideology makes him an outlier in Taiwanese society. It was also somewhat extreme for his industry, even given its general alignment with the pan-blue KMT camp. Still, it served him well in his work guiding Chinese tour groups. His frequent criticisms of the DPP, of Taiwan independence activism and democratic governance, and of Japan's colonial administration and present leadership were certainly a form of theater. But what he left unsaid was at least as important. His elisions of KMT human rights abuses, illegal land appropriations, widespread public opposition to unification with China, and the well-documented and inexorable increase in Taiwanese national identification were not only a practical matter of tour management but also a personal, political choice with profound impact on guests' perception of Taiwanese history and contemporary public opinion.

It is difficult to know how differently Jerry would present his opinions to a nontourist audience of Taiwanese people—I can only speculate as to whether he would talk about "Japanese devils" and "our Premier Wen Jiabao." What seems clear, however, is that his hyperbolic semipublic performances of Chinese nationalism were consistent enough with his own personal stance.

Ethnic Elisions

The guide rarely mentioned the names of post-1949 Taiwan's most salient quasi-ethnic divisions, that of the mainlander (*waishengren*) and Taiwanese (*benshengren*). This is not surprising, as these terms are Taiwan-specific and can produce a politically charged affect of opposition and discomfort, which the guide usually tried to avoid. Instead, he spoke more in terms that would be comprehensible to Chinese tourists, for example, "old soldiers."

The guide also made a point of introducing the tourists not only to Taiwan-born descendants of mainlanders but also to resident Chinese nationals. Examples include the Chinese immigrant at the Kenting seafood stall, married to a Taiwanese, as well as salespeople at other sites on the east coast. He did this, he told me in one-on-one conversation, to make the tourists feel more at home.

Remarkably, when referring to indigenous Taiwanese, the guide frequently used ethnic terms that are heard *only* in China and not in Taiwan, including "High Mountain ethnicity" (*gaoshanzu*; the PRC's official designation) to refer to all of Taiwan's many indigenous groups, as well as "minority nationalities" (*shaoshu minzu*). He also occasionally referred to them as the unique hybrid term "High Mountain indigenous" people (*gaoshan yuanzhumin*), as indigenous people (*yuanzhumin*; the most standard usage in Taiwan), and sometimes by their individual tribal names, such as Amis or Truku. While his usage was inconsistent, it indicated his cognizance and flexible deployment of PRC ethnic designations.

The tourists themselves did not express any interest in indigenous issues or history. As Sun said, "We have ethnic minorities in the mainland too, but I don't know too much about them either." To Sun and the others, indigenous peoples were just another component, not particularly significant, of the Han-dominated multiethnic menagerie of "Chinese nationalities."

Blurring Business and Leisure

At the start of the tour, Sun told me that he and his colleagues were sent by his Taiwanese boss as an incentive for good job performance as well as to gain a better understanding of Taiwan, where their company was headquartered. Sun and his colleagues stayed within the confines of the tour group and its itinerary for nearly the entire duration, apart from joining a company dinner in Kaohsiung and making their own shopping trip. The morning after their dinner, their Taiwanese colleagues delivered several boxes that were labeled as Taiwanese confectionaries for them to bring back to China.

While the construction workers' primary purpose indeed seemed to be leisure, they still took the opportunity to conduct some business and material exchange. The only conclusion that can be inferred from this is that other Chinese visitors who are counted as leisure tourists also likely mixed work and pleasure. This turns out to be at least as true for independent tourists who are not bound to tight tour schedules.

Intragroup Interaction

Our tour group neatly divided into three pieces: The five Subei construction workers, the Shanghainese family of four, and the guide and driver. As an individual traveler and an unusual "Western" presence on such a trip, I floated freely between these subgroups. When visiting larger sites, after the guide completed his basic introduction, we typically split into two parts—the family and the construction workers, whom I shared time with evenly when I was not speaking with the guide or site vendors or staff. During lunch and dinner, all guests, including the family and children, usually shared a table. The guide and driver would eat separately after seating us and explaining anything exceptional about the meal. As we ate, we usually discussed the food, the sites, and our impressions of the tour and of Taiwan. More infrequently, we would talk about our personal backgrounds.

The guests were mostly polite to one another and took care to ensure that everyone had enough to eat of each dish. The construction workers were also patient with the children, who would occasionally make a mess or a loud noise, eat food out of sequence, or rapidly spin the table's serving wheel in ways that inconvenienced other diners. Explicit discussion of political topics never took place between the family and the construction workers. However, in smaller groups, for example, during breakfast or while watching TV with the construction workers, Taiwanese politics came up as a topic of common conversation. The guide's refrain "Taiwan is too democratic" was noted and repeated. As the only "foreigner" on this trip, and indeed the only foreigner any of my fellow tourists had ever spoken with, I was often asked to provide my "American" opinion on these questions. I tactically chose stances that I presumed would be inoffensive to them, to the point of occasionally overcompensating by criticizing US politicians. In this way, not entirely unlike Jerry, I became a performer as well, avoiding conflict by saying things I thought the guests would want to hear while maintaining sufficient consistency with my own ideology.

Shopping for Unification

KMT imagery pervaded most of our shopping destinations. Well-known brand-name stores such as the Chinese-invested pineapple cake shop Vigor Kobo, as well as smaller eateries and shops like the Beiping Restaurant and the Alishan lunch stop/tea shop, placed signed photos of President Ma and Mayor Hau in prominent positions. At no point did we see anything similar with DPP or other opposition leaders.

The most striking example of party influence was of course provided at the KMT-operated jade store in Hualien, which not only featured portraits of both KMT and CCP leaders but also employed staff who claimed that "buying [their] vases [would] help support peaceful unification." The guide had indirectly primed this store's sales pitch for several days by claiming that the former DPP administration had cut veterans benefits, by repeatedly pointing out veterans hospitals and residential complexes along the roadside, and by introducing us to mainland veterans whenever possible. On the bus, he claimed that 25 percent of profits from the shop would be distributed to veterans who no longer received state support. However, the salespeople made no such claim. When I asked them individually, they said that they did not know details but that the store and the KMT certainly "support our troops." Unlike Jerry, they made their sales pitch by presenting the store or the KMT not as a veterans welfare agency but as a commercial avenue to realize the political unification of China and Taiwan.

As pointed out in chapter 2, to "peddle politics through business" (*yi shang cu zheng*) has been part of China's strategy to financially entice Taiwanese to support unification at least since the Hu Jintao era (S. Kastner 2006). This shop, however, was a novel example of the converse—using politics to peddle business—in this case, deploying discourses of unification and ethnonational affiliation to entice Chinese tourists to further enrich the KMT. Remarkably, no one in my group bought anything, precisely due to the apparent similarity of this store's hard sell approach to those prevalent in China.

Other shopping stops routinely emphasized ethnocultural commonalities between China and Taiwan while also sporting KMT iconography. Examples include the Alishan tea shop, whose products featured a photo and signature of President Ma on the box, as well as Teresa Teng's music, which was said to have universal appeal to Chinese people on both sides of the strait. While these stores used assumed affiliations to stimulate sales, they stopped short of claiming that tourist spending supported a wider political project. However, Vigor Kobo's status as a Chinese-Taiwanese joint venture did allow Jerry to present it as an example of the "peaceful development of cross-strait relations."

Throughout this particular tour, Chinese tourist spending was directed toward KMT and KMT-supporting businesses, unevenly benefiting Taiwan's private sector, to the detriment of non-KMT-aligned interests. I found the explicitness of this partisanship surprising, even if it was consistent with the positions of travel industry trade association executives who expressed support for the KMT and affiliated politicians in interviews, as discussed in chapter 2.

On the basis of this tour experience, the contours and affective contents of which are generally consistent with my interviews with other tourists, it seems fair to conclude that the group tour structure generally reproduced the effect of being in China for most tourists. This effect was consistent throughout the trip, despite its many unscripted and unpredictable moments. Put another way, cross-strait group tourist sites, and the spaces in between, were effectively stage-managed and mediated to avoid expressions of dissonance or conflict between the pro-unification ideologies of most Chinese guests and the anti-unification sentiments of most Taiwanese hosts. Even when they walked through the streets of Taiwan unescorted, these tourists remained experientially ensconced in "one China."

THE VARIETIES OF INDEPENDENT TOURIST EXPERIENCE

In May 2012, Han Han, China's most popular blogger, published a post titled "Winds of the Pacific" (Taipingyang zhi feng), about his recent trip to Taiwan:

> I don't want to delve into the politics. As a writer from the mainland, I just feel lost. A pervasive feeling of loss. The society I grew up in spent a few decades teaching us to be violent and vengeful, and then a few more decades teaching us to be selfish and greedy. Our parents destroyed our culture, our ethics, our ability to trust, our faith and consensus, but failed to build the utopia that was promised. We may have no choice but to keep doing the same things. As a writer, I have to constantly worry about whether my words will step on some line somewhere. I assume people have ulterior motives when they treat me with warmth. Other than self-survival and competition, we have lost interest in everything else. This is how we have come to define ourselves. . . .
>
> Yes, I have to thank Hong Kong and Taiwan, for protecting Chinese civilization. Even when we have the Ritz Carlton and the Peninsula, Gucci and Louis Vuitton, wives of local officials with more money than their leaders, movie budgets 20 or 30 times theirs, the World's Fair and the Olympics, but, on the streets of Taipei, I didn't feel any bit of pride. Whatever we have, they already had; whatever we are proud of, their taxpayers will never approve; whatever we should be proud of, we've already lost.[1]

Despite his disclaimer, Han's post is nothing if not political. He may skirt the question of Taiwan independence, but he uses the island imaginary as a tinted mirror for what the People's Republic of China (PRC) could be but is not, or was but is no longer. Filled with anecdotes of the kindness of strangers—the taxi driver who returned a phone that Han had dropped in the backseat or the eyewear store owner who guilelessly gave Han's friend a free pair of contact lenses—Han's post treats Taiwan not as a renegade province under the thumb of the United States or as an exotic tourist destination, but as a rhetorical device for an indirect critique of the Chinese Communist Party's (CCP) role in the corruption of "Chinese values." Han's taxi driver was not just a taxi driver—in the retelling, the cabbie came to represent the supposed generous spirit of all Taiwanese people. Except, in Han's reading, the driver's generosity was not so much Taiwanese as it was *Chinese*, free of the corrupting influence of the CCP. Han therefore suggests that he was helped not by a Taiwanese as much as by a more authentic Chinese subject. Taiwan's history as a Japanese colony and US protectorate, as well as its many other specificities and contingencies, are elided in this account.

Han's account contrasts strikingly with that of Liping, a nineteen-year-old woman from Henan Province. In July 2013, Liping attended a talk about dissident artist Ai Weiwei by a professor from Hong Kong University held at Taipei's famed Eslite Bookstore. Liping had never heard of Ai, despite his international renown and his contribution to the design of the Beijing 2008 Summer Olympics' "Bird's Nest" stadium, a symbol of national pride. She returned from Taiwan to China with a newfound appreciation for the limits of her knowledge about her own country.

I had first met Liping a few weeks before her trip while I was browsing in the small Shanghai art museum where she volunteered. During our initial casual conversation, in which she asked routine questions about what I was doing in China, she told me that she would be going to Taiwan soon as an independent tourist. After explaining my research and eliciting her interest and consent, the conversation quickly transitioned into a semi-structured interview. During her trip we stayed in touch through the instant messaging app WeChat and had another follow-up interview on her return to Shanghai: "There was so much I learned that I didn't know about, about Taiwan, about mainland China. I didn't know about these artists being under house arrest. I didn't know that Taiwan had such a vibrant arts scene . . . well, I knew about Eslite before I went there—it's a famous place for us—but I didn't realize how many books I'd see that I didn't know about or that there'd be these talks on people like Ai Weiwei. Wow, he's really extraordinary."[2]

Liping's reflection sounded almost too neatly dramatic to be true. More than Han's account, which more or less recapitulated a conventional story about Taiwan as a purer part of China, Liping's tale could be spun as an example of the CCP's worst nightmare, as a sign that independent tourists would inevitably find their way into scenes and spaces that would subvert hegemonic party narratives. Yet, Liping's tale was but one of many I recount in this chapter, which focuses as much on ambiguity and contradiction as on coherent, progressive stories of "awakening" or "uncovering" a hidden truth.

The following account is composed of observational and interview data collected between June 2012 and April 2015. While I made efforts to ensure a range of ages, genders, and sending regions in the sample, it makes no claims to being an exhaustive or even representative survey. Instead, I wish to highlight and discuss the *variety* and *diversity* of independent tourist narratives and interpretations of Taiwan's political history and trajectory and to tease out factors that likely affected their perceptions and statements. In so doing, I trace the social circuits and territorial narratives remade through the practices of independent tourism.

Interview subjects were recruited through a variety of online and off-line channels. Online, I participated in social networks and instant messaging software platforms, including Facebook, WeChat, Line, Skout, and Couchsurfing. Through the posts of friends on these sites, but more frequently via new contacts with no known prior connections to my own social networks, I recruited roughly half of my interview subjects. The remainder were found off-line via a variety of venues and channels, including direct recruitment at airports, tourist sites, or cultural events; introductions from mutual Taiwanese friends and acquaintances; and snowballing introductions from past interview participants. It is worth noting that the diversity of their perspectives speaks as much about the different spaces within Taiwan as it does about the diversity of the class, generational, and educational backgrounds of the tourists themselves. For this reason, I include basic biographical details about the tourists and the background to the interviews, as appropriate and available, to help situate their stories and provide interpretive context.

Like the ethnography of a group tour in chapter 4, my raced, gendered, and nationalized positionality affected the conduct and interpretation of these interviews. The physical settings, as well as the recruitment sites, also influenced the outcomes. For example, interviewees at independent music festivals or indigenous folk shows tended to be younger than the mean. Some attended such events along with Taiwanese acquaintances or had particular interest in Taiwanese cultural or performing arts. At these events, recruitment sometimes proceeded during group conversation within a mixed group of Chinese tourists and Taiwanese attendees, which may have prompted responses meant to be more accommodating of Taiwanese sentiment.

For example, as related in chapter 3, during a mid-concert interview in Dulan, Mingqi, a twenty-two-year-old female college student from Chengdu, Sichuan, described Taiwan as "an island in the Pacific." This phrasing made no reference to its proximity to mainland China or its cultural and national legacy, purported or otherwise. That Mingqi, a PRC citizen, spoke to me in the language of a Taiwanese nationalist showed a remarkable familiarity with local territorial terminology. Her geographical framing, which centered Taiwan and ignored China, was right at home in this venue.

But meetings in pro-Taiwan spaces or introductions from Taiwanese personal acquaintances did not guarantee respondents would necessarily exhibit a conciliatory or Taiwan-centric attitude. For example, Zhimin, a forty-four-year-old male urban planning professor from Shanghai Tongji University introduced to me by his Taiwanese colleague, a personal acquaintance, provided perhaps the most primordial and violent rationale for unification I heard in any interview:

> Taiwan is basically free and independent now. And I can see why they'd want to stay that way. Life here is nicer, more comfortable, cleaner, warmer. . . . It's probably better for Taiwan now to maintain the status quo, and that's good for China because, eventually, Taiwan and mainland China will have to reunite. Why? It's in Taiwan's ultimate interests, it's in the interests of all Chinese people worldwide. There's a resource war coming. There's just not enough water or energy to support the whole world's population. There's going to be great conflict, even war ahead. There will be two main sides, the US, Europe, and Japan versus China and the Chinese people of the world. Taiwan will need to ally with mainland China on this one. They will, it's just a question of whether it's sooner or later. It's in their interests, it's in their blood. When this showdown happens, all the Chinese people of the world will feel this struggle [*douzheng*] in their blood.[3]

While the apocalyptic tone of Zhimin's vision was exceptional, his contention that temporary maintenance of the status quo followed by eventual unification was both inevitable and preferable to immediate unification or independence was shared by several other wealthy and well-educated informants with no connection to my social networks and who had few if any Taiwanese friends. For example, Ping and Lu, a late-twenties professional couple from Shanghai, whom I had first recruited at Dulan's Water Running Up site and followed up with later in a café in their luxury Taipei hotel, explained:

> LU: Taiwan is a pretty nice place now I think. Life here doesn't seem as fast-paced as in Shanghai. It's comfortable, people are friendly. I feel relaxed here, not stressed. . . .
>
> PING: Yes, I agree. Maybe this sounds strange to say, but I actually think it's good that Taiwan is more or less free to be on its own right now,

different from the mainland. It makes Taiwan a nicer place to be, and eventually when Taiwan unifies with China, that means it'll be better for China too, since we're all one family anyway. It doesn't need to happen now, or in the next ten or even twenty years, but it will happen, there's no doubt about it. . . . I don't think it really matters what people in Taiwan want. Taiwan is so small anyway.[4]

Other people recruited via random online channels divulged interpretations of the Chinese Nationalist Party (KMT) that, while increasingly unpopular with contemporary Taiwanese youth, shared affinities with small subcultures of Republic of China (ROC) nostalgia on the mainland. For example, Lijun, a twenty-six-year-old female accountant from Guangzhou, speculated about how different modern Chinese history might have been had the KMT defeated the CCP and wondered if China might still be as authentically Chinese as she felt Taiwan is today: "People here seem more honest. The street names in Taipei have these kinds of Confucian attitudes in them. The Eight Virtues [*ba de*], loyalty and filial piety [*zhongxiao*] and so on. This place is more Chinese than China. I think the KMT has preserved Chinese culture much better here. There was no Cultural Revolution here . . . and there are temples everywhere. Sometimes I think that the KMT should make a deal with the CCP and offer to come back and raise China's cultural level."[5] Lijun's analysis dovetailed neatly with the KMT's hegemonic discourse. While a minority opinion, hers would have pleased President Ma Ying-jeou, who championed Taiwan as the standard-bearer of Chinese culture.

The remainder of this chapter is flexibly structured around emergent keywords and tourist types and further plumbs the evident variety of interpretation reflected in the above remarks.

Taiwan as "Small, Fresh, and New"—and Japanese?

Nearly all respondents under thirty-five years old described Taiwan in general, and in particular its bed-and-breakfast inns and youth culture event spaces, as *xiaoqingxin*, a Chinese neologism that defies concise translation into English. Like the related term "petit bourgeois" or "little capitalist" (*xiaozi*), this term is frequently used by middle-class Chinese youth but relatively little heard in Taiwan. Literally, it is a contraction of the words for "small," "fresh," and "new." *Xiaoqingxin* first entered the Chinese lexicon to describe indie pop music that evokes a warm, carefree mood, often with feminine vocal textures (Ding 2012).

Typical Chinese-language examples are the songs of Taiwanese musicians Cheer Chen or Soda Green. The term was later extended to refer to literature, including the works of Japanese writer Haruki Murakami, as well as clothing with minimalist or floral designs and natural fabrics.

Xiaoqingxin quickly transcended its initial sensory modalities, expanding from sound to image and eventually on to describe the affective qualities of *spaces*. These include not only retail shops and bed-and-breakfasts but also particular regions and even the entire whole of Taiwan. For example, said Ju, a clothing retail worker from Hangzhou, "Taiwan is so *xiaoqingxin*. I feel like I can really relax here."[6] A similar sentiment was shared by Lu, the Shanghai-based professional quoted earlier: "I really like the east coast. It gives me such a *xiaoqingxin* feeling. It's natural, relaxed, comfortable. I think I'll go there more often for vacations." Sometimes *xiaoqingxin* was used pejoratively, particularly by men. "The food here is good, but the hotels are a little bit, a little bit too . . . cute . . . *xiaoqingxin*. This is a destination that more women will enjoy," said a thirty-eight-year-old male accountant from Beijing.[7]

While *xiaoqingxin* was among the most frequently used adjectives for Taiwan by independent tourists, rarely if ever did my interviewed group tourists say *xiaoqingxin*. While some of the words that group tourists used included "warm" (*wenxin*), "comfortable" (*shufu*), "friendly" (*qinqie*)—words that do not conflict with *xiaoqingxin*—few ever used *xiaoqingxin* itself. While this can be partly attributed to generational differences—particularly evident in their different music tastes and fashion sensibilities—it is also likely due to the very different spaces they experienced and produced within Taiwan. The mass-market hotels of the group tourist circuit presented stark stylistic contrasts with the smaller inns favored by many independent tourists. Even more memorable than the hotels, the obligatory commission-based shops responsible for the bulk of tour operator profits were often large, pushy, and hastily constructed. They were not at all "small and fresh," as opposed to many of the smaller boutique outlets and pop-up stores along the east coast or in commercial areas that were more popular with younger shoppers, such as Taipei's university districts or Taitung's Dulan.

Incipient *xiaoqingxin*-ification of Taiwanese spaces and shops was a cause of concern for some Taiwanese culture workers, who feared the gentrification of established centers of new youth culture, like Shida, the area around National Taiwan Normal University, which had incubated Taiwan's underground music scene in the 1990s and 2000s. By the late 2000s, Shida had become a site of struggle between entertainment venues, night market vendors, local resident associations, and real estate developers bidding on "urban redevelopment projects" (Frazier 2012). Underworld, Shida's landmark live music space, was forced to close in 2013 due to newly aggressive enforcement of old permit violations. In its place arose a new lifestyle outlet derided by Claire, a Taiwanese singer-song-writer and independence activist: "Underworld, and Shida in general, used to be so exciting. Now Underworld is closed and the area around is filling up with all these *xiaoqingxin* stores. I don't know, maybe they're aimed at Chinese tourists. Sometimes I feel like I don't even recognize this neighborhood anymore."[8] For tourists with relatively extensive international travel and cultural experience, the cute, or *kawaii* ("cute" in Japanese), aspects of the *xiaoqingxin* aesthetic also evoked Taiwan's complicated relationship with Japan. This is a sensitive issue for Chinese visitors, but not one about which each was equally aware. For example, Jing, a twenty-eight-year-old solo female tourist, expressed shock when I asked her how she felt about Japan's colonial legacy:

> ME: Do you see any Japanese influence in Taiwan?
>
> JING: I see a lot of fashion trends here that seem to come from Japan, but clearly Taiwan is Chinese. I mean, it's always been a part of China.
>
> ME: Even during the period of Japanese rule?
>
> JING: Taiwan was colonized by Japan? Really? Are you sure? Why didn't I know about that?
>
> ME: Yes, for fifty years. Who did you think was administering Taiwan in the early twentieth century, or during World War II, or the war between the KMT and CCP?
>
> JING: I don't know. I guess I thought it was just always part of the Republic of China. But you're saying it was Japan? Wow. Really, I had no idea. How could I not know that?[9]

Jing, who was college educated and worked for an international marketing company based in Shenzhen, China's wealthiest city, on the border with Hong Kong, had already spent three full days in Taipei and visited landmarks built during the Japanese period, including the Presidential Office. Following this trip, she returned twice to Taiwan to explore the east coast, which she described in a WeChat conversation: "So slow and beautiful and sunny and *xiaoqingxin* . . . it's almost like a different country. It's kind of like what I imagine Hawaii to be like."

Other visitors were more cognizant of Japan's influence on Taiwan and used it to provide an interpretive and comparative frame. For example, Chiyun, a thirty-seven-year-old male accountant and the colleague of a Chinese acquaintance, described Taipei's Ximending shopping district in the following terms: "It looks kind of like Shinjuku, with all the signs and flashing lights and Japanese brands everywhere. Then again, we have all this flashiness [*huali*] in our shopping districts too. But still, maybe because the only other overseas [*haiwai*] place I've been to besides Taiwan is Japan, this sort of looks a bit like that. Plus I can tell that people here still sort of identify with Japan . . . like, Lee Teng-hui. He still speaks Japanese all the time, right? I don't know why."[10]

Without the presence of a tour guide like Jerry to redirect the conversation, Chiyun's contrast of Taiwan with Japan became simultaneously banal and politically charged—banal because it discusses mere visual surfaces and is based on limited personal experiences, as he had no other overseas place to compare it to. Yet, his quick subsequent mention of Lee, who is widely reviled in China, touched on a key geopolitical and cultural legacy of Taiwanese leaders that he found discomforting. This tension is familiar to other Chinese tourists who grapple with the contradiction between fondness for contemporary Japanese youth and fashion culture and resentment over past Japanese colonial occupations and military invasions. These legacies are instrumental to narratives of national humiliation, especially those that use Taiwan and Japan in service to patriotic education. This tension animated the account of Zhimin, the Shanghai professor who predicted a future global race war and environmental apocalypse. He reflected:

> Taiwan seems a lot closer to Japan. It's like the people here wish they were Japanese. I've been to both of them a lot. You know, I'm an urban planning professor, so I can see how Taiwanese urban spaces are a lot like Japan's, and of course there are old Japanese buildings all over the place. . . . Right now it makes sense that Taiwan would feel closer to Japan. Japan is still richer and more advanced than China, and Taiwan was colonized by it. But we're bigger, we're stronger, we've got a more ancient history. Taiwan will have to come around and return eventually.

Many independent tourists observed Taiwan's resemblances to Japan. Even those like Jing, who was naive about Taiwan's colonial history, still noticed the influence of Japan's youth and fashion cultures. Yet, very few group tourists, both in my Shanghai group tour and in my other interviews and conversations at tourist sites, commented on Japan and Japanese influence. I propose the following two-fold explanation for this discrepancy: First, independent tourists come from a more limited set of wealthier cities and have other higher barriers to entry. This attracts a class of people who are more likely to have traveled to or otherwise gained deeper firsthand impressions of Japan. Second, group tour guides typically centered China and displaced Japan in their representation of Taiwan's history. As one example, guide Jerry did frequently talk about the Japanese colonial administration in critical terms, but his primary ethnic narrative focused on similarities and continuities between Taiwan and China. In chapter 3, I noted similar behavior from Frank, who did not otherwise present himself as an aggressive Chinese nationalist. Other tour guides generally confirmed in interviews that they invoked Japan only when necessary and aimed to keep China at the center of their narration of Taiwanese history.

For independent tourists, there is a further layer of irony to the blurring of Japan and China as cultural origin-points of contemporary Taiwan: many of the more "civilized" qualities that the independent tourist Han attributes to a purer version of Chinese culture could just as easily be ascribed to colonial and contemporary Japanese cultural influence, and often are by Taiwanese themselves. But Han, like many group tourists, was sufficiently invested in the Chinese national narrative to not even consider this concordance.

"Warm," "Friendly," "Civilized" —and Feminine?

The affective power of Han's popular blog post, which opens this chapter, is predicated on a presentation of Taiwan as a place that has preserved the "warmth" and "friendliness" of "traditional Chinese culture." A variety of my Chinese tourist informants likewise reported Taiwan to be a warm (*wenxin*), friendly (*reqing*), and civilized (*wenming*) place. "Warm" and "friendly" are everyday words in Taiwan, but "civilized" has a sharply political implication in contemporary China, where it has been used as a keyword in nationwide campaigns to produce citizen-subjects that dutifully comport themselves toward meeting the biopolitical objectives of the Chinese state (Tomba 2009). This of course recalls much older discourses in imperial China that contrasted civilized metropolitan subjects with the barbarian outsiders (Callahan 2005). Civilizational discourse found further purchase in more recent campaigns that aimed to "improve" the "quality" (*suzhi*) of Chinese at home and while abroad as tourist "ambassadors" (Chio 2010).

Tourists spoke about Taiwan's supposedly civilized qualities in different ways. Some supported Han Han's thesis that Taiwanese were simply more authentic Chinese. Others, however, invoked a more developmentalist discourse that presented Taiwan as having achieved a more advanced cultural level, with higher-"quality" people, and as therefore more "civilized" than China, even if its physical infrastructure already lagged behind that of China's first-tier cities. In almost all such cases, these tourists used Taiwan as an example for China to learn from, even if they acknowledged that Taiwan might have lost its relative economic advantage.

Younger respondents used loaded terms like "civilized" less frequently than middle-aged or older respondents. For example, a forty-six-year-old male accountant observed, "Taiwanese seem more civilized in general than people in the mainland. They talk more softly and don't litter trash on the streets. In fact, it's pretty amazing that Taipei is as clean as it is given how hard it can be to find a trash can around here."[11] A twenty-three-year-old recent female graduate from Nanjing University made a similar observation without explicitly using the word: "The pace of life here is a lot more relaxed. People don't seem as worried about their careers. I see cafés everywhere, bars. Maybe it's because there's no better jobs for them to do here besides those . . . so that many of the people here go to the mainland to find work. But maybe it's worth it for the people here who can stay. People here are friendlier and more leisurely. I'm going to have to come back more often when my stress level gets too high."[12]

Like the *xiaoqingxin* qualities discussed above, the warmth and friendliness of Taiwanese people was often gendered in the accounts of both male and female tourists, who often commented on the softness (*wenrou*) of the visual presentation and speech patterns of Taiwan's women and even some of its men.[13] Few respondents hazarded any effort at causal explanation beyond a simple geographical determinism in which Taiwan's island topography and safer urban environments were supposed to engender a kind of gentility. By comparison, many of them conjectured that China's rapid modernization, migration patterns, family planning enforcement, and communist ideology had bred out the traditional femininity of its women. For example, Zhu, a male manager at a logistics company, observed: "Women here are so soft. They're not fierce [*qianghan*] like our women, particularly Shanghainese women. I guess Taiwan didn't have such a quick modernization, or it modernized earlier, and so women don't need to fight so hard to get ahead professionally. Or maybe, because there are bigger families here . . . the women are more traditional?"[14]

The supposedly "soft" attributes of Taiwanese women were not universally praised; some tourists found it phony, affected (*zuozuo de*), or irritating and said they preferred the "directness" of women in the mainland. It is also worth noting the irony in their perception of Taiwanese women as being more traditionally feminine, given that Taiwan would rank as the second-most "gender-equal" society in the world, far higher than China, if measured by the United Nations Gender Inequality Index (J. Liu 2013).

Military fantasy further layers the way that the geo-coding of gender can repress Taiwanese subjectivity and resurface as a mode of wish fulfillment for male protagonists. For example, Zhimin, the apocalyptic professor from Shanghai, said, "Can you imagine the men here fighting? I know there's still conscription and forced military service, for now, but the guys here are too gentle. They wouldn't stand a chance against our men." Here, a patriarchal militarism asserted the inevitability of Taiwan's domination.

"Free," "Democratic," and Falling Behind?

Taiwan's democratic system was assessed variably by the tourists I interviewed. Some agreed with the guide and group tourists of chapter 4 that Taiwan is "too democratic." Others suggested that Taiwan is not truly democratic and that the elections are a sham and controlled by domestic corporate or external—usually US—interests. Others expressed admiration for Taiwan's spirited election culture. Few of them saw any essential contradictions between democratic practice and Chinese ethnonational identity, although they usually highlighted the imagined "impossibility" of a similar system working in contemporary China. Many of them offered critical observations of the role of the media in election campaigns. For example, a thirty-three-year-old male civil engineer from Xiamen, said: "I've been to Taiwan five times in the last two years and it seems like there's always an election going on. There are noisy electioneering trucks, fireworks, billboards . . . TV shows with critics ruthlessly attacking the politicians. How can people here keep up with it all? It's impressive that these people [pundits] who analyze and criticize can be so incisive, but I think it's not good for Taiwan's image as a whole. The attacks on politicians are so personal. And if the president is called a dog or whatever, what does that say about Taiwan as a country?"[15]

Another, Zhihao, argued that China's political system was superior to not only Taiwan's but also that of the United States and that self-interested Taiwanese would be forced to realign:

> I think that Taiwan's political system on the whole probably makes Taiwan a nicer place to live right now than the mainland, but in the long term it's not competitive. We can build things so much faster—highways, buildings, industry. There's no way Taiwan can keep up with that, and it's not just because Taiwan is small. You see too that the US superpower is also falling behind China. Our system is just better, more efficient, faster. And it's more culturally suited to Chinese people [*Zhongguoren*] too. We've been an empire in the past, and Confucian. And we just do things differently, and you see even Africa and all these other poor countries want to do business with us now and not the US. Taiwanese people will eventually see this. They're practical and want to be prosperous. They won't look to the US for support forever. The US won't be able to keep up anyway.[16]

The thrust and nuance of Zhihao's analysis was typical of most independent tourists I spoke with. Unlike many group tourists, he had spent enough time observing Taiwan to note that most people in Taiwan have no desire to be annexed by China nor to adopt its political system. But he still supported a goal of eventual unification and believed that Taiwanese would inevitably find that it was in their self-interest to agree with him.

There were exceptions to this narrative, including people who posited that China could learn from Taiwan's media and election system. Some of these reflections were couched in a kind of nostalgia for a pre-communist China. For example, Jing, whom we met earlier, said, "If the ROC still governed China, it would probably be like Taiwan is today—both Chinese and democratic." Another respondent, introduced to me by her American Airbnb host, acknowledged that there might be something culturally novel or distinctive about Taiwan's grassroots democratization: "I've read a little about Taiwan's democratization and also the 228 Incident. Maybe it's because I stayed in the Airbnb of a foreigner and she had this book on her shelf about it and also all these antinuclear banners on the wall. It seems like some Taiwanese are really proud of their political system. It's too bad that some of them use that to think they aren't Chinese or part of China. That's a bit too much. But still, the CCP will probably have to learn from the KMT if it wants to keep power."[17] These last responses are basically consistent with those of Lu and Ping, the Shanghai-based professional couple, who thought that it was in China's long-term interest for Taiwan to stay autonomous and democratic for a few more decades before uniting with China.

Youth Music Culture

Many independent tourists came to Taiwan to explore its pop and other music scenes, which have been popular in China at least since the 1980s (T. Gold 1993). Taiwan's festivals and live music houses quite literally perform culture and politics on a multidimensional stage, affording Chinese visitors an opportunity for more spontaneous and unmediated interaction and engagement than at designated tourist sites. Components of this tourist circuit include Taipei's live music venues; pilgrimages to annual festivals throughout the island, such as Spring Scream in Kenting; and journeys throughout the year to towns like Dulan that are known for local folk music cultures.

Witch House, a small independent music venue and café near National Taiwan University, is a Taipei hot spot noted in a number of online Chinese tourism blogs. According to Bully, the bookings manager, by 2012 the space had become popular with young Chinese independent tourists even during the daytime, when there were no scheduled live performances: "They show up just to take selfies. There are so many of them, we see them all the time now. Every day, really. Probably more come just to take photos than to actually see the shows."[18]

Other popular live music venues included the Wall and Revolver, both located in university districts. Dulan, a much more remote destination, drew a more committed and selective set of music and culture tourists than the capital.

Spring Scream and Spring Wave, held in the southern beach town of Kenting during the national Tomb Sweeping Holiday in early April, are two of Taiwan's best-known annual music festivals. Other draws include electronic music events scheduled throughout the year, such as Earth Fest and Green Ecstasy. Many of the tourists I interviewed at the Kenting events were Chinese university students who came to visit their classmates on exchange at Taiwanese universities and timed their trips around the holiday festivals.

Spring Scream, the longest-running independent rock festival in Taiwan, if not all of Asia, was founded in 1995 by two Taiwan-based American expatriates, Jimi Moe and Wade Davis. Spring Scream catalyzed Kenting's transformation from a sleepy beach village into a tourist destination and helped launch many Mandarin-speaking acts that later became popular in China. Still run by its original founders, although in many ways overshadowed by newer, larger, corporate-sponsored pop or electronic music festivals such as Spring Wave, Spring Scream draws primarily independent Taiwanese bands.

While Spring Scream is not itself an explicitly political event, it and other nodes of Taiwan's independent music scene have long been cultural incubators for political activism, including pro-independence and pro-environmental advocacy. The most famous personal example of musical and political convergence may well be Freddy Lim, the lead singer for the death metal band Chthonic and cofounder of the former Taipei music venue, The Wall (along with Jimi Moe). A cultural and political entrepreneur, Lim founded the Formoz rock festival, staged pro-independence music events in front of the Presidential Office during the Chen Shui-bian presidency, and served as the director of Amnesty International's Taiwan chapter. In 2015, he cofounded the New Power Party with other Sunflower Movement–affiliated figures, won a hotly contested legislative seat in the January 2016 elections, and was reelected in 2020. Another example of the overlap between politics and music is the group Radicalization (Jijin Zhenxian), a music and design collective specializing in pro-independence and pro–direct action clothing and paraphernalia. Its most popular T-shirt—a black background with white bilingual text reading "Fuck the government, Ziji guojia ziji jiu [Save your own country]"—became iconic during the Sunflower Movement. Its products, both authentic and counterfeit, are sold at many street rallies and music festivals, including Spring Scream.

Starting in 2007, Spring Scream took place in a reserved section at Eluanbi Lighthouse, a national park on the southern tip of Taiwan frequently visited by Chinese tourists—my August 2014 "Southern Jiangsu VIP" tour group was no exception. During the festival weekend, about half of the park was roped off for ticketed revelers and guarded by festival staff and volunteers. Tourism proceeded as usual within the rest of the park outside the festival grounds, with the usual assortment of buses, guided groups, and smaller numbers of independent tourists. Of the fifteen tourists I spoke with in the park in 2015, few knew about the festival inside, although they were curious about the excitement and commotion they could hear spilling into the rest of the park.

At one of the festival stages, a punk band led the crowd in a brief "Fuck China!" chant. A few paces away was Radicalization's booth, selling its growing stable of political gear, including a T-shirt whose back read (in English) "Taiwan is not a part of China" and whose front read (in Chinese) "The interior of Taiwan is Nantou" (*Taiwan de neidi shi Nantou*), a political geographic joke that poked fun at Taiwanese performers who, when catering to the China market, refer to China as the "interior" instead of Nantou County, which marks the geographical center of Taiwan Island.[19]

All of the Chinese festival attendees I interviewed were under thirty years old. Many were college students visiting classmates who were on exchange programs in Taiwan. None of them wanted to talk politics, and several of them were confused and disappointed that they had accidentally bought tickets for the older and smaller Spring Scream, the name of which continues to be conflated by the media with all of Kenting's many happenings that holiday weekend, instead of the larger and more pop music-oriented Spring Wave.

Despite the overt political language of some of the performers and booths, the vast majority of music and vending celebrated themes of peace and love and fun and community spirit. All the tourists that I interviewed chose to highlight these gentler qualities of the event and Kenting's beach holiday appeal. For example, Yiming, a twenty-two-year-old male student from Guangzhou who was visiting his Taichung-based schoolmates for spring break, said, "This festival is sort of different than what takes place back in the interior. I can tell that this event has been going on a while. People know each other. It's friendly and safe. People aren't trying to sell me stuff. . . . Well, there's beer, but it's not advertised all over the place, and it's cheap! I don't know. I think this is the real Kenting spirit."[20]

Another respondent, Zhang, observed a kind of "cliquey" quality to Spring Scream's culture and linked this to Taiwan's island geography: "Yes this is fun enough, but I feel like it's hard to really fit in to this festival without playing guitar and singing or something. It's inward-looking, kind of like I feel Taiwan is. Maybe it has something to do with Taiwan being a small island."[21]

Zhang himself came from a wealthy, mobile, and educated family from Guangdong Province and had traveled to Japan, Thailand, and Europe before Taiwan. To him, Taiwan seemed insular and noncosmopolitan, despite the large number of international and expatriate attendees visible at Spring Scream during our interview. Perhaps this view indeed owed to the focus on local culture and identity evident throughout the festival.

At Spring Scream and other music events, few tourists I spoke with explicitly objected to the expression of "local" (*bentu*) sentiment, but at Mono Circus, a small electronic music festival held for the first time in Nantou County in June 2015, I observed a twenty-two-year-old Inner Mongolian male tourist nearly get into a fistfight with festival co-organizers who refused to humor his casual assertion, made over beers, that "We are all Chinese people." My interview with the tourist, who had learned about the festival by a chance meeting with an attendee on a train, turned into an attempt to demonstrate to me that Taiwan has belonged to China since the Ming dynasty.

With Kenting's Spring Scream drawing Chinese tourists across the strait, the "soft power" of Taiwan's music culture industry did not go unnoticed by pro-unification forces. July and August 2015 saw the first "Cross-Strait Youth Scream" event on Guanyinshan beach in Xiamen, Fujian. The website of one of the two organizing agencies, Jiuzhou Culture Broadcasting Center, an outfit run by China's Taiwan Affairs Office and dedicated to "opening cross-strait cultural exchanges," described the event as a "new platform for cross-strait youth to express their love of cross-strait peace, freedom, and trendiness [*ziyou shishang*] and quest for a musical life."[22] The alleged participation of former Taiwan government officials, including an ex-official of the Mainland Affairs Council, drew criticism from Democratic Progressive Party legislators and briefly garnered newspaper headlines in Taiwan (Hung and Yang 2015). None of the Chinese tourists or Taiwanese musicians or fans I interviewed in 2015 had even heard of this event, much less planned to attend it. Meanwhile, the two founders of Spring Scream expressed bemused displeasure on their Facebook pages about yet another unauthorized appropriation of their event name.

An Apolitical Rejoinder: The Banality of Family Visitation

I turn now from the culturally and politically pregnant themes of the previous sections to something more banal but important and understudied: a significant number of independent visitors to Taiwan include relatives of (usually female) Chinese nationals who have married Taiwanese. Strictly speaking, these people were not leisure tourists per se, but on the basis of my repeated trips to Taipei Songshan Airport to conduct randomized interview subject recruitment at different times of day, they represented a considerable number of the people visit-

THE VARIETIES OF INDEPENDENT TOURIST EXPERIENCE

ing under permit regimes designed for independent tourists. There has been little attention paid to these familial visits, although concerns about unauthorized use of independent tourist permits to facilitate travel for other kinds of purposes, including espionage or eventual labor migration, had been raised by politicians and pundits (Cole 2010; V. Chao 2011).

The twelve such visitors that consented to interviews included eight parents and four siblings of Chinese women who had married into Taiwan. The majority of these visitors spent over two weeks in Taiwan, longer than typical leisure tourists, but used little of that time for sightseeing. While all eight of the parents were visiting Taiwan for the first time, they expressed much more interest in spending time with their daughters than in visiting local tourist sites. All of them shared positive impressions of Taiwan, more or less in line with the "warm, friendly, and civilized" themes outlined above. The siblings expressed little interest in moving to Taiwan, let alone much confidence in its economic future. A sixteen-year-old brother offered a typical response: "I'm going to go back to Tianjin to start a trading company. There's a lot more going on back home. It's kind of boring here and not as modern as I expected."[23]

Such visitation is a functional continuation of the mobility reforms of the late 1980s and the 1990s, when both Chinese and Taiwanese administrations finally permitted visitation between family members. However, all of the twelve interviewees used the newer travel permits aimed at independent tourists, which, they explained, were much easier to obtain. In institutional and regulatory terms, this demonstrates another, likely unintentional instrumentality of tourism development—the nominal opening of independent leisure tourism extended and co-opted older forms of permitted travel.

If what they said is taken at face value, then rather than validating the fears of more strident Taiwanese nationalists who fear job loss to Chinese migrant or immigrant workers and the possible growth of a pro-unification voting bloc, these Chinese visitors expressed no desire to stay in or affect Taiwan in any way, apart from visiting their relatives. Their attitude provides an important if mundane counterpoint to the tensions explored in this book—in short, a significant number of Chinese visitors simply did not care all that much about "politics" and were largely indifferent to difference.

The Political Indeterminacy of Independent Tourism

This chapter has recounted and analyzed a diverse set of interview and ethnographic data to extract keywords and themes in the experiences recounted by individual Chinese travelers. Particular themes included Taiwan as "small, fresh, and new"; warm, friendly, and civilized; and free and democratic. Many of these traits and qualities interwove with discussions of Taiwan's Japanese colonial heritage and China's own economic modernization and political development. Such themes were articulated variably, and occasionally explosively, in the spaces of Taiwan's sometimes-radical music culture.

On average, the independent tourists I interviewed expressed a wider range of opinions than group tourists. While the vast majority supported China's claims to Taiwan, several suggested that Taiwan's current de facto independence would be good for both Taiwan and China in the long run, assuming an ultimate trajectory of unification. Several, such as Mingqi in Dulan, were content to allow Taiwanese to determine their own political future. Some independent tourists underwent politically and aesthetically transformative experiences, like Liping, the young art museum volunteer who first learned about dissident artist Ai Weiwei at a Taipei bookstore. Others used Taiwan to imagine an idealized, nostalgic version of a purer Chinese world, like the blogger Han. Some brave younger students entered into the more visceral, messier fray of events like Spring Scream, which mixed the playful appeal of independent music with pro-independence politics.

The territorial narratives of these tourists are diverse and resist easy typologies. On the one hand, even many of those who appreciated Taiwan's current de facto independence still hoped for or assumed the inevitability of unification with China. On the other hand, many of those who expressed the most sympathy or support for Taiwan independence had engaged with Taiwanese friends at music and other cultural events, suggesting that the interpersonal circuits formed through the practice of independent tourism had the capacity for territorial resocialization. That said, it is just as possible that tourists' pre-trip ideologies may have influenced the places and people they chose to visit.

In some of these cases, freed from the constraints of group tourism, independent tourists stepped away from the standard sites and temporarily transcended their tour book itineraries. However, others, including the family tourists interviewed at Songshan Airport, claimed to have barely even left the house and showed little interest in anything distinctively "Taiwanese." Taiwan's heterotopic qualities allowed them to draw from and project a wide variety of territorial imaginaries, which said as much about the tourists themselves and where they came from as it did about Taiwan.

What conclusions can be drawn from this chapter's discussion of the attitudes, behaviors, and travel circuits of independent tourists? Some Taiwan independence advocates have suggested that opening the gates to increased independent tourism would cause security breaches and economic threats. While my research was not designed to uncover such threats, my results suggest that many family visitors cared little about "politics." Meanwhile, there was also scant evidence to support the claims of Ma Ying-jeou and others who suggested that Taiwan's democratic values would somehow be absorbed by Chinese tourists and thereby lead to social and political transformation across the strait.

Independent tourism therefore functions as a disorganized political technology of state territorialization that produces multiple, divergent imaginaries of Taiwan and China. In some cases, it caused what might be termed a territorial resocialization in which tourists changed their pre-trip stances toward Taiwan and even reimagined themselves as different kinds of Chinese subjects. In other cases, it consolidated a Chinese subjectivity and confirmed a priori hopes for territorial "unification," even if it subtly adjusted or deferred the desired timeline or mechanisms for such an outcome.

As for Taiwanese hosts, many said they preferred independent tourists to group tourists and actively avoided group tourist shopping destinations. But others, such as the activist musician, Claire, expressed dismay about the commercial and aesthetic impacts of independent tourists. While such impacts can be observed in the commercial territorializations of the tourist industry anywhere, in the case of Taiwan, it is often still inflected through a politics of opposition to China's territorial claims. Chapter 6 examines how Ma's continued push for China-centric economic policies, including tourism development, did not just trigger the profound renewal of such oppositional politics, but prefigured a radically different future for Taiwan.

WAVES OF TOURISTS, WAVES
OF PROTEST, AND THE END
OF "ONE CHINA"

Between 2008 and 2014, inbound Chinese tourism transformed from a purported breakthrough achievement of the Ma Ying-jeou administration into an unspoken but implicit target of the largest protest in Taiwanese history. This protest, the Sunflower Movement, was sparked by a trade deal with China that included major tourism provisions. What began as a student-led occupation of parliament climaxed with a rally of nearly half a million supporters in front of the Presidential Office, which saw the controversial trade bill successfully quashed and withdrawn from parliament after twenty-four days. Later the same year in Hong Kong, the Umbrella Movement, a call for democratic reforms, grew into a seventy-nine-day street occupation of three different urban sites, making it then the biggest protest movement in Hong Kong's history. Its demands for "genuine universal suffrage" and open elections were not met, but Hong Kong's political society was permanently transformed.

Only two years after these uprisings, the Taiwanese tourism industry staged its own protest of ten thousand participants in the face of a steep drop in Chinese tourism. This decline in tourism was likely directed by the Chinese government in retaliation to the Democratic Progressive Party's (DPP) landslide win in the 2016 presidential and legislative elections. This election represented a decisive rejection of Ma's China-centric policy and accorded with the position advocated by Sunflower activists and their allies. In response to the drop in their revenues, China-oriented tourism industry cartels demanded a financial bailout and called for changes to Taiwan's new cross-strait policy. Their implicit demand was for the new president, Tsai Ing-wen, to accept the 1992 Consensus and the "One China" principle, positions that had become unacceptable to the majority of Taiwanese.

This chapter, informed by participant-observation and interviews conducted from within these protests and election campaigns, traces the wild twists and turns of this dramatic political arc to narrate the wider shifts that took place during and after the ethnographic episodes of chapters 3–5. While a full accounting of the Sunflower and Umbrella Movements and of the political situation in Hong Kong as a whole is beyond the scope of this book, I provide brief overviews here to allow for a cogent and colorful comparative argument.[1]

Although the sovereign status of Hong Kong is fundamentally different from that of Taiwan, the Umbrella Movement was in many ways a response to similar concerns about Chinese political influence. As put by Sunflower activist Chen Wei-ting, "The driving force behind the two movements was the Chinese Communist Party . . . I realize that we are facing similar problems" (Tsoi 2014). The popular slogan "Today Hong Kong, tomorrow Taiwan" exemplified shared concerns and responses. Umbrella activists employed tactics that resembled, outscaled, and outlasted the Sunflower Movement's, even if they did not win any policy concessions. Unique, however, to Hong Kong was a series of protests against Chinese tourists that both preceded and immediately followed the mass movement, suggesting that reactions to tourism can be read as a barometer of public feeling toward mainland China. It also suggests that discontent was fueled in part, as I will argue, by tourism-driven sociopolitical friction.

A central puzzle I address in this chapter is why Chinese tourism was not an overt point of contention for Taiwan's Sunflower Movement but was much more at issue in and around the Umbrella Movement. This may appear counterintuitive at first glance, because the Sunflower Movement was sparked by a trade deal that included major tourism provisions, while the Umbrella Movement's major demands were for universal suffrage and election reforms that had no direct connections to Chinese tourism. This situation makes more sense when contextualized by the variable impacts of Chinese tourism on both destinations, as well as by structural differences in the abilities of Taiwanese and Hong Kongers to determine their own political fate.

The remainder of the discussion examines the implementation and representation of the People's Republic of China's (PRC) retaliatory cuts to outbound tourism, its instrumentalization of Taiwan's tourism industry as a tool of political warfare, and the effects of these campaigns on Taiwan's electorate. I explain how Taiwan's tourism industry protest, which implicitly demanded that Taiwan's new president accept a domestically unpopular "One China" principle, evinced a remarkable geopolitical convergence with China's territorial project, yet failed to sway the outcome of the 2020 election, in which the DPP retained the presidency by an even wider margin.

Chinese Tourism and Taiwan's Sunflower Movement

The rise and fall of cross-strait tourism corresponds with the 2008 beginning and 2016 end of the Ma administration. Ma's early administration instigated a succession of trade deals with China and a rapid increase in Chinese tourism, one of the marquee early "successes" of his China-focused policy. But a few years later, Ma had become notoriously unpopular, and his presidency was left in tatters by a popular revolt against a key policy goal, the passage of the Cross-Strait Services Trade Agreement (hereafter referred to as the Services Trade Agreement). This free trade agreement would have significantly liberalized cross-strait investment and the ownership of politically sensitive sectors, including tourism. Had it been ratified, the agreement would have wrought the biggest structural change to the cross-strait tourism economy since the opening of leisure tourism in 2008.

While the intensity of the public backlash against the Services Trade Agreement was astonishing, it did not come out of nowhere. Ma had ascended to the presidency in an electoral landslide, after eight years of the embattled DPP administration of Chen Shui-bian. However, Ma lost momentum following a series of blunders and the failure of his China-centric policy to tangibly improve Taiwan's economy. He barely won reelection in 2012 against the DPP's Tsai, a legal scholar who served as head of the Mainland Affairs Council (MAC) under Chen and earlier helped negotiate Taiwan's accession to the World Trade Organization under President Lee Teng-hui. By late 2013, even though his approval rating had fallen to just 9 percent, Ma continued to pin his legacy on the consolidation of closer ties with China. During these years, Taiwan's civil society remobilized and built capacity for new nongovernmental organization (NGO) and student-led social movements, which organized uneasily alongside the DPP, sometimes in concert and sometimes in conflict (Ho 2014).

Although Ma promised that economic growth and political stability would follow from the signing of trade deals with China, by 2014 few economic dividends were evident to the majority of Taiwanese, increased tourist numbers notwithstanding. Taipei housing had become unaffordable for many residents (Y.-L. Chen 2015) and new college graduates faced limited job prospects and low salaries (Dou and Luk 2014). Given the Chinese Nationalist Party's (KMT) large parliamentary majority, however, it was hard to anticipate any major policy reorientation. No one could have foreseen that an arcane trade deal would become the flash point.

The Services Trade Agreement was negotiated and signed behind closed doors in Shanghai on July 21, 2013, by representatives from Taiwan's semiofficial agency for cross-strait engagement, the Straits Exchange Foundation, and its Chinese counterpart, the Association for Relations Across the Taiwan Straits. The agreement would have opened eighty sectors of China's economy to Taiwanese investment and sixty-four sectors of Taiwan's economy to Chinese investment, including hotels, tourism, publishing, and medical services. It was one in a series that followed the Economic Cooperation Framework Agreement (ECFA), a deal for increased economic integration between Taiwan and China that had been signed in 2009 (Hsieh 2011). Both ECFA and the Services Trade Agreement were presented by the Ma administration as boons for Taiwan's economy, despite the government's own Chung-Hua Institution for Economic Research estimating in 2013 that the latter would deliver only a 0.025–0.034 percent increase in Taiwan's annual gross domestic product.

The Services Trade Agreement would have allowed an unlimited number of mainland Chinese companies to incorporate sole proprietorships, joint ventures, partnerships, and branches for hotels and restaurants and is designated for "sightseeing" (*guanguang*) purposes. As for travel agencies, it would have permitted China–based companies to establish up to three "commercial presences" within Taiwan, putting them in direct competition with domestic operators. Going in the other direction, the agreement would have permitted an unlimited number of Taiwanese companies to conduct similar activities in mainland China. While permission for an unlimited number of Taiwanese companies to operate in China versus a limit of three Chinese companies to operate in Taiwan may appear advantageous to Taiwan at first glance, the much larger scale and capitalization of China's operators constituted a serious competitive threat to Taiwan's industry. Yet, according to Yao Ta-kuang, the head of the Travel Agent Association of the Republic of China (ROC), Taiwan's tourism trade associations generally supported the agreement because they assumed that more bilateral trade and investment would grow the industry as a whole.[2]

From its inception, critics and activists decried the treaty's secretive negotiation as an example of undemocratic and underhanded politics. They expressed particular concern for the impact that greater Chinese penetration of Taiwan's economy would have on the island's small- and medium-sized businesses, media culture, and freedom of expression. Advocates of Taiwanese sovereignty and democracy argued that this trade bill had ominous implications for national security and self-determination. Others suggested that a deeply unpopular president had no mandate to enact such major legislation. Throughout, Ma himself was the primary target of popular discontent in his capacity not only as ROC president but also as chairman of the KMT, a dual role that empowered him to use his party's internal disciplinary mechanisms to force KMT legislators to support the bill.

Yet, despite such criticisms, and a hunger strike conducted by several DPP members with social activist backgrounds, the general public was not paying much attention yet. Even the DPP leadership had taken an ambiguous stance, beset by internal divisions, lacking a clear cross-strait economic policy agenda, and caught between the clashing interests of capital and grassroots voters. Although the DPP caucus had demanded a thorough review of the Services Trade Agreement, most individual legislators declined to take a strong position against the treaty. Possible conflicts of interest abounded—rumors of personal or business relationships between not only KMT but also prominent DPP figures and Chinese interests were not uncommon, especially about politicians who had proved willing to make compromises to boost industrial sectors including tourism and hospitality (R. Lin 2012a).

This ambivalence began to evaporate on March 17, 2014, the day that KMT legislators reneged on a June 2013 agreement with the DPP to conduct an item-by-item legislative committee review of the Services Trade Agreement. Instead of conducting the procedure as promised, the committee convener unilaterally declared that the review period had already ended after a mere thirty seconds and that the bill would soon be submitted to a plenary session. Had the chamber not been stormed the following evening, it was all but certain that the KMT-dominated legislature would have passed the bill for a signature from President Ma.

On the night of March 18, a motley crew led by activists from the Black Island Nation Youth Front (Heise Daoguo Qingnian Zhenxian), a loosely organized student political action committee formed the previous year, stormed the assembly hall of the Legislative Yuan. The several hundred occupiers repelled police efforts to eject them, escorted out the few officers on duty, and barricaded the doors with seats tied together with rope. The movement found its moniker after a supportive local florist donated a case of fresh sunflowers to the front lines, meant metaphorically to cast light on the opaque "black box" (heixiang) trade deal negotiations.

The broad geopolitical implications of a protest against ostensible KMT collusion with China were not lost on 1989 Tiananmen Square protest leaders Wang Dan and Wu'er Kaixi, both long based in Taiwan, who briefly entered the Legislative Yuan on March 19 to announce their support for the students. Lower-profile figures inside the Legislative Yuan included several locally enrolled students from Hong Kong and mainland China, who had entered the building with their classmates. "Yes, I'm not supposed to be here, but I'm curious what this is all about—this couldn't happen in China!" a nineteen-year-old female finance student from Henan told me on March 20.

The courtyard and streets outside the Legislative Yuan, in central Taipei, soon swelled with supporters and an increasingly sophisticated collection of new student and civic groups, encompassing food distribution networks, provision of blankets and raincoats for nights with cold and wet weather, mobile recharging and Wi-Fi access centers, and free speech zones. Academics from across Taiwan held outdoor classes, and a protester tent city with distinctive neighborhoods mushroomed in the adjacent lanes and alleyways.

Despite the domestic media's initial focus on minor property damage, public opinion quickly swung behind the movement leaders' call for the Services Trade Agreement to be sent back for review, with even pro-blue media outlets such as TVBS polling a majority of Taiwanese as supportive of the movement's goals. Growing popular support empowered occupation leaders to expand their demands. With the legal scholar Huang Kuo-chang and NGO representatives occupying decisive roles in an emergent strategy group, the demand for a review of the Services Trade Agreement extended to a demand for the government to create an oversight body for the public review of all future cross-strait agreements. Huang argued that because existing law, based on an anachronistic ROC constitution, still treated the "Mainland Area" and the "Taiwan Area" as separate jurisdictions within the same country, there was no proper legal procedure for a review of a treaty-like instrument such as the Services Trade Agreement. He maintained that short of writing a new constitution—no easy task—an oversight body would at least draw more public input into the drafting and passage of cross-strait agreements.

After peaking in a massive public rally in front of the Presidential Office on March 30 with approximately five hundred thousand participants, the Sunflower Movement started to wind down on April 6 after Wang Jin-pyng, the Speaker of the Legislative Yuan and a political foe of Ma despite their many shared years of service to the KMT, declared that the contentious bill would not be passed before a supervisory mechanism was put in place, as demanded by movement participants. By April 10, the Sunflower activists inside the legislature cleaned up the chamber and left the building, holding a tightly choreographed public ceremony in the street outside to conclude the occupation and thank their supporters.

Although the DPP took a backseat to the protesters throughout the Sunflower Movement and gave them only tacit support, the party had much to gain from the hobbling of Ma and the KMT. Still unpopular, the KMT soon suffered an unprecedented and perhaps permanently crippling defeat in the "nine in one" midterm local elections on November 29, 2014. Despite ample campaign coffers, KMT mayoral candidates were defeated in their traditional northern strongholds of Taipei, Taoyuan, and Hsinchu, turning the conventional wisdom about Taiwan's electoral geography on its head. Popular DPP incumbents were handily reelected in the south. The DPP earned 47.6 percent of the nationwide vote compared to the KMT's 40.7 percent, not including Taipei, which elected an independent tacitly allied with the DPP-led pan-green coalition, but who maintained a cagey distance, like many of the Sunflower activists who joined in to support his campaign.

The KMT's loss followed the Sunflower Movement and a widespread perception of the disappointing and unevenly distributed economic benefits that had followed from Ma's attempts to hitch Taiwan's wagon to a now slowing Chinese economy, even as the number of Chinese visitors to Taiwan surged (Huang 2014). In the twilight of his presidency, Ma's dream of a "peace treaty" with China based on a "One China" principle disintegrated, especially after China's president Xi Jinping reiterated in September 2014 that "One Country, Two Systems" is the only model for cross-strait political relations acceptable to the PRC. In light of the simultaneous unrest in Hong Kong, a territory intended to showcase the successful implementation of the "One Country, Two Systems" scheme to Taiwan, the two leaders' collective cross-strait efforts may be remembered not as achieving political unification, but rather as the precipitous electoral collapse of the KMT.

Although tourism provisions constituted a major part of the Services Trade Agreement, tourism attracted far less attention from Sunflower activists than provisions regarding other sectors such as publishing, medical services, and telecommunications. In my dozens of formal and informal interviews with activists within and around the Legislative Yuan, few people mentioned tourism as a major motivating factor for their protest participation. Still, the importance of tourism was acknowledged by some of the movement's highest-profile spokespeople. For example, during his court trial on March 25, 2015, protest leader Chen Wei-ting asked, "What would Taiwan be like now if we hadn't organized those protests? All these industries—publishing, telecoms, tourism—would have been bought up by large Chinese interests" (M. Gold 2015).[3]

More potent than the specific effects on tourism or even on more sensitive sectors was a widely shared perception that the legally dubious attempts to pass the trade agreement were an example of the unaccountability and opacity of collusion between the KMT and the Chinese Communist Party (CCP). Sunflower activists characterized party-to-party negotiations and agreements as an existential threat to Taiwan's democracy, de facto independence, and viability as a nation-state. These are of course issues constantly at play in the government's and the tourism industry's ambiguous performances of Taiwan as a part of China.

As opposed to what would unfold later in Hong Kong, it seems fair, however, based on a counterfactual inference, to speculate that the Sunflower Movement and the ensuing political transition may have spared Chinese tourists from the more direct attention of pro-Taiwan independence or anti-China demonstrators. Although Taiwanese nationalists counterdemonstrated against pro-PRC activists at iconic sites such as Taipei 101, they never targeted Chinese tourists with an aggressive direct action campaign. Indeed, Lai Fang-cheng, the convener of the most visible group of independence demonstrators, the Taiwan Independence Revolutionary Army, took pains to represent his group as "sane and dignified" and nonviolent, as noted in chapter 3.

Rather than cast Chinese tourists as (un)witting proxies of the PRC, Sunflower and allied activists directly targeted the policies and legislative maneuvers of the KMT, which they portrayed as aligning with the CCP to the detriment of the Taiwanese people. This approach worked to mobilize students and other members of civil society who might otherwise have remained apathetic or weakly supportive of the DPP, whose politicians had taken an ambiguous stance toward cross-strait economic policy, in part due to considerations of their constituents' business interests.

Therefore, in a paradoxical fashion, by indirectly stoking the fears of activists, tourism's political instrumentality (as manifest in the Services Trade Agreement) and the post-Ma drop in inbound Chinese tourism arguably neutralized the potential for tourism to provoke direct street conflict between activists and Chinese visitors. As suggested by the following case of Hong Kong, if popular support for the Sunflower Movement had not put the brakes on Ma's cross-strait policy, it is not unlikely that frustrated activists may have targeted Chinese tourists as an outlet for frustrations about Taiwan's trajectory vis-à-vis China.

"Today Hong Kong, Tomorrow Taiwan"? A Comparison and Conjuncture

"Today Hong Kong, tomorrow Taiwan" was a slogan that, although coined before the Sunflower Movement, spread ever more vigorously during the occupation as a warning to Taiwanese civil society. It implied that the "One Country, Two Systems" scheme—a PRC policy framework originally developed to apply to Taiwan but implemented first in Hong Kong and Macao (Cooney 1997)—would not serve Taiwan's interest (Tsoi 2014). The phrase popped up on stickers throughout the indoor and outdoor spaces of the Sunflower Movement, was exhorted during talks and lectures in free speech zones, and debated in popular media outlets. The slogan found renewed purchase a few months later during the 2014 Umbrella Movement.

The Umbrella Movement was triggered by the Beijing authorities' August 2014 refusal to permit civil nominations for the election of the chief executive of the

Hong Kong Special Administrative Region. This decision denied Hong Kong voters the ability to freely elect their own leaders, forcing them to choose instead between three candidates preselected by a committee that was ultimately controlled by the leadership in Beijing. The decision darkened an already gloomy political and economic mood, encapsulated by a popular song and spin-off slogan, "The city is dying, you know." A "declinist culture meme," this song sprang from the hit local television show *When Heaven Burns* and proliferated throughout spaces of resistance well before the advent of the Umbrella Movement (Garrett 2013a, 115). The show's theme song was adopted as the anthem of the Anti–Moral and National Education Campaign (Huang and Rowen 2015), a student-led protest in 2012 against CCP-directed Chinese nationalist indoctrination, before reappearing during the Umbrella Movement.

It is remarkable that a place with as dense and vigorous a human landscape as Hong Kong could have already then been said to be dying, especially given the "Chinese tourist wave" (Siu, Lee, and Leung 2013) that had hit the city, which brought over a quarter billion arrivals of Chinese tourists after 2003. But the concentrated economic gains extracted from skyrocketing property values and blockbuster sales of milk powder and other commodities to mainland Chinese visitors were tainted by widespread fears about threats to Hong Kong's culture and quality of life. Instead of thanking China for this "gift," many locals instead complained of rising prices and trashed public spaces (Siu, Lee, and Leung 2013).

Furthermore, like Taiwan, Hong Kong faced rising income inequality, and young activists and international diplomats (Bush 2014) alike speculated that collusion between local oligarchs and the CCP might be driving these political and economic woes. Hong Kong was among the most unequal economies in the world (Hu and Yun 2013) by many measures, including a 2011 Gini coefficient of 0.537—well above the 0.4 marker used by analysts to suggest the potential for social unrest. Activists seized on these fears to galvanize street-level and electoral campaigns for more autonomy and social justice measures (Garrett 2013b; Garrett and Ho 2014).

These calls coincided with small protests staged against Chinese tourists in popular shopping districts, as well as widely circulated graphic depictions of these tourists as locusts raiding Hong Kong's limited resources (Garrett and Ho 2014). Nativist and localist movements thus rippled out in greater force as the "Chinese tourist wave" broke over Hong Kong. They included diverse ideological elements, including nascent ethnonationalism and independence advocacy, as well as calls for structural economic adjustments and enhanced social welfare programs (Veg 2017). These protests drew a significant amount of official opprobrium and media condemnation despite their relatively low attendance (Garrett 2014).

A manifesto of sorts, read by some protesters and vociferously criticized by Hong Kong's administration, had been Lingnan University professor Chin Wan's book *On the Hong Kong City-State* (2011). Chin's book, which called explicitly for Hong Kong independence, treated Chinese tourists and migrants as the most significant threat to the territory's society and institutions. Chin's analysis is especially remarkable for its concern that democratic reforms within China would actually work against the possibility of increased autonomy for Hong Kong, as such reforms would likely take a populist-nationalist turn and accelerate the "mainlandization" of Hong Kong, making Hong Kong not only economically and politically but also culturally indistinct from the rest of China. This is a strikingly different interpretation than that of Taiwan's Ma administration, which argued that cross-strait tourism would promote democracy in China and therefore somehow serve Taiwan's interests.[4]

City University of Hong Kong professor Thomas Cheng concurred that tourism and the backlash against it was part and parcel of the emergence of "radical politics" in Hong Kong, even if he did not share Chin's concerns about democratization in the PRC:

> Naturally when more than 40 million tourists from Mainland China visit Hong Kong every year, the territory becomes very crowded, causing resentment among the locals. While tourism is a major pillar of the economy, most Hong Kong people do not feel they have benefitted directly from it. Instead they believe that this influx has caused considerable inconveniences. Commercial premises in districts most frequented by tourists tend to command higher rents, driving up prices and forcing the relocation of small businesses serving the locals. Mainland tourists' massive purchases of baby formula caused a shortage of supply for mothers with infants, resulting in an uproar and embarrassment for the HKSAR [Hong Kong Special Administrative Region] government. Some Hong Kong people are upset that workers at expensive luxury goods outlets treat Mandarin-speaking customers better. (J. Cheng 2014, 219)

Prior to the Umbrella Movement, these tensions manifested in various contentious episodes, including the "Liberation of Sheung Shui," a protest that targeted not only individual leisure tourists but also the so-called parallel traders (*shui huo*), mainland Chinese smugglers who used tourist permits to enter Hong Kong in order to purchase commodities for resale in China. This vigorous trade led to product shortages and price increases for area residents. In fact, the parallel traders of Sheung Shui, an area near the mainland border, were the first to be called "locusts" by the local press (Bad Canto 2012). The "liberation" was carried out by a loosely organized group of people, first acquainted online, who later met in person to make placards and shout slogans while marching through Sheung Shui shopping centers. The event provoked significant state opprobrium for the display of the British flag by some participants, which Beijing-friendly media outlets portrayed as a direct insult to the legitimacy of PRC rule over the former British colony. Other similar actions followed on Canton Road, in a more central location frequented by wealthier mainland shoppers (Garrett 2014).

Beyond the sincere calls for universal suffrage and genuine democracy, much of the affective force of the Umbrella Movement was indeed stoked by fears of "mainlandization." Indeed, the vast majority of young protesters I interviewed while I resided within the occupation zones opposed what they explicitly described as the cultural and political "mainlandization" of Hong Kong. They supported increased political autonomy and even independence in many cases. Many protesters appreciated the sense of linguistic familiarity and cultural kinship they felt in the protest zones. For example, a twenty-six-year-old journalist said, "It's nice to be here with each other, with just Hong Kong people. I don't think I've heard so much pure Cantonese in weeks," as we sat together folding origami umbrellas. "This is like the Hong Kong of my youth," agreed a forty-five-year-old salon worker. She clarified that she was referring not only to the high proportion of "locals" but also to the general everyday qualities of civility, order, and hygiene that she did not associate with mainland China.

Despite this, demonstrators generally treated the occasional visitor from mainland Chinese to the occupation zones with a mix of excitement, ambivalence, and guarded respect. The Umbrella Movement, as well as the resumption of anti-tourist protests, thus demonstrated that mainland tourism to Hong Kong had prompted a dual dilemma for the CCP's territorial program—not only did it spark resistance, but for a time it even threatened to incorporate a few brave tourists into its multiplying protests.

Once the brief window of cultural openness and possibility for cross-border solidarity pried open by some Umbrella demonstrators had closed, anti-tourist actions quickly recommenced, including new "liberations" of shopping areas closer to the mainland border, including the New Territories neighborhoods of Yuen Long, Tuen Mun, and Sha Tin. These were bolstered by the emergence of several new nativist or localist groups, including Hong Kong Indigenous, as well as the increased popularity that other allied localist groups like Civic Passion had gained through their participation in the occupation sites. Hong Kong Indigenous was in fact formed by two Umbrella activists who described the movement and its nonviolent tactics as a "complete and utter failure" (Tsoi and Wong 2016). In this respect, the Umbrella Movement, coupled with the unyielding response of the CCP and Leung Chun-ying's administration, contributed to the further polarization and radicalization of Hong Kong society, which looked set to escalate with further increases in tourism.

After the Umbrella Movement, some CCP-allied Hong Kong lawmakers noticed such tensions and took steps to address them. At a March 2015 meeting of the National People's Congress in Beijing, Michael Tien, a leader (with Regina Ip) of the pro-Beijing New People's Party, observed: "It started out as a so-called congestion problem, crowd problem, tourism problem. It has now escalated to become a political problem, because those who object to the scheme are chanting slogans of wanting independence. That is a very different matter; it has now alerted the highest echelons" (Sim 2015). Several weeks later, China's Ministry of Public Security announced that residents in Shenzhen, neighboring Hong Kong, would be restricted to one visit to Hong Kong per week, as a measure to curb parallel trading (Li and Lin 2015).

Although the CCP showed some willingness to mitigate tourism impacts, it continued to squeeze Hong Kong civil society and democracy advocates by reinterpreting the Basic Law to retroactively disqualify newly elected legislators on the grounds of being insufficiently patriotic. Many activists were imprisoned for various offenses, including student activist Nathan Law, the youngest legislator to be elected in Hong Kong's history, who was jailed for his role in the Umbrella Movement. What became known as mainlandization thus accelerated after the Umbrella movement ended, with tourism-related tensions again serving as both barometer and proximate cause.

The mainlandization of Hong Kong was observed closely by Taiwanese before, during, and after the Umbrella Movement.[5] Early in the Umbrella Movement, Sunflower activists demonstrated in solidarity with their Hong Kong counterparts.[6] After student demonstrators in Hong Kong were met with police tear gas on September 28, 2014, Taiwanese activists, including Sunflower icon Chen Wei-ting, stormed the Hong Kong trade office in Taipei. They decried police brutality and demanded a halt to all talks with China. They and 1989 Tiananmen Square protest veterans later staged demonstrations in Liberty Square. Lau Ka-yee, a women's rights activist from Hong Kong, told the crowd, "Taiwanese often say that today's Hong Kong will be tomorrow's Taiwan. However, I think: 'Today's Hong Kong is today's Taiwan' is closer to the truth. People need to gain a sense of urgency" (Lii 2014). Several Taiwanese activists soon flew to Hong Kong to demonstrate in solidarity, and many Hong Kong activists expressed support for Taiwan's social movements to me in interviews. "If this doesn't work, maybe we'll try to emigrate to Taiwan," was a half-serious refrain I heard directly from many Umbrella activists after I arrived in Hong Kong on September 30.

Sunflower leader Lin Fei-fan's reflection on the Umbrella Movement, published in *Foreign Policy* as "Today's Hong Kong, Today's Taiwan" (2014), encapsulated the concerns of many Taiwanese and also noted the role of tourism:

> The main goal of the "one country, two systems" policy by which China governs Hong Kong is to provide a template for Taiwan, but the developments of recent years clearly show China placing increasingly tight restrictions on Hong Kong's self-governance. It's not just that China has reneged on its promise that Hong Kong's system would remain "unchanged for 50 years." A more serious problem is that conflicts within Hong Kong society have proliferated. The wealth disparity there cannot be solved via existing structures, and the huge influx of mainland tourists, as well as mainlanders who become Hong Kong residents, have also created even more social problems. Taiwan faces similar concerns. We have seen that Taiwan and the Chinese government have signed a number of trade agreements exposing Taiwan to industrial outsourcing, falling salaries, increases in the disparity between rich and poor, national security risks, and other crises.

In this passage, Lin nods toward Hong Kong's problems with Chinese tourism, implying that Taiwan could face similar social strife.

Yet, apart from a raft of critical reports on social and popular media, Taiwan saw little to no specifically anti-Chinese tourist activism. There are spatial factors at play, such as Taiwan's much greater land area, meaning that far fewer tourists were spread out over a far larger range and caused relatively less disruption to the everyday lives of residents. A further factor is institutional and geopolitical: it is easy to speculate that, without the social pressure-release valve of the Sunflower Movement and the institutional capacity for reform and redirection soon exercised via the ballot box—and, for better or worse, the ensuing drop in inbound Chinese tourism—some radical Taiwanese activists would have followed their Hong Kong counterparts and targeted Chinese tourists as proxies for the PRC and the KMT.

The DPP Wins and the Tourism Industry Gets Weaponized

The DPP swept to victory in the November 2014 midterm and January 2016 general elections, winning not only the presidency but, for the first time ever, a legislative majority with 68 out of 113 total seats. They were complemented by five seats won by the New Power Party, which had grown out of the Sunflower Movement and espoused a more strident pro-independence and social justice platform.

The DPP's landslide came on the heels of eight years of an extraordinarily unpopular Ma administration that had championed tourism from China, emphasized the "Chinese" in the ROC and the KMT, and attempted to recover an anachronistic legal representation of the ROC as sovereign over all of China. The popularity of the Sunflower Movement, the failure to pass the Services Trade Agreement, and the election of Tsai and a DPP-majority legislature signified Taiwan's shift away from political and economic reliance on China and toward the development of relations with other territories.

Tsai, the DPP chair, had campaigned on a cautious approach to cross-strait issues, positioning her somewhere in the middle of the China-centric economic policy of Ma and the more assertively pro-independence stance of Chen Shuibian in his second term. Tsai consistently promised to "maintain the [cross-strait] status quo," which implied support for maintaining the Chinese tourist trade. At a travel industry event in September 2015, Tsai had vowed not to limit tourist numbers, stating, "Many people think the DPP does not welcome Chinese tourists. This is definitely not true." She did call for improved tour quality and a proportional increase in independent tourist arrivals, a position that was fairly similar to that of the KMT (Yeh et al. 2015).

Tsai's moderate stance suggested that the PRC's deployment of tourism as a political and economic incentive for cooperation—as well as a tactical threat— had already achieved some degree of consolidation. Indeed, it had already proved effective even with local DPP politicians. For example, Kaohsiung mayor Chen Chu, who had been imprisoned decades earlier for participation in pro-democracy movements (Jacobs 2012), visited China in 2013 in part to stimulate more tourist arrivals after the earlier slowdowns. The year prior to Chen's visit, about 60 percent of international tourists in Kaohsiung had come from China, twice as high a percentage as the 2012 national average (R. Lin 2012a). Chen's trip was motivated by previous controversies, which implicated tourists and the travel industry. In 2009, following a visit from the Dalai Lama and the Kaohsiung Film Festival's screening of a documentary about exiled Uyighur leader Rebiya Kadeer, who the PRC had labeled a terrorist, Chinese tourist numbers collapsed. Occupancy rates at Kaohsiung hotels dropped from 60 percent to 30 percent, and department store and restaurant revenues plummeted. This led to "heavy pressure from local tourism operators" on Mayor Chen (M. Chan 2013). Taiwanese legislators and leaders launched a goodwill tour to court back the industry, and local officials cut public funding for the Kaohsiung Film Festival as a sign of contrition (R. Lin 2012b).

Although Tsai declared her support for Chinese tourism, she did not champion it in the same way that Ma had. On the contrary, after her election, she suggested that Taiwan should diversify its economic focus beyond China, and her transition team quickly began exploring trade agreements with other countries, including Japan. Tsai also developed the New Southbound Policy, renewing an earlier Lee-era initiative to promote bilateral trade and investment with Southeast Asian nations, and loosened travel restrictions for inbound tourists from a number of countries in the region.

Meanwhile, rumors swirled that Chinese authorities would cut outbound tourist numbers in retaliation for the Taiwanese electorate voting in the DPP. Sowing confusion over the cause and conduct of the cuts seemed to be part of the strategy. The likelihood of such diffuse yet direct retaliatory measures had been communicated earlier to me by a former high-level Ma cabinet official, who preferred to remain anonymous.[7] According to Wu Pi-lian, a committee member in the Travel Quality Assurance Association and president of Cheng An Travel Service, Chinese tourism companies were not given direct commands, but had been led to "infer the implicit orders" of government officials, according to a March 5, 2016, report in *China Post*:

> "According to what we know, their superiors would, after completing half a thought, say, 'Do you understand what I mean?' And the listeners would say, 'Yes, we do,'" Wu said. During the meetings, provincial-level government officials and the tour operators had reached an understanding over the details of the plan through the use of applause, she said. "The authorities would say something like, 'What are you thinking in terms of numbers? What is more reasonable?' And the people listening would not dare to name a number," Wu said. "(The officials would say,) 'Do you think that 800 is reasonable?' And no one would reply. Then the officials would say, 'If you think that this is feasible, let us have a round of applause.'" (E. Lin 2016)

Other travel agents corroborated this story. For example, Ko Mu-chou, head of Sunrise Travel Service, confirmed that his Chinese industry partners revealed that their respective provincial government authorities had instructed them to limit group tours. One unnamed province's tourism bureau had initially allowed each agency to send ten to thirty group tours monthly, but reduced that range to only one to three groups by December 2015, according to a report published December 23, 2015, in the online outlet *Initium*. Roget Hsu, the former secretary-general of Taiwan's Travel Agent Association, was quoted in an October 26, 2016, report by Voice of America Chinese as saying that in January of that year, Chinese travel agencies had "verbally informed" Taiwan travel agencies that they "would be limiting the number of tourists, and the number of Chinese group tours [would] be cut by one-quarter or one-third. Not only that, the number of independent tourists would also be affected."

The rumors prompted concern from government officials and industry leaders and ultimately a denial from both the Taiwan Tourism Bureau and Chinese authorities. Tourist numbers had undeniably dropped ahead of the election, but a Beijing official attributed this to tourists choosing to stay away due to the "highly politicized atmosphere," according to a Reuters report from January 13, 2016. Whether this particular episode was due to tourist "choice" or state or corporate policy is hard to determine conclusively. Other tensions notwithstanding, the drop was not unlike those that preceded earlier presidential elections, during which tourist numbers were kept down and return flights from China to Taiwan were heavily discounted, leading to broad speculation that the CCP was encouraging China-based Taiwanese businesspeople to return home to vote, presumably for the KMT (J. Kastner 2011).

Tourist numbers had in fact rebounded somewhat by late January, shortly after the election, and the Tourism Bureau publicly claimed that China was not officially cutting tourist numbers (Chen, Shu, and Wu 2016). Taiwan Affairs Office (TAO) spokesperson An Fengshan said in a February 2016 press conference that the initial drop in Chinese tourists was due to "market behavior [*shichang xingwei*]" and that further steps would depend on the "development of cross-strait relations and market changes."[8] However, the TAO's attribution of apolitical "market behavior" to China's tourism cuts became utterly untenable after Tsai's May 20, 2016, inauguration speech, which acknowledged the "historical fact" of the 1992 talks between ROC and PRC representatives but accepted neither the "One China" principle nor the 1992 Consensus. Tsai's speech was heavily criticized in the Chinese media. In the following two months, the Taiwan Tourism Bureau recorded a drop of 30 percent in Chinese group tour arrivals.

Although Chinese officials initially played coy about the cause and conduct of the cuts, China's TAO later blamed the Tsai administration. "Whoever caused the situation should end it," said the office's spokesperson Ma Xiaoguang on September 14, 2016. By that time, the number of Chinese group tourists dropped by 51.2 percent and total Chinese tourist arrivals were down by 36 percent compared to the same period the previous year, according to the Taiwan Tourism Bureau (Wu 2016). By February 7, 2017, TAO spokesperson An averred that for Taiwan not to recognize the 1992 Consensus had harmed the "vital interests [*qieshen liyi*]" of people on both sides of the strait—especially Taiwan's—because the number of Chinese tourists to Taiwan was steadily declining. A reporter noted that the number of Chinese tourists to Taiwan hit a new low even as Taiwan authorities relaxed travel restrictions on individual tourists. To that, An responded that there had indeed been a decline in the number of Chinese tourists to Taiwan, "and the reason for the decline in figures is clear for the world to see" (Liu and Hou 2017).[9]

Well before the TAO clarified its position, Taiwan's government had already anticipated the drop and prepared a response. In an interview published by the *Washington Post* on July 21, 2016, President Tsai said, "We do witness reductions in [the] quantity [of Chinese tourists], but overall, we are still evaluating the impacts brought upon the tourism industry. However, on the whole, we also hope for higher diversity in the source of tourists . . . our tourism industry will be developed into a more diverse model that suits tourists from different sources and adapts to different tourists." While China-focused tourism entrepreneurs worried loudly, some other observers suggested that the shifts would turn out for the wider public's benefit. "At present, the benefits of Chinese tourists in traveling to Taiwan are not shared with the majority but are instead concentrated in the hands of the minority," observed the tourism scholar Chen Junan in a report published on March 7, 2016, by BBC Chinese.[10]

The DPP administration decided to target Southeast Asian tourists via the New Southbound Policy and prepared emergency bridge loans of 30 billion NTD (US$960 million) for travel agents affected by the cuts. Still, party leaders noted an apparently coordinated campaign to use tourism for political ends. At the September 8, 2016, Taiwan Tourism Forum, Tsai Chi-chang, deputy Speaker of the Legislative Yuan, said, "For quite some time, Chinese tourists have been used as an instrument of China's United Front tactics. Although we've had constant reminders of this, it still goes on."[11]

News of the cuts rippled throughout popular and social media, with high-profile international outlets like the *New York Times* and *Time* magazine quoting vendors who complained of disappearing tour groups. It seemed that not only the cuts but also the ensuing media spin was part of the play. Stories in Chinese state-controlled media, including a May 26, 2016, report from Xinhua, depicted Taipei taxi drivers as suffering severely from the cuts and quoted several who demanded that Tsai Ing-wen accept the 1992 Consensus to save their livelihoods.

On September 12, 2016, over ten thousand tourism workers took to the streets of Taipei for a first-ever industry protest. The event was organized and publicized by a variety of industry groups, including the Tourism Industry Self-Help Association, the Mainland Tourist Bus Drivers Alliance, the Travel Agent Association, and even the Taiwan Beef Noodle Soup Association. I joined them for the walk from the Huashan 1914 cultural district to the Presidential Office, donning their free stenciled white T-shirt and white hat to stave off the light rain. Like their slogans on the hats and shirts, their printed placards focused on livelihood issues: "We want jobs, we want to survive, we want food on our tables!"

and "No job, no life." In addition to tax relief, their list of twelve demands included the elimination of entry permit fees for Chinese tourists and permit-free entry for short transit stays of under seventy-two hours.

Preprinted banners stopped short of calling for the "One China" principle, but the language on them implied ethnonational affinity if not unity: "The two sides (across the Taiwan Strait) belong to the same family" (*Liang'an, yi jia qin*). Taipei mayor Ko Wen-je, who had initially been supported by many Sunflower activists, later employed a similar phrase to pursue relations with PRC city leaders.

Every single protest participant I queried directly—over twenty people, including guides, drivers, and office staff—insisted that their primary goal was to press Tsai to accept the "One China" principle and the 1992 Consensus in order to rescue their industry. They said that they and their colleagues did not print such positions on the signs or call for them in the speeches because they did not want to appear "too political."

The protest was extensively covered within China, with the following account, published on September 13 on the *Global Times* website, a representative example:

> Mr Hsin Jin-Long, the Chairman of the Mainland Tourist Drivers Alliance, said that for drivers like him who specialize in ferrying Mainland tour groups, it is really difficult to make ends meet, with some drivers not even having a single tour group in a month. He said: "There is only one problem in the tourism industry now, and that is the 1992 Consensus." Towards Tsai Ing-Wen, he asked: "Is accepting the 1992 Consensus that difficult? Is it more important than the livelihoods of people?"
>
> Another driver with more than 10 years' experience, Mr Chang Guo-Chun said that, previously, there were at least seven to eight Mainland tour groups each month. Now, there is only one group once every few months. He said: "Nobody knows where the next group is. I can't even afford to buy cigarettes."

Despite all the noise, the industry's position began and remained firmly in the national minority. A May 2016 poll by Taiwan Think Tank found that over 78 percent of respondents suggested that Taiwan's government should increase tourism from other countries rather than accept the 1992 Consensus. Only 13.5 percent supported the 1992 Consensus. Well after the protests, by late 2017, a poll conducted by the Cross-Strait Policy Association suggested that Tsai's stance, to "maintain the status quo" but not accede to the 1992 Consensus, remained the most popular position of any major Taiwanese politician.

While China's cuts certainly hurt the livelihood of Taiwanese tour guides and drivers and imperiled the many hastily constructed hotels that had mushroomed during the Ma-era Chinese tourist boom, the majority of Taiwan's economy remained non-reliant on tourism. That this cross-strait media storm occurred despite tourism's relatively small contribution to Taiwan's economy underscored its uncanny political salience: even at its peak in 2015, tourism (including government spending and revenues from all sending regions, *including* domestic) only accounted for 1.8 percent of Taiwan's gross domestic product, ranking Taiwan 163rd out of 184 surveyed countries (World Travel and Tourism Council 2016).

In the meantime, the drops emboldened online activists and designers to unleash a flurry of satirical ads that celebrated the disappearance of Chinese tourists. "Welcome to Taiwan, without Chinese!" read the captions on a series of photos of idyllic, people-free landscapes first released on the PTT online bulletin board system. The memes quickly went viral, prompting Tourism Bureau deputy director general Wayne Liu to disavow them as not official. Liu explained in a public statement: "Tourism is a happy industry, and it should use positive ways to promote Taiwan. Otherwise, it would only harm Taiwan."

While the overall economic impact of Tsai's New Southbound Policy will be debated for years to come, its tourism measures appear to have played a major part in compensating for the drop in Chinese visitors, at least in terms of total tourist arrivals if not total spending, which remains impossible to accurately estimate. "Taiwan will maintain its policy of welcoming mainland Chinese tourists . . . but due to political factors that impact mainland tourists coming to Taiwan, our government will plan for the worst and prepare for the best," said Chiu Chui-cheng, deputy minister of the MAC, at a news briefing in late December 2016. Likely due to reductions in visa restrictions, the establishment of new air routes, and the promotion of targeted marketing campaigns, visitation from Thailand grew by 57 percent, Vietnam by 34 percent, and the Philippines by 24 percent from 2015 to 2016. Visitors from Japan and Korea grew by 16 percent and 34 percent, respectively, according to the Taiwan Tourism Bureau online database. Despite the drop in Chinese tourist arrivals, Taiwan received nearly 10.7 million total visitors in 2016, an increase from 10.4 million in 2015.

Many travel agency representatives and commentators remained nonplussed by this market shift. During the September 2016 protest, Taiwan's Travel Agent Association spokesperson Ringo Lee said, "Even if the number of tourists from South Korea increases by 100 percent, it could still not make up for the 5 or 10 percent decrease in the number of tourists from the Chinese mainland" (Tan 2016). Others suggested that Chinese tourists spend much more—as much as twice the amount—as their Southeast Asian counterparts. Such claims continued echoing for months in Chinese state media. For example, in a report published on May 20, 2017, Xinhua quoted National Chengchi University professor Chiu Kunshuan: "The increase in the number of Southeast Asian tourists cannot make up the gap left by Chinese mainland tourists, but the DPP is ignoring this state of affairs and argues that the 'quality' of tourism has increased and the air has become cleaner with fewer mainland visitors. This kind of attitude is worrying."

Tourism and the Fiery Crash of the 1992 Consensus

On July 18, 2016, only a few months after the election, a drunk Taiwanese tour bus driver set his vehicle on fire, killing himself, the guide, and twenty-four Chinese tourists. The image of the inferno was indelible. The story received nearly around-the-clock news coverage. The bodies of eight tourists were found crowding near the emergency exit, which had been locked, a common but illegal practice to prevent thefts. Coming in the middle of a media storm about the drastic drop in inbound tourist numbers, the tragedy triggered a cross-strait and domestic reckoning about tourist affairs.

Before the cause of the blaze was determined, commentators speculated that the rushed itineraries of cut-rate cartelized tours might have fatigued the driver and led to safety risks. Tour buses were thoroughly inspected for safety across the island. The *Global Times*, a Chinese tabloid, warned in an editorial, "If Taiwan does not seriously reflect and improve, mainland Chinese tourists would be playing with their lives if they go there again." China's TAO activated an emergency response mechanism and sent a team to Taiwan. "We are highly concerned with the life and property safety of our . . . compatriots," said spokesperson Ma Xiaoguang (Mckirdy 2016).

As inbound tourism continued dropping, a team of eight mayors from the KMT's pan-blue coalition soon went to China on a "self-help relief" mission (*zili jiuji*). They reached agreements with Chinese officials and tour companies to market trips only to counties and cities that elected KMT or KMT-aligned politicians who had avowed their support for the 1992 Consensus. Dividing Taiwan into a strange half-donut shape, the "1992 Consensus tour" would by necessity begin in Taoyuan, now administered by a DPP mayor but still the site of the airport, then head over the central mountains to the blue stronghold of Hualien for a trip to Taroko Gorge, before cutting back north to New Taipei City but not Taipei City, which despite no longer being run by a KMT leader, still featured a number of the most "Chinese" sites, like the National Palace Museum. It would then go to central Nantou County before swinging through Changhua on the way back to the airport.[12] These so-called blue tours did not find much of a market, according to my queries with their Taiwanese ground handlers, but their very existence indicates that tourism was, for a time, producing two Taiwans in yet another sense.

The political potential of 1992 Consensus–based tourism realized its last gasp in the November 2018 nine-in-one local elections, when the KMT trounced the DPP in multiple mayoral races. Most surprising was the loss of the longtime pan-green stronghold of Kaohsiung to charismatic former legislator Han Kuo-yu, who campaigned even more aggressively on the promise of China's riches, particularly via tourism, than Ma Ying-jeou had. His key slogan emphasized the potential benefit of the traffic of not only commodities *to* but bodies *from* China: "Goods go out, people come in, Kaohsiung gets rich" (*Huo chu de qu, ren jin de lai, Gaoxiong fa da cai*). Repeatedly intoning this slogan, which rhymes in Mandarin, Han's campaign pinned Kaohsiung's fortunes to the tourism trade.

Even before Han took office, tourist attractions, hotels, and taxis noted a significant uptick in business. "Sentiment seems to have returned after the midterm election," said the chairman of the Kaohsiung Association of Travel Agents, who predicted the imminent resumption of charter flights for Chinese group tourists, as quoted in a January 13, 2019, story in the *Nikkei Asian Review*. Two months later, in March, China TAO spokesperson An Fengshan announced that tourists would be encouraged to travel to Kaohsiung. In a press conference that May, his colleague Ma Xiaoguang said, "After last year's nine-in-one elections, with more and more county and city mayors expressing support for the 1992 Consensus, mainland tourists to Taiwan are an obvious indicator of warming [relations]."[13]

The DPP's fortunes looked dismal after its poor performance in the midterm elections. It was Xi Jinping himself who inadvertently tossed the party a lifeline by insisting in a speech on January 1, 2019, that the best way to uphold the "One China" notion of the 1992 Consensus was to implement a "One Country, Two Systems" approach similar to that of Hong Kong. Tsai nimbly responded to Xi's blunt and apparently tone-deaf approach by asserting, with wide popular support, that Taiwan would never accept a "One Country, Two Systems" arrangement.

Han went on to clinch the KMT nomination for the presidency, but the supposed post-midterm election "warming" period for and through tourism proved short-lived. China's Ministry of Tourism and Culture announced that it would stop issuing permits to residents of forty-seven different Chinese cities to travel to Taiwan. In an online statement, the ministry implicitly blamed its move on the Tsai administration: "In view of the current cross-strait situation, such visits will be temporarily restricted until further notice." Taiwan's MAC responded by condemning Beijing's "breaking the travel agreement made between people on the two sides of the Taiwan Strait. . . . We deeply regret the unilateral suspension of individual visits and free travel by mainland tourists to Taiwan." The move, in line with the previous failed ban on individual tourism in 2016, seemed designed to support the KMT through the usual carrot-and-stick approach. "If Han Kuo-yu wins, I am sure the mainland will immediately resume the visa applications," said Lin Chinfa, the former chairman of the Beijing chapter of the Association of Taiwan Investment Enterprises on the Mainland (Chung, Zuo, and Lo 2019).

The promise of profits from Chinese tourism was one of the few inducements left in the KMT's electioneering arsenal. It proved wholly insufficient to compensate for Han's plummeting popularity, which followed widespread fatigue with his erratic and populist style, a series of personal scandals, and the incongruity of his platform with broader domestic and regional transformations. Fortuitously timed for Tsai and the DPP was Hong Kong activists' resumption and escalation of protest against the Beijing government, triggered by the near passage of a law to extradite accused criminals to the mainland, aggravated by police brutality, and later expanded to include renewed demands for genuine universal suffrage. These protests again coincided with further actions against parallel traders. Fearing prosecution or worse, dozens of Hong Kong activists fled to Taiwan on tourist visas, provoking a discussion within Taiwan about the constitutionality of offering them political asylum. In the meantime, the special administrative region's plight became a regular talking point for Tsai and her party.

As the number of Chinese tour groups and independent visitors continued crashing ahead of the January 11, 2020, presidential and legislative elections, their presence was partially replaced by politically minded visitors from Hong Kong, who arrived to witness elections and use them as an opportunity to amplify their own demands for democratic reform. "I'm a Hong Konger. Thanks to Taiwan for being a model. We also want universal suffrage," was the message on one of many placards held high by mask-wearing black-clad demonstrators near DPP headquarters.

Hong Kong protest imagery lit up the DPP's final election eve rally. The stage flashed the slogan "Hong Kong to Taiwan is not far, one ticket away. Taiwan to Hong Kong is not far, one ballot away" (*Xianggang li Taiwan bu yuan, yi zhang jipiao de juli. Taiwan li Xianggang bu yuan, yi zhang xuanpiao de juli*). As photographs of Hong Kong protesters appeared on-screen, Tsai announced, "The young people of Hong Kong have used their lives, blood and tears to demonstrate to us that one country, two systems is not feasible. Tomorrow it is our young people's turn to show them that the values of democracy and freedom can overcome all difficulties." Scores of Hong Kongers in the crowd, whether on temporary tourism permits or seeking long-term asylum, shouted their support and solidarity.

The next day, Tsai was reelected by the largest margin in Taiwanese electoral history, and the DPP retained its majority in the legislature. Scores of Hong Kong demonstrators, most wearing a uniform of all-black clothes and face masks, joined the DPP victory rally in the streets around party headquarters, hoisting and waving "Liberate Hong Kong" flags. I did not see a single ROC flag in the crowd or at the massive DPP rally the night before, in striking contrast to their spectacular profusion at the Han rally one night earlier. Tsai gave a tacit nod to Hong Kongers when she declared in her victory speech that Taiwan would honor the right for demonstrators to protest peacefully. In her first postelection international interview, with the BBC, she squarely asserted, "We are an independent country already and we call ourselves the Republic of China (Taiwan)," committing her to the *Huadu* camp that supports the maintenance of Taiwan's de facto independence as the ROC, and driving the final nail into the coffin of the 1992 Consensus.

With Tsai's convincing reelection win in the face of aggressive posturing from the PRC, it became evident that any renewal of tourism, let alone other cross-strait engagements, would only be promoted through a reframed territorial narrative, even if the "status quo" remained unchanged. As Tsai put it to BBC journalist John Sudworth in an interview published on January 14,

> The situation has changed. The ambiguity can no longer serve the purposes it was intended to serve. Because [for more than] three years we're seeing China has been intensifying its threat . . . they have their military vessels and aircraft cruising around the island. . . . And also, the things happening in Hong Kong, people get a real sense that this threat is real and it's getting more and more serious. . . . We have a separate identity and we're a country of our own. So, if there's anything that runs counter to this idea, they will stand up and say that's not acceptable to us. . . . We're a successful democracy, we have a pretty decent economy, we deserve respect from China.

Still, she maintained a commitment to the pursuit of stable relations, stating, "[For] more than three years, we have been telling China that maintaining a status quo remains our policy. . . . I think that is a very friendly gesture to China."

Chinese state media response indicated no rethinking of PRC strategic direction. The *Global Times*, whose hyperbolic stances signal the limits of acceptable party-state discourse, published an editorial on January 11 that insisted that Tsai and the DPP "wantonly hyped up the so-called threat from the Chinese mainland while slandering Han's mainland connections." Flying in the face of polls measuring Taiwanese people's support for self-determination, it asserted that "the Taiwan society has formed a collective consciousness to oppose Taiwan secession among Taiwan people."

Within Taiwan, calls for change were voiced by some KMT figures worried about the party's future electoral viability. Han soon faced and lost a recall campaign raised by Kaohsiung residents disgruntled by his taking a three-month leave of absence to campaign for the presidency. Even Ma Ying-jeou himself lamented that China had produced a "misunderstanding," saying its leadership "placed too much emphasis on 'one China' and forgets there is the component 'each side having its own interpretation.'" The head of the KMT Youth League, who was born one year after 1992, suggested that the party should move away from its pro-unification stance and conceded that Taiwan had "achieved consensus in refusing to acknowledge the legitimacy of the 1992 consensus" (Yang and Chung 2020). This was a position not dissimilar from Tsai's earlier calls to form a "Taiwan Consensus," from which its citizens would determine their own future.

Despite a decisive election, ambiguities and ironies in Taiwan's territorial representation remained unresolved in all camps. The amended ROC constitution still claimed sovereignty over, yet distinguished between, the "Taiwan Area" and the "Mainland Area" and called, as before, for their eventual unification. Tsai promised throughout both of her campaigns to maintain the "status quo" and not to amend the relevant parts of the constitution, even as many of her supporters continued to press her to call for de jure independence. The overlapping claims of the ROC and the PRC in the South and East China Seas remained unresolved with each other, as well as with those of other claimant states. The KMT still named itself "Chinese Nationalist Party," even after having run its 2016 presidential election campaign under the slogan "One Taiwan."

Even so, with the landslide election of 2020, it looked as if the more plural of the two "Taiwans" had grown in discursive prominence to eclipse the other in the face of the red sun across the strait. A few weeks later, in the cross-strait "diplomatic and economic 'grey zone' between open hostility and peaceful friction" (Templeman 2019), the region and the wider world were rocked by a new viral force, not a local border-perforating catastrophe like a bus crash, but the global border-reinforcing cataclysm of COVID-19, which brought all cross-strait traffic to a standstill and thrust Chinese tourism and Taiwan's contested sovereignty to the center of world attention.

EPILOGUE

One China, Many Taiwans demonstrates that as much as tourism served to signify China's global integration, its conduct remained constrained by the geopolitical imperatives of its governing party-state. That tourism did not achieve political unification with Taiwan, and in fact provoked a backlash, illuminates the limits of and contradictions between tourism's intertwined instrumentalities for capital accumulation and state territorialization.

The COVID-19 pandemic not only effectively ended cross-strait tourism but also put all of global tourism on an indefinite hiatus. Although Taiwan, at the time of writing, has come out relatively unscathed from the pandemic, it has found itself in as geopolitically precarious a position as ever. This epilogue examines the pandemic's impacts in the Taiwan Strait, before reflecting on the role of tourism and territory in realizing and reconfiguring life in Taiwan, China, and beyond.

Taiwan, Tourism, and COVID-19

On December 31, 2019, as election tourists from Hong Kong descended on Taipei, an "unexplained viral pneumonia" was reported in Wuhan. That day, well before Chinese officials or the World Health Organization (WHO) acknowledged human-to-human transmission of COVID-19, Taiwan's medical authorities began formulating a comprehensive response, including monitoring and quarantines, increased mask production, and eventual border closures, first for visitors from

Wuhan and Hubei Province, then for all of China, and finally for nearly all international arrivals.

Although WHO officials denounced border closures, tourists and travelers were among the first targets for preventive measures against the spread of the virus, first within China and then elsewhere. When the virus spread outside Wuhan, the ascription of disease origin took on a local, national, and often racist tenor. Hotels across China refused to house travelers from Hubei, until the central government coordinated a list of venues that would take them in and even offered to repatriate ones who had already left the country. As for other countries, many simply banned arrivals from China and a growing list of other sending regions, before formulating other public health responses. Chinese and Asian tourists and residents alike found themselves targeted as potential viral vectors, in Australia, Europe, and elsewhere. After the epidemic spiraled out of local cadre control, China's central party leadership implemented draconian lockdowns. Although these severe measures eventually contained the outbreak within China, they came at a great human cost. Many other countries were slow to respond and suffered severe socioeconomic disruptions and tragic losses of life.

For Taiwan, China's earlier election-season tourism cuts suddenly looked like a blessing in disguise. The move may have inadvertently spared Taiwan from wider infection, speculated transportation and communications minister Lin Chia-lung in a February 11, 2020, interview with SET News. Although reduced numbers of Chinese tourists may have helped mitigate the first wave, far more crucial were other factors, including past experience with SARS, extreme wariness of China (Schubert 2020; Leonard 2020), and an alert public health administration bolstered by universal health coverage, designed in part based on the counterexample of the United States' uneven and expensive system (Scott 2020). An additional counterintuitive factor, acknowledged even by Taiwanese medical authorities, may have been Taiwan's exclusion from direct participation in the WHO, which led leaders to take a highly precautionary approach (Lin, Wu, and Wu 2020; Watt 2020). As put by foreign minister Joseph Wu, "We were not able to get satisfactory answers either from the WHO or from the Chinese CDC, and we got nervous and we started doing our preparation" (Watt 2020).[1]

After the contagion brought much of the world economy to a standstill and even early epidemic control success stories like Singapore and South Korea succumbed to repeated waves of infection, Taiwan stood alone in 2020 as an economically developed and democratically governed state that anticipated a health crisis and contained the virus. Through this, the exceptional state of Taiwan emerged in some ways as the most normal country in the world.

Taiwan's officials recast their successful public health management as the "Taiwan model" and put it to work to enhance the national image, expand space for international participation, and assert Taiwan's sovereignty and distinction from China (Rowen 2020). The Taiwan model was later pitched as a tourist attraction in its own right. In a May 2020 Chinese-language press release presenting a three-step plan to safely reopen tourism, Minister Lin said that Taiwan's successful response to the epidemic would serve as the "best kind of marketing for international tourism, and [we] believe Taiwan will be the fastest country in Asia, if not the world, to restore tourism; our nation's people can share Taiwan's success in containing the epidemic to quickly restore our economic prospects."[2]

The success of the Taiwan model was challenged in the summer of 2021, when Taiwan experienced its first wave of infection after a year with no cases of local transmission. As with tourism, the drama played out on the battlefield within and between the many Taiwans in the orbit of "One China," as struggles over the provenance of and access to vaccines became ever higher pitched. Although Tsai Ing-wen's administration had ordered twenty million vaccines from international suppliers prior to the domestic outbreak, their arrival was held up not only due to delays in production and delivery, which had been suffered by many other countries, but also due to the very familiar clash of territorial prerogatives: Taiwan's access to BioNTech-Pfizer mRNA vaccines remained controlled by Shanghai Fosun, the China-based company that had acquired distribution rights for "Greater China," which included Taiwan. According to Taiwanese officials who attempted to negotiate a purchasing contract, the company requested that Taiwan designate itself as a part of China in order to complete the purchase and then later declared that the vaccines would be unavailable anyway. Meanwhile, Chang Ya-chung, a pro-unification academic who went on to run for Chinese Nationalist Party (KMT) chair, claimed that a Chinese organization called Beijing Cross-Straits Eastern Culture Center had offered to donate its own Sinopharm vaccines, as other KMT figures offered to fly to China to negotiate purchase agreements. Such offers were not taken up by the Tsai administration, which noted the demonstrated lower efficacy of existing Chinese-made vaccines and continued overseeing the development, testing, and rollout of new Taiwan-made vaccines. Meanwhile, Taiwan's private sector, less constrained than state officials, stepped in, with prominent figures such as Taiwan Semiconductor Manufacturing Company's Morris Tsai and Foxconn's Terry Gou and the Buddhist Tzu Chi Charity Foundation successfully pursuing direct purchase agreements with BioNTech-Pfizer's offices in Germany (Hioe 2021).

Between the nationwide soft lockdown and an accelerated vaccination program, Taiwan went from triple- to single-digit daily caseloads between May and August 2021. Still, with the global tourism industry all but shut down, and with Taiwan caught between a new round of tension and uncertainty between China and the United States, whose leadership blamed China for the outbreak, the future of travel and the use and limitations of territory and borders remained open questions.

At a different conjuncture, the pandemic might have engendered greater efforts toward regional if not national collaboration. It unfolded instead in a time rattled by talk of a new cold war, with Hong Kong subject to a sweeping new "national security law" promulgated from Beijing and activist Joshua Wong figuring his city as a twenty-first-century Berlin (Escritt 2019). Its liberation, argued Taiwanese sociologist Wu Jieh-min (2020), required a US guarantee of Taiwan's defense as the front line of democracy. The two great powers appeared poised to accelerate their economic decoupling and harden their borders, rendering the fate of Taiwan and its twenty-four million people even more uncertain in what otherwise looked like a moment of triumph.

Tourism and the "Good Life"

One China, Many Taiwans has shown how cross-strait tourism performed the territory of Taiwan in multiple and complex ways. Not only did these performances often transform guests' and hosts' understandings of themselves and each other—they also played a part in transforming the territoriality of Taiwan and "One China." In less than a decade, the promotion of "reconciliation" by way of tourism gave way to popular resistance to the irredentism of the People's Republic of China (PRC). As a result, the so-called 1992 Consensus of "One China, each with its own interpretation" was already all but dead even before the COVID-19 pandemic dealt the final blow to cross-strait tourism.

For many group tourists, a sense of having never left China was achieved through pre-trip priming, tightly regimented itineraries, and skillful territorial translation by local guides and vendors. This produced a profound disjuncture between PRC tourists' identification with their Taiwanese hosts as idealized Chinese subjects and Taiwanese hosts' alienation from their guests. On the one hand, in many cases PRC tourists praised Taiwanese for their kindness and good manners, attributing such charms to an idealized Chinese essence. On the other hand, Taiwanese people became less likely to identify as Chinese and avoided PRC tourists.

For some independent tourists with the time, means, or interest to observe or participate in more heterogenous spaces, other Taiwans, and even other Chinas, were possible. This also held true for Hong Kongers seeking sanctuary from an increasingly totalitarian PRC, as well as others able to cross its threshold. Taiwan was a place where a blogger like Han Han could conceive a Chinese nationalist critique of the Chinese Communist Party, where a Shanghai-based student like Liping could discover dissidents at the Eslite Bookstore, where someone such as myself could climb a ladder into the legislative occupation that became the Sunflower Movement, and where the exiled Hong Kong Causeway Bay bookseller Lam Wing-kee could open a new bookstore free from censorship and fear of kidnapping.

Like its world-leading public health governance, Taiwan's spaces for realizing new ways of being in the world are produced in part by its precarity, its contested politics, and its senses of in-betweenness. The same could be said for Hong Kong, where such qualities afford its "impossible challenge and the source of its emancipatory potential," for it to "not just stand at the midpoint of competing poles but produce alternative ways of being," as the journalist Wilfred Chan (2020) reflected poignantly. In this respect, the fates of the two territories have converged even if the prescription designed for both—"One Country, Two Systems"—diverged if not collapsed completely. How to secure the means of reproduction for such alternative ways of being remains a crucial and challenging question for both territories, each in its own way. Still, this is a concern that Taiwan for now appears more safely placed to address, and it has begun extending a welcome mat for some political refugees fleeing its neighbor. The rest of the world might consider learning from such acts of hospitality.

As Nina Caspersen observed in her sprawling comparative study of "unrecognized states," "Non-recognition does not determine the political system, but it does constrain it" (2012, 99). In some ways, constraint is not such a bad thing. Its pressures can be productive, as shown by Taiwan's creative adaptations. The crisis of derecognition from the UN and the United States did help to push a largely bloodless transition to multiparty electoral democracy in the 1980s. Such pressure has also propelled succeeding social movements, including the Sunflower Movement and transitional justice projects (Ho 2018, 2019a; Rowen and Rowen 2017).

"Independence will solve everything," a slogan I spotted on a T-shirt worn by a Taiwan Independence Revolutionary Army demonstrator at Taipei 101, exemplifies a potent sentiment in Taiwan that might be considered a case of "cruel optimism." This phrase has been memorably figured by Lauren Berlant as "the condition of maintaining an attachment to a significantly problematic object" (2011, 24). In Berlant's telling, attachments to dreams of wealth, beauty, freedom, and so on, undermine their realization, obviating humbler efforts at collective action that might realize a provisional "good life." In the case of the demonstrator's slogan, the attachment is to a notion of state sovereignty that is manifestly unable to resolve transboundary governance problems, let alone threats of violent annexation.

Like activists, tourists are no strangers to the sentiments of cruel optimism, as illustrated by the cliché "I'd always regret not going to X, but having gone to X is something to regret always." Tourists seek pleasure and freedom of movement even as they are constrained, complicated, and undermined by the imperatives of the industry that moves them—tourism's utopian desires propel its heterotopic manifestations and contradictory outcomes. The optimistic affects of tourism are so much crueler when considered alongside the well-known paradox that, at least for destinations that run on the promise of pristineness, the more popular they become, the more they undermine their own conditions of reproduction.

Taiwan is not the only place performed and transformed by tourism, nor the only destination experienced and produced multiply and contradictorily by guests, hosts, and everyone in between. In Taiwan and elsewhere, tourism's promise of the "good life" by way of endless economic expansion was shattered, perhaps permanently, by COVID-19. However the global tourism industry may be reconstructed, it faces a further challenge from climate change, mass extinctions, and immiseration accelerated by many of its own practices (Fletcher et al. 2020).

Up until the COVID-19 pandemic, tourism was among the most celebrated drivers of the endless growth potential of late capitalist globalization (Bianchi 2009; Fletcher 2011; Harvey 2020). The threat to economic production and social reproduction caused by everyday tourism *and* its sudden cessation highlights the risks of an international order predicated on mobilities long taken for granted. These mobilities will need to be refashioned in a world in which tourism will continue to simultaneously serve and destabilize the interests of capital and territory, its valences of geopolitical, environmental, and social (in)security evermore visible.

Beyond Taiwan and China, as other regions form and reform, as flows of bodies and capital reconfigure states and nations, and as rising tides and changing climates reshape borders between land and sea, tourism's capacities to perform and transform territory will rearticulate in destinations yet to be realized.

Appendix

Methodology

One China, Many Taiwans contends that tourism is a mode of territorial social-ization and that it and the institutions and industries that shape it can perform bordering functions with profound geopolitical effects. Such functions and their effects can be analyzed by examining tourist experience and expression before, during, and after trips, for tourism's staging of state territory takes place across temporal as well as spatial boundaries. Predeparture planning, the journey, and the return all afford opportunities for national performance and memorialization. Utterances, photographs, stories about self and other, domestic and foreign, in-ternal and external—at "home," "abroad," and "in between"—all belong in a study of tourism and territory.

To examine how tourism performed and transformed the territoriality of Taiwan and "One China," I conducted qualitative research between and across borders—in Taiwan for a total of four years between 2012 and 2020; in Shanghai and Hong Kong for two months each in 2013 and 2014, respectively; and during the many flights in between. Methods include multisited, mobile ethnography at tourist and protest sites; semi-structured interviews with tourists, tourism indus-try workers, state officials, industry representatives, and citizens; and content analysis of a wide variety of documents.

To ascertain how Taiwan was presented to Chinese tourists, I had to tour Tai-wan with them. This meant not only visiting popular sites but also joining groups tours, engaging in conversations with fellow visitors, observing guide explanations, reading itinerary descriptions, and engaging with vendors and staff at sites, restaurants, and hotels. My fieldwork included repeated site visits, several day tours of Taipei, and a full eight-day around-the-island group tour that departed from Shanghai.

As a fluent Chinese-speaking US national with a non-Chinese appearance, I occasionally became something of a minor tourist attraction myself while conducting participant observation, which at least served to draw more interview subjects. More seriously, the relationship between Taiwan and the United States complicates the relationship between both polities and China. Therefore, my positionality necessitated linguistic adaptation to the territorial conventions of tourists and Taiwanese alike.

To dive deeper after casual conversations with countless tourists, I conducted semi-structured interviews with tourists on tour, tourists who were preparing to leave for Taiwan, and tourists who had already returned to China. These more formal interviews included sixty Chinese tourists in Taiwan, thirty-six political activists or protest-site visitors (including both Taiwan and Hong Kong), twenty Taiwanese tourist industry workers and representatives, and four Taiwanese civil servants and politicians. Based on respondent availability, interview lengths ranged from ten to seventy-five minutes. Most were conducted on-site or in offices, while others took place in nearby parks or cafés. Many more conversations with various types of interlocutors were had in more casual contexts and recorded in field notes.

The sample generally aimed for diversity in age, gender, income, and professional background, but was not meant to be exhaustive or strictly representative. Recruitment took place during tourist participant-observation and through personal contact networks and used snowballing methods with multiple origin points. Given the multisited, mobile aspect of my methods, these points spanned the whole of Taiwan over the course of several years of research, providing for a broad set of people who did not share the same social networks or backgrounds. When possible, I conducted follow-up phone or text interviews after their departure.

To relate the sentiments of Chinese tourists with those of Taiwanese tourism industry workers, I also conducted interviews with Taiwanese guides, vendors, site managers, hotel staff, and bus drivers. My years of residence in Taiwan as a student and journalist between 2001 and 2005, and time spent working in China in the tourism industry between 2006 and 2008, prior to the commencement of this project, helped me extend my sample beyond people recruited in the field and allowed for more diverse responses.

To examine the political factors affecting tourism management, I conducted interviews with Taiwanese state officials and tourism industry leaders. Agencies included the national-level Taiwan Tourism Bureau (under the Ministry of Transportation and Communications) and the Mainland Affairs Council (under the Executive Yuan). I also conducted interviews in Shanghai in 2013 with officials at Taiwan's quasi-official tourism-focused consulate, the Taiwan Strait Tourism Association. On the industry side, I conducted several interviews with past and present travel industry trade association leaders. These interviews revealed considerable overlap and blurring between state and industry rhetoric, practice, and operations, as noted in chapter 2.

Concurrent and later research included extensive analysis of regional print, radio, TV, policy documents, and online popular and social media. To both inform and supplement the interviews and ethnography described above, a wide variety of documents were collected and analyzed, including but not limited to (1) Republic of China and People's Republic of China state tourism policy, announcements, and statistics; (2) Taiwanese and Chinese travel industry documents, including sales and marketing materials, tour itineraries, and guide training guidelines; (3) forms and other documents that facilitate and regulate cross-strait travel, including entry/exit permits, passports, and mandatory identification papers; (4) Chinese-language guidebooks and Internet sites about Taiwan travel; (5) print, TV, and blog posts about cross-strait travel, whether produced by Chinese tourists or Taiwanese; and (6) Taiwanese public opinion polls regarding national identity, sovereignty, and tourism.

Field notes and interview results were compared and contrasted with ethnographic content analysis of tourist documents to assess how travel permits, tourist itineraries, site descriptions, and other tourist media produce, cite, confirm, delimit, or undermine discursive boundaries between Taiwan and China. This included attention to cartographic representations in various state documents (including entry permits and forms) and industry documents (including guidebooks and tour itineraries). All of these data sets supported and informed one another—interview questions were refined on the basis of data gleaned from document collection and participant observation, while interview results provided new directions for directed attention during participant observation. This approach allowed for triangulation of data sources and more careful and comprehensive analysis.

This methodology is reflexive about its political effects, which are addressed throughout the text. Even when applying a critical social scientific spirit toward tourism, territoriality is a hard habit to break. There is no shortage of scholarship predicated on foundational divisions between domestic and international tourism or inbound versus outbound tourism. Indeed, a significant slice of the tourism studies literature is concerned with crafting typologies of tourists based on their sending country or region (Wong and Lau 2001; Mok and Defranco

2000; and Guo et al. 2006 are just a few China-specific examples). These analyses can not only obscure the complexity and heterogeneity of tourists but also discursively produce state territory, a performative process that I aim to demystify here. I do not mean to suggest that all such aggregations or simplifications are devoid of any utility—Dutch passport holders, for example, may very well behave quite differently in general while on tour than Chinese—but I simply wish to point out the state-centric epistemology of much applied tourism research and its subjectivating, territorializing, and disciplinary effects (see also Oakes 2011). While perhaps of value when used carefully by planners, such discourses can not only reify states and borders but also reproduce, wittingly or not, the violence, erasures, and elisions implicit in their service.

Indeed, if tourism is no simple leisure activity, neither is its scholarship. For this reason, I have argued not only that tourist practice should be viewed as a component of state territorialization but that "tourism studies" itself has geopolitical effects (Rowen 2021). The work of "area studies," broadly viewed, is at least as culpable (Sakai 2009). In the case of Taiwan, an ongoing project to legitimate "Taiwan studies" as a field of scholarly practice distinct from "China studies" imbues its knowledge production with a territorial function precluded by Taiwan's earlier role as a proxy site for a generation of Sinologists shut out from China (Harrison 2006). With the passing of that period, Taiwan studies has further institutionalized through workshops, conferences, and journals. As adjacent fields extend their attention to its object of knowledge, and as prospects for critical scholarship in proximate regions such as Hong Kong and China look increasingly constrained if not outlawed outright, Taiwan becomes an ever more invigorating site for study. I hope this book conveys some of its vitality and appeal.

Notes

INTRODUCTION

1. I follow the International Union of Tourism Organization's broad definition of a tourist as "any person visiting a country, region or place other than that in which he or she has their usual place of residence" (Williams 1998, 4). This is similar to but more generalized than Valene L. Smith's definition of a tourist as a "temporarily leisured person who voluntarily visits a place away from home for the purpose of experiencing a change" (1977, 2). Either of these definitions is adequate for the case of Chinese nationals who are traveling to Taiwan.

2. Personal communication, 2012.

1. HOW TAIWAN BECAME AN EXCEPTIONAL TERRITORY

1. Taiwan's complicated "ethnic" demographics are vital to understanding both its political geography and the political economy of its tourism sector. According to Taiwan's Ministry of the Interior, approximately five hundred thousand, or roughly 2 percent, of Taiwan's present-day population are Austronesian peoples (*yuanzhumin*, or "indigenous," "aboriginal," or literally "original residents"), whose ancestors arrived far earlier than subsequent waves of immigrants from China. The ethnic composition of the remainder of the population is typically described as split between the majority Taiwanese (*benshengren*) and mainlanders (*waishengren*). The Taiwanese are composed primarily of the descendants of pre-twentieth-century south Fujianese (*minnan*, or Hoklo) settlers and secondarily of the Hakka, who despite having different sociolinguistic backgrounds are often treated as *benshengren* in political analysis due to their pre-twentieth-century arrival (for one example, see Shen and Wu 2008). The mainlanders consist of the descendants of more recent arrivals from throughout China who came with the KMT with the 1945 occupation of Taiwan and the mainland military defeat that followed in the late 1940s.

2. Throughout his political career, Ma was frequently accused of spying on Taiwanese students during his studies as part of his obligations as a KMT-supported overseas scholar (Schafferer 2002).

3. UN General Assembly, Resolution 2758, Restoration of the lawful rights of the People's Republic of China in the United Nations, October 25, 1971. https://digitallibrary.un.org/record/192054.

4. Although there have been various efforts to bridge or transcend the blue-green divide via the establishment of new parties (which are sometimes color coded as purple or white), they have so far gained little traction.

5. This episode came just a year after China had forced Taiwan's team to replace its ROC badges with KMT logo badges, which had been approved years earlier under the "Chinese Taipei" Olympic scheme, in order to compete in the 2016 Paralympics in Rio de Janeiro.

6. Personal communication, February 7, 2016.

2. THE RISE OF CROSS-STRAIT TRAVEL AND TOURISM

1. Interview, January 30, 2015.

2. Interview, January 28, 2015.

3. Due to ROC Tourism Bureau report formatting, figures that include "visitor pur-pose" arriving from "mainland China" also include non-Chinese nationals as well, but these account for under 2 percent of the total number of arrivals. As for Chinese nation-als arriving from airports outside of China, this group is simply uncountable due to a characteristically anachronistic quirk of ROC record keeping that designates all people who are both ethnically "Chinese" and non-ROC citizens as "overseas Chinese" (*huaq-iao*). This term can include non-PRC citizens who apply as "overseas Chinese" for spe-cial visas or travel permits. Further, the "exhibition" and "medical treatment" categories were not tabulated until 2012.

4. The figures' basis in tourist self-reporting was confirmed in interviews with Tour-ism Bureau officials.

5. Interview with Tourism Bureau official, March 29, 2014.

6. Interview with Mr. Yu, head of Cola Travel, April 24, 2014.

7. Interview, January 30, 2015.

8. Interview, February 6, 2014.

9. Interview with Johnson Tseng, January 30, 2015.

3. TAIWAN AS TOURIST HETEROTOPIA

1. I am grateful to Scott Writer for first referring me to this book as well as pointing me to the writer Han Han's Taiwan travelogue, discussed in Chapter 6.

2. Interview, July 2, 2012.

3. Depending on context, glosses for the *wen* in *tongwen, tongzhong* can include ei-ther "culture" or "language."

4. Interview, July 5, 2012.

5. Interview, July 7, 2012.

6. The twenty-four-hour Eslite branch shut down in early 2020, just weeks after the opening of Causeway Bay Bookstore by Hong Kong political exile Lam Wing-kee.

7. This figure was provided in an interview with Taipei 101 spokesperson Michael Liu, March 30, 2014.

8. Interview, May 22, 2014.

9. Follow-up interview with Michael Liu, April 2, 2014.

10. Interview, May 26, 2014.

11. Interview with Chen De-sheng, March 20, 2014.

12. Interview, April 18, 2015.

4. CIRCLING TAIWAN, CHINESE TOUR-GROUP STYLE

1. This name and others in this chapter and Chapter 5 have been changed.

2. I overheard dozens of Chinese tourists similarly denigrating destinations in Shan-gri-La (Zhongdian), Yunnan, among other places, in 2011 and earlier.

3. Taiwan's west coast offers a world-class high-speed rail line, used by very few group tourists.

4. "Ethnic groups" is used for instance by the DPP as part of its "Four Great Ethnic Groups" rubric (sometimes adding a fifth, "new migrants"). Such usage may be super-seding the older territory-based distinction between *waishengren* and *benshengren*.

5. THE VARIETIES OF INDEPENDENT TOURIST EXPERIENCE

1. Han's original blog post is no longer accessible, but it has been preserved at Guan-cha, https://www.guancha.cn/WenZhai/2012_05_13_73785.shtml, as well as on several Taiwanese websites. The passage I quote is taken from a translation by Chieh-Ting Yeh that appeared in a May 2012 post on the website Tea Leaf Nation.

2. Interview, July 26, 2013.

3. Interview, July 28, 2012.

4. Interview, July 20, 2012.

5. Interview, June 10, 2015.

6. Interview, February 2, 2014.

7. Interview, July 20, 2012.

8. Interview, August 8, 2014.

9. Interview, April 25, 2014.

10. Interview, February 10, 2014.

11. Interview with Baixi, July 12, 2012.

12. Interview with Amu, July 10, 2012.

13. I have even been told on several occasions while conducting research in China or with Chinese tourists that my own Taiwanese accent presents as "girly" or "effeminate" (*diadia de*), pushing me to experiment with different speech patterns.

14. Interview, May 5, 2014.

15. Interview with Hao, March 4, 2014.

16. Interview, March 3, 2015.

17. Interview with Mei, June 1, 2014.

18. Interview, July 27, 2012.

19. Taking this joke to the next level, Radicalization and its associates organized a new festival, Inland Rock, in Nantou on September 19, 2015.

20. Interview, April 4, 2015.

21. Interview, April 4, 2015.

22. http://www.jiuzhouwenhua.com/c48485.jsp, last accessed February 4, 2016.

23. Interview, August 2, 2012.

6. WAVES OF TOURISTS, WAVES OF PROTEST, AND THE END OF "ONE CHINA"

1. For fuller accounts of these movements, see Veg 2015; Rowen 2015; J. Chan 2014; K. Chan 2015; Ho 2019a.

2. Interview, January 28, 2015.

3. Although many protesters faced trial toward the end of the Ma administration, most charges against them were dropped shortly after Tsai was inaugurated.

4. Ma administration officials frequently speculated that cross-strait tourism might precipitate significant cultural or political change in China. For example, in a letter to the *National Interest*, Thalia Lin (2014), then executive officer of the Taipei Economic and Cultural Office (the de facto ROC consulate) in the United States, argued, "37 percent of the eight million tourists to visit Taiwan in 2013 were mainland Chinese. As time passes, Taiwan's success will definitely enlighten and make a positive impact on the general public of the Mainland."

5. An alternate, reciprocal take on this geographical quasi-equation was anticipated by a pro–Moral and National Education scholar in Hong Kong, Sonny Lo, who defined "Taiwanization" in the following way: "The 'Taiwanization' of Hong Kong means that the territory's chief executive would be not only directed by universal suffrage but also outside the control of Beijing" (2008, 13). This idiosyncratic usage, which frames an entire book about the feasibility of using Hong Kong's system as a model for Taiwan, equates Taiwanization with "democratization" and implies its undesirability for Beijing.

6. The Sunflower Movement, and Taiwan's democracy in general, served as something of a beacon to Hong Kong activists, causing concern among critics of the movements. For example, pro-government Hong Kong legislator Regina Ip reflected on the "inspirational relationship" between the Sunflowers and the Umbrellas in a 2014 *South China Morning Post* editorial about how best to "counter pernicious external influences." Such

"pernicious influences" included not only the Taiwanese activists and academics who visited the occupation sites in Hong Kong but also the very (American and Taiwanese) idea of public nomination, which is "much harder to eradicate." Ip's article reflected Beijing's general drive to paint the protests as the product of "foreign forces" and thereby disclaim responsibility for listening to the demands of Hong Kong's student activists. Ip had a personal stake in this issue, having championed the failed passage of the "antisubversion" Article 23 in 2003, ultimately triggering a protest movement against that bill and in 2012 against a Moral and National Education campaign, which had consolidated activists and served as predecessor to the Umbrella Movement.

7. Personal communication, January 2016.

8. Author's translation.

9. Author's translation.

10. Author's translation.

11. Author's translation.

12. For a map of the "1992 Consensus tour," see http://www.taihainet.com/news/tw news/bilateral/2016-10-02/1808413_2.html.

13. Author's translation.

EPILOGUE

1. As with the rise and demise of inbound Chinese tourism, Taiwan's window to the WHO coincided with the presidency of Ma Ying-jeou. In January 2009, with the assent of the PRC, the WHO invited Taiwan to establish a direct point of contact to exchange information on health emergencies. It also allowed Taiwanese officials to log in to the WHO's Event Information Site, where it could examine advisories shared between member states. Furthermore, the WHO promised that it would send experts to Taiwan in the event of a health emergency. A few months later, with only a few weeks' notice, the WHO director general invited Taiwan, as "Chinese Taipei," to join the meeting of the World Health Assembly (WHA) as a nonvoting observer, which did allow for personal contacts to be made and for information to be shared. After the KMT lost the presidency in 2016, Taiwan was no longer invited to the meetings of the WHA. No explanation was provided (P.-K. Chen 2018). This exclusion perhaps turned out to be yet another blessing in disguise for COVID-19 management.

2. Author's translation.

References

Abrams, Philip. 1988. "Notes on the Difficulty of Studying the State (1977)." *Journal of Historical Sociology* 1 (1): 58–89. https://doi.org/10.1111/j.1467-6443.1988.tb00004.x.

Adams, Kathleen M. 1998. "Domestic Tourism and Nation-Building in South Sulawesi." *Indonesia and the Malay World* 26 (75): 77–96. https://doi.org/10.1080/1363981 9808729913.

——. 2021. "What Western Tourism Concepts Obscure: Intersections of Migration and Tourism in Indonesia." *Tourism Geographies* 23 (4): 678–703. https://doi.org/10 .1080/14616688.2020.1765010.

Anderson, Benedict. 2006. *Imagined Communities*. 2nd ed. London: Verso.

Andrade, Tonio. 2008. *How Taiwan Became Chinese: Dutch, Spanish, and Han Colonization in the Seventeenth Century*. New York: Columbia University Press.

Arlt, Wolfgang G. 2006. *China's Outbound Tourism*. London: Routledge.

Asia Times. 2005. "Taiwan Welcomes Direct Air Link Talks," December 9, 2005.

Bad Canto. 2012. "'Liberate Sheung Shui Station': Hong Kong Netizens Act against Smugglers." September 15, 2012. https://badcanto.wordpress.com/2012/09/15/liberate -sheung-shui-station-hong-kong-netizens-act-against-smugglers/.

Balibar, Étienne. 2002. "What Is a Border?" In *Politics and the Other Scene*, 75–86. London: Verso.

Barclay, Paul D. 2017. *Outcasts of Empire: Japan's Rule on Taiwan's "Savage Border," 1874–1945*. Oakland: University of California Press.

Beckershoff, André. 2014. "The KMT-CCP Forum: Securing Consent for Cross-Strait Rapprochement." *Journal of Current Chinese Affairs* 43 (1): 213–41. https://doi.org /10.1177/186810261404300108.

Bedford, Olwen, and Kwang-Kuo Hwang. 2006. *Taiwanese Identity and Democracy: The Social Psychology of Taiwan's 2004 Elections*. New York: Palgrave Macmillan. https://doi.org/10.1057/9781403983558.

Berlant, Lauren. 2011. *Cruel Optimism*. Durham, NC: Duke University Press.

Bianchi, Raoul V. 2009. "The 'Critical Turn' in Tourism Studies: A Radical Critique." *Tourism Geographies* 11 (4): 484–504. https://doi.org/10.1080/14616680903262653.

Billig, Michael. 1995. *Banal Nationalism*. London: SAGE Publications.

Blum, Susan D. 2001. *Portraits of "Primitives": Ordering Human Kinds in the Chinese Nation*. Lanham, MD: Rowman & Littlefield.

Bouris, Dimitris, and Irene Fernández-Molina. 2018. "Contested States, Hybrid Diplomatic Practices, and the Everyday Quest for Recognition." *International Political Sociology* 12 (3): 306–24. https://doi.org/10.1093/ips/oly006.

Bradsher, Keith. 2006. "Facing Crisis, Taiwan Announces Flights to China." *New York Times*, June 14, 2006.

Brighenti, Andrea Mubi. 2010. "On Territorology: Towards a General Science of Territory." *Theory, Culture & Society* 27 (1): 52–72. https://doi.org/10.1177/02632764093 50357.

Bunten, Alexis Celeste. 2015. *So, How Long Have You Been Native? Life as an Alaska Native Tour Guide*. Lincoln: University of Nebraska Press.

Bush, Richard C. 2005. *Untying the Knot: Making Peace in the Taiwan Strait*. Washington DC: Brookings Institution Press.

——. 2014. "Hong Kong: Examining the Impact of the 'Umbrella Movement.'" December 3, 2014. https://www.brookings.edu/testimonies/hong-kong-examining-the-impact-of-the-umbrella-movement/.

Butler, Judith. 1993. *Bodies That Matter: On the Discursive Limits of "Sex."* New York: Routledge. https://doi.org/10.4324/9780203760079.

Callahan, William A. 2004a. *Contingent States: Greater China and Transnational Relations*. Minneapolis: University of Minnesota Press.

——. 2004b. "Diasporic Tycoons, Outlaw States, and Beijing Bastards: The Contingent Politics of Greater China." *East Asia* 21 (1): 65–74. https://doi.org/10.1007/s12140-004-0010-2.

——. 2005. "Nationalism, Civilization and Transnational Relations: The Discourse of Greater China." *Journal of Contemporary China* 14 (43): 269–89. https://doi.org/10.1080/10670560500065629.

——. 2009. "The Cartography of National Humiliation and the Emergence of China's Geo-body." *Public Culture* 21 (1): 141–73. https://doi.org/10.1215/08992363-2008-024.

Caspersen, Nina. 2012. *Unrecognized States: The Struggle for Sovereignty in the Modern International System*. Cambridge, UK: Polity Press.

Chan, Johannes. 2014. "Hong Kong's Umbrella Movement." *Round Table: The Commonwealth Journal of International Affairs* 103 (6): 571–80. https://doi.org/10.1080/00358533.2014.985465.

Chan, Kin-man. 2015. "Occupying Hong Kong." *Sur Journal* 12 (21). https://sur.conectas.org/en/occupying-hong-kong/

Chan, Minnie. 2013. "DPP Star Chen Chu Kicks Off Mainland China Visit." *South China Morning Post*, August 10, 2013.

Chan, Wilfred. 2020. "The Infinite Heartbreak of Loving Hong Kong." *Nation*, May 2020.

Chang, Bi-yu. 2015. *Place, Identity, and National Imagination in Post-War Taiwan*. Abingdon, Oxon: Routledge.

Chang, Maukuei. 2003. "On the Origins and Transformation of Taiwanese National Identity." In *Religion and the Formation of Taiwanese Identities*, edited by Paul R. Katz and Murray A. Rubinstein, 23–58. New York: Palgrave Macmillan. https://doi.org/10.1057/9781403981738_2.

Chang, T. C. 2021. "'Asianizing the Field': Questioning Critical Tourism Studies in Asia." *Tourism Geographies* 23 (4): 725–42. https://doi.org/10.1080/14616688.2019.1674370.

Chao, Chien Min. 2003. "Will Economic Integration between Mainland China and Taiwan Lead to a Congenial Political Culture?" *Asian Survey* 43 (2): 280–304. https://doi.org/10.1525/as.2003.43.2.280.

Chao, Linda, and Ramon H. Myers. 1994. "The First Chinese Democracy: Political Development of the Republic of China on Taiwan, 1986–1994." *Asian Survey* 34 (3): 213–30. https://www.jstor.org/stable/2644981

Chao, Vincent Y. 2011. "Over-Enthusiastic PRC Tourist Raises Security Concern." *Taipei Times*, July 9, 2011.

Charney, Jonathan I., and J. R. V. Prescott. 2000. "Resolving Cross-Strait Relations between China and Taiwan." *American Journal of International Law* 94 (3): 453–77. https://doi.org/10.2307/2555319.

Chen, Ping-Kuei. 2018. "Universal Participation without Taiwan? A Study of Taiwan's Participation in the Global Health Governance Sponsored by the World Health Organization." In *Asia-Pacific Security Challenges*, edited by Anthony J. Masys and Leo S. F. Lin, 263–81. Cham: Springer International Publishing. https://doi.org/10.1007/978-3-319-61729-9_12.

Chen, Wei-ting, Wei Shu, and Lilian Wu. 2016. "Rumors of China Cutting Visitor Numbers to Taiwan False: Bureau." *Channel News Asia*, January 18, 2016.

Chen, Yi-Ling. 2015. "The Factors and Implications of Rising Housing Prices in Taiwan." Brookings Taiwan-U.S. Quarterly Analysis. July 15, 2015. https://www.brookings.edu/opinions/the-factors-and-implications-of-rising-housing-prices-in-taiwan/.

Cheng, Isabelle, and Dafydd Fell. 2014. "The Change of Ruling Parties and Taiwan's Claim to Multiculturalism before and after 2008." *Journal of Current Chinese Affairs* 43 (3): 71–103. https://doi.org/10.1177/186810261404300304.

Cheng, Joseph Yu-shek. 2014. "The Emergence of Radical Politics in Hong Kong: Causes and Impact." *China Review* 14 (1): 199–232. https://muse.jhu.edu/article/543358.

Chin Wan. 2011. *On the Hong Kong City-State*. Hong Kong: Enrich Publishing.

China Times. 2010a. "Taipei, Beijing to Open Reciprocal Tourism Offices." February 11, 2010.

——. 2010b "Cross-Strait Tourism Offices to Open in April." February 26, 2010.

Ching, Leo T. S. 2001. *Becoming "Japanese": Colonial Taiwan and the Politics of Identity Formation*. Berkeley: University of California Press.

Chio, Jenny. 2010. "China's Campaign for Civilized Tourism: What to Do When Tourists Behave Badly." *Anthropology News* 51 (8): 14–15. https://doi.org/10.1111/j.1556-3502.2010.51814.x.

——. 2014. *A Landscape of Travel: The Work of Tourism in Rural Ethnic China*. Seattle: University of Washington Press.

Chun, Allen. 1994. "From Nationalism to Nationalizing: Cultural Imagination and State Formation in Postwar Taiwan." *Australian Journal of Chinese Affairs*, no. 31: 49–69.

Chung-Hua Institution for Economic Research. 2013. Liang'an fuwu maoyi xiehui jingji yingxiang pinggu baogao. http://www.ecfa.org.tw/Download.aspx?No=39&strT=ECFADoc.

Chung, Jake. 2015. "Beijing to Exempt Taiwanese from Entry Permits." *Taipei Times*, June 19, 2015. https://www.taipeitimes.com/News/front/archives/2015/06/19/2003621042.

Chung, Lawrence, Mandy Zuo, and Kinling Lo. 2019. "Beijing's Ban on Solo Travellers to Taiwan Could Cost Self-Ruled Island US$ 900 Million by January." *South China Morning Post*, July 31, 2019. https://www.scmp.com/news/china/politics/article/3020787/beijing-halt-individual-travel-permits-taiwan-over-rising.

Clark, Cal. 2008. "The Statehood of Taiwan: A Strange Case of Domestic Strength and International Challenge." In *The "One China" Dilemma*, edited by Peter C. Y. Chow, 81–96. New York: Palgrave Macmillan.

Closs Stephens, Angharad. 2016. "The Affective Atmospheres of Nationalism." *Cultural Geographies* 23 (2): 181–98. https://doi.org/10.1177/1474474015569994.

Cole, J. Michael. 2010. "'Tourist' May Have Been Guided by PRC." *Taipei Times*, July 18, 2010.

Cooney, Sean. 1997. "Why Taiwan Is Not Hong Kong: A Review of the PRC's 'One Country Two Systems' Model for Reunification with Taiwan." *Pacific Rim Law & Policy Association* 6 (3): 497–548.

Cresswell, Tim. 2010. "Towards a Politics of Mobility." *Environment and Planning D: Society and Space* 28 (1): 17–31. https://doi.org/10.1068/d11407.

Damm, Jens. 2011. "Taiwan's Ethnicities and Their Representation on the Internet." *Journal of Current Chinese Affairs* 40 (1): 99–131. https://doi.org/10.1177/186810261104000104.

D'Amore, Louis J. 1988. "Tourism—a Vital Force for Peace." *Annals of Tourism Research* 15: 269–83. https://doi.org/10.1016/0160-7383(88)90087-4.

Dawley, Evan N. 2019. *Becoming Taiwanese: Ethnogenesis in a Colonial City, 1880s–1950s*. Cambridge, MA: Harvard University Asia Center.

Derrida, Jacques. 2000. *Of Hospitality*. Stanford, CA: Stanford University Press.

Ding, Xiaoxing. 2012. "Dangdai chuanboxue shiye de xiaoqingxin xianxiang yanjiu." Master's thesis, Zhejiang University.

Dirlik, Arif. 2018. "Taiwan: The Land Colonialisms Made." *Boundary 2* 45 (3): 1–25. https://doi.org/10.1215/01903659-6915545.

Dou, Eva, and Lorraine Luk. 2014. "In Taiwan, Foxconn Sparks Debate over College Grad Salaries." *Wall Street Journal*, May 15, 2014.

Edensor, Tim. 2000. "Staging Tourism: Tourists as Performers." *Annals of Tourism Research* 27 (2): 322–44. https://doi.org/10.1016/S0160-7383(99)00082-1.

——. 2001. "Performing Tourism, Staging Tourism: (Re)producing Tourist Space and Practice." *Tourist Studies* 1 (1): 59–81. https://doi.org/10.1177/146879760100100104.

——. 2008. *Tourists at the Taj: Performance and Meaning at a Symbolic Site*. London: Routledge.

Escritt, Thomas. 2019. "My Town Is the New Cold War's Berlin: Hong Kong Activist Joshua Wong." *Reuters*, September 9, 2019. https://www.reuters.com/article/us-hongkong-protests-germany/my-town-is-the-new-cold-wars-berlin-hong-kong-activist-joshua-wong-idUSKCN1VU0X4.

Eskildsen, Robert. 2005. "Taiwan: A Periphery in Search of a Narrative." *Journal of Asian Studies* 64 (2): 281–94. https://doi.org/10.1017/s0021911805000781.

Farmaki, Anna. 2017. "The Tourism and Peace Nexus." *Tourism Management* 59: 528–40. https://doi.org/10.1016/j.tourman.2016.09.012.

Fauna. 2012. "Mainland Chinese Tourists Deface Plants in Taitung, Taiwan." China-SMACK, 2012. http://www.chinasmack.com/2012/stories/mainland-chinese-tourists-deface-plants-in-taitung-taiwan.html.

Fitzgerald, John. 1995. "The Nationless State: The Search for a Nation in Modern Chinese Nationalism." *Australian Journal of Chinese Affairs*, no. 33: 75–104.

Fletcher, Robert. 2011. "Sustaining Tourism, Sustaining Capitalism? The Tourism Industry's Role in Global Capitalist Expansion." *Tourism Geographies* 13 (3): 443–61. https://doi.org/10.1080/14616688.2011.570372.

Fletcher, Robert, Ivan Murray Mas, Macià Blázquez-Salom, and Asunción Blanco-Romero. 2020. "Tourism, Degrowth, and the COVID-19 Crisis." POLLEN: Political Ecology Network, March 24, 2020. https://politicalecologynetwork.org/2020/03/24/tourism-degrowth-and-the-covid-19-crisis/.

Foucault, Michel. 1986. "Of Other Spaces." *Diacritics* 16 (1): 22–27.

——. 1988. "Technologies of the Self." In *Technologies of the Self: A Seminar with Michel Foucault*, edited by Luther H. Martin, Huck Gutman, and Patrick H. Hutton, 16–49. London: Tavistock.

——. 2009. *Security, Territory, Population: Lectures at the Collège de France 1977–78*. Edited by Michael Senellart. Translated by Graham Burchell. Basingstoke: Palgrave Macmillan. https://doi.org/10.1057/9780230245075.

Franklin, Adrian. 2004. "Tourism as an Ordering: Towards a New Ontology of Tourism." *Tourist Studies* 4 (3): 277–301. https://doi.org/10.1177/1468797604057328.

Franklin, Adrian, and Mike Crang. 2001. "The Trouble with Tourism and Travel Theory?" *Tourist Studies* 1 (1): 5–22. https://doi.org/10.1177/146879760100100101.

Frazier, David. 2012. "Dodgy Dealings." *Taipei Times*, July 25, 2012.

Friedman, Sara L. 2015. *Exceptional States: Chinese Immigrants and Taiwanese Sovereignty*. Oakland: University of California Press.

Garrett, Daniel. 2013a. "Superheroes in Hong Kong's Political Resistance: Icons, Images, and Opposition." *PS: Political Science & Politics* 47 (1): 112–19. https://doi.org/10.1017/S1049096513001637.

——. 2013b. "Visualizing Protest Culture in China's Hong Kong: Recent Tensions over Integration." *Visual Communication* 12 (1): 55–70. https://doi.org/10.1177/147035 7212447910.

——. 2014. "Framing the Radicals: Panic on Canton Road (I)." China Policy Institute Blog, February 26, 2014. https://blogs.nottingham.ac.uk/chinapolicyinstitute /2014/02/26/framing-the-radicals-panic-on-canton-road-i/.

Garrett, Daniel, and Wing-chung Ho. 2014. "Hong Kong at the Brink—Emerging Forms of Political Participation in the New Social Movement." In *New Trends of Political Participation in Hong Kong*, edited by Joseph Yu-shek Cheng, 347–83. Hong Kong: City University of Hong Kong Press.

Gellner, Ernest. 1983. *Nations and Nationalism*. Oxford, UK: Blackwell.

Gillen, Jamie. 2014. "Tourism and Nation Building at the War Remnants Museum in Ho Chi Minh City, Vietnam." *Annals of the Association of American Geographers* 104 (6): 1307–21. https://doi.org/10.1080/00045608.2014.944459.

Gold, Michael. 2015. "Taiwan Activists Fan China Fears as Protest Trial Opens." *Reuters*, March 25, 2015.

Gold, Thomas B. 1993. "Go with Your Feelings: Hong Kong and Taiwan Popular Culture in Greater China." *China Quarterly* 136: 907–25. https://doi.org/10.1017/S03 05741000032380.

Gregson, Nicky, and Gillian Rose. 2000. "Taking Butler Elsewhere: Performativities, Spatialities and Subjectivities." *Environment and Planning D: Society and Space* 18 (4): 433–52. https://doi.org/10.1068/d232.

Guo, Yingzhi, Samuel Seongseop Kim, and Dallen J. Timothy. 2007. "Development Characteristics and Implications of Mainland Chinese Outbound Tourism." *Asia Pacific Journal of Tourism Research* 12 (4): 313–32. https://doi.org/10.1080/10941 660701760995.

Guo, Yingzhi, Samuel Seongseop Kim, Dallen J. Timothy, and Kuo-Ching Wang. 2006. "Tourism and Reconciliation between Mainland China and Taiwan." *Tourism Management* 27 (5): 997–1005. https://doi.org/10.1016/j.tourman.2005.08.001.

Harrison, Mark. 2006. *Legitimacy, Meaning, and Knowledge in the Making of Taiwanese Identity*. New York: Palgrave Macmillan.

——. 2015. Taiwan's choice. *Asia and the Pacific Policy Society*. http://www.policyforum .net/taiwans-choice/.

Harvey, David. 2020. "Anti-Capitalist Politics in the Time of COVID-19." Davidharvey. org, March 19, 2020. http://davidharvey.org/2020/03/anti-capitalist-politics-in -the-time-of-covid-19/.

Hazbun, Waleed. 2004. "Globalisation, Reterritorialisation and the Political Economy of Tourism Development in the Middle East." *Geopolitics* 9 (2): 310–41. https:// doi.org/10.1080/14650040490442881.

Herington, Jonathan, and Kelley Lee. 2014. "The Limits of Global Health Diplomacy: Taiwan's Observer Status at the World Health Assembly." *Globalization and Health* 10 (71): 1–9. https://doi.org/10.1186/s12992-014-0071-y.

Hickey, Dennis V. 1997. "U.S. Policy and Taiwan's Bid to Rejoin the United Nations." *Asian Survey* 37 (11): 1031–43. https://www.jstor.org/stable/2645739

Hioe, Brian. 2021. "The Politics of Taiwan's COVID-19 Response." *Diplomat*, September 10, 2021. https://thediplomat.com/2021/09/the-politics-of-taiwans-covid-19-response/.

Ho, Ming-sho. 2014. "The Resurgence of Social Movements under the Ma Ying-jeou Government: A Political Opportunity Structure Perspective." In *Political Changes in Taiwan under Ma Ying-jeou*, edited by Jean-Pierre Cabestan and Jacques deLisle, 100–119. Abingdon, Oxon: Routledge.

——. 2015. "Occupy Congress in Taiwan: Political Opportunity, Threat, and the Sunflower Movement." *Journal of East Asian Studies* 15: 69–97. https://doi.org/10.1017/S1598240800004173.

——. 2018. "Taiwan's Anti-Nuclear Movement: The Making of a Militant Citizen Movement." *Journal of Contemporary Asia* 48 (3): 445–64. https://doi.org/10.1080/00472336.2017.1421251.

——. 2019a. *Challenging Beijing's Mandate of Heaven: Taiwan's Sunflower Movement and Hong Kong's Umbrella Movement*. Philadelphia: Temple University Press.

——. 2019b. "Taiwan's Road to Marriage Equality: Politics of Legalizing Same-Sex Marriage." *China Quarterly* 238: 482–503. https://doi.org/10.1017/S0305741018001765.

Ho, Yung-Ching, Chuang Shih-Chieh, and Huang Chien-Jung. 2012. "Research on Brand Recognition of Sun Moon Lake: The Example of Mainland Chinese Tourists." *Journal of Island Tourism Research* 5 (1): 52–71.

Hom, Stephanie Malia. 2015. *The Beautiful Country: Tourism and the Impossible State of Destination Italy*. Toronto: University of Toronto Press.

Horton, Chris. 2017. "What's in a Name? For Taiwan, Preparing for the Spotlight, a Lot." *New York Times*, August 16, 2017. https://www.nytimes.com/2017/08/16/world/asia/taiwan-chinese-taipei-sports-universiade.html.

Horton, Chris. 2019. "Why reporting on Taiwan isn't easy, in one photo: Taiwanese audience in Republic of China afro wigs cheer the arrival of team Chinese Taipei." Twitter, August 30, 2017. https://twitter.com/heguisen/status/902865844748746752?s=20&t=9lb3Yii4TLskIlM9DbpaKg.

Hsiao, Frank S. T., and Lawrence R. Sullivan. 1979. "The Chinese Communist Party and the Status of Taiwan, 1928–1943." *Pacific Affairs* 52 (3): 446–67. https://doi.org/10.2307/2757657.

Hsieh, Pasha L. 2011. "The China–Taiwan ECFA, Geopolitical Dimensions and WTO Law." *Journal of International Economic Law* 14 (1): 121–56. https://doi.org/10.1093/jiel/jgr009.

Hsing, You-tien. 1998. *Making Capitalism in China: The Taiwan Connection*. New York: Oxford University Press.

Hsu, Jenny W. 2009. "Government's Tourism Policy Ineffective, DPP Says." *Taipei Times*, November 1, 2009. http://www.taipeitimes.com/News/taiwan/archives/2009/11/01/2003457376.

Hu, Fox, and Michelle Yun. 2013. "Hong Kong Poverty Line Shows Wealth Gap with One in Five Poor." *Bloomberg Business*, September 30, 2013. https://www.bloomberg.com/news/articles/2013-09-29/hong-kong-poverty-line-shows-wealth-gap-with-one-in-five-poor.

Huang, Jewel. 2006. "MAC Finds Support for Chinese Tourists Rising." *Taipei Times*, December 23, 2006. https://www.taipeitimes.com/News/taiwan/archives/2006/12/23/2003341565.

Huang, Min-Hua. 2014. "Taiwan's Changing Political Landscape: The KMT's Landslide Defeat in the Nine-in-One Elections." *Brookings East Asia Commentary*, December 8, 2014.

Huang, Shu-mei, and Ian Rowen. 2015. "Raising Umbrellas in the Exceptional City: Encounters with the 'Other' in Liminal Spaces." *Journal of Archaeology and Anthropology* 83: 25–56. https://doi.org/10.6152/jaa.2015.12.0003.

Hughes, Christopher R. 2011. "Negotiating National Identity in Taiwan: Between Nativization and De-sinicization." In *Taiwan's Democracy: Economic and Political Challenges*, edited by Penelope B. Prime, John W. Garver, and Robert Ash, John W. Garver, and Penelope B. Prime, 51–74. Abingdon, Oxon: Routledge. https://doi.org/10.4324/9780203809044.

Hung, Rui-chin, and Ming-yi Yang. 2015. "Ex-Government Official Planning Chinese Festival." *Taipei Times*, April 16, 2015.

Jackson, Dominic. 2018. "Madonna Wraps Herself in ROC Flag to Close Out Concert in Taipei." *Shanghaiist*, May 5, 2018. http://shanghaiist.com/2016/02/05/madonna _wraps_herself_in_roc_flag_d/.

Jacobs, J. Bruce. 2005. "'Taiwanization' in Taiwan's Politics." In *Cultural, Ethnic, and Political Nationalism in Contemporary Taiwan: Bentuhua*, edited by John Makeham and A-chin Hsiau, 17–54. New York: Palgrave Macmillan. https://doi.org /10.1057/9781403980618_2.

——. 2012. *Democratizing Taiwan*. Leiden: Brill.

Jacobs, J. Bruce, and I-hao Ben Liu. 2007. "Lee Teng-hui and the Idea of 'Taiwan.'" *China Quarterly* 190: 375–93. https://doi.org/10.1017/S0305741007001245.

Jafari, Jafar. 1989. "Tourism and Peace." *Annals of Tourism Research* 16 (3): 439–43. https://doi.org/10.1016/0160-7383(89)90059-5.

Johnson, Nuala C. 1999. "Framing the Past: Time, Space and the Politics of Heritage Tourism in Ireland." *Political Geography* 18 (2): 187–207. https://doi.org/10.1016 /S0962-6298(98)00072-9.

Karl, Rebecca E. 1998. "Creating Asia: China in the World at the Beginning of the Twentieth Century." *American Historical Review* 103 (4): 1096–1118. https://doi.org /10.2307/2651199.

Kastner, Jens. 2011. "Politics Seen in Cheap China–Taiwan Flights." *Asia Times Online*, December 8, 2011. http://www.atimes.com/atimes/China/ML08Ad01.html.

Kastner, Scott L. 2006. "Does Economic Integration across the Taiwan Strait Make Military Conflict Less Likely?" *Journal of East Asian Studies* 6: 319–46.

Kerr, George. 1965. *Formosa Betrayed*. Boston: Houghton Mifflin.

Kim, Samuel Seongseop, Dallen J. Timothy, and Hag-Chin Han. 2007. "Tourism and Political Ideologies: A Case of Tourism in North Korea." *Tourism Management* 28 (4): 1031–43. https://doi.org/10.1016/j.tourman.2006.08.005.

Kolstø, Pål. 2006. "The Sustainability and Future of Unrecognized Quasi-States." *Journal of Peace Research* 43 (6): 723–40. https://doi.org/10.1177/00223433060 68102.

Lee, Joy. 2014. "Tourism Income Reaches High in 2013: Bureau." July 10, 2014. http:// www.chinapost.com.tw/taiwan/national/national-news/2014/07/10/412049 /Tourism-income.htm.

Lee, Ying, and Hsiu-tzu Lin. 2009. "Hoteliers Lash out at Chinese Tourists." *Taipei Times*, July 5, 2009. https://www.taipeitimes.com/News/front/archives/2009/07/05/20 03447896.

Leifer, Michael. 2001. "Taiwan and South-East Asia: The Limits to Pragmatic Diplomacy." *The China Quarterly*, no. 165: 173–85. https://www.jstor.org/stable/3451111.

Lemke, Thomas. 2007. "An Indigestible Meal? Foucault, Governmentality and State Theory." *Distinktion: Journal of Social Theory* 8 (2): 43–64. https://doi.org/10.1080 /1600910x.2007.9672946.

Leonard, Andrew. 2020. "Taiwan Is Beating the Coronavirus. Can the US Do the Same?" *Wired*, March 2020.

Li, Chien-pin. 2006. "Taiwan's Participation in Inter-governmental Organizations: An Overview of Its Initiatives." *Asian Survey* 46 (4): 597–614. https://doi.org/10.1525 /as.2006.46.4.597.

Li, Fion, and Liza Lin. 2015. "China Limits Shenzhen Visits to Hong Kong to Curb Day Trips." *Bloomberg*, April 13, 2015. https://www.bloomberg.com/news/arti cles/2015-04-13/china-limits-shenzhen-visitors-to-hong-kong-to-curb-day -trippers.

Light, Duncan. 2001. "'Facing the Future': Tourism and Identity-Building in Post-Socialist Romania." *Political Geography* 20 (8): 1053–74. https://doi.org/10.1016/S0962-6298(01)00044-0.

Lii, Wen. 2014. "Protesters Storm HK Office in Taipei in a Display of Solidarity." *Taipei Times*, September 30, 2014. http://www.taipeitimes.com/News/front/archives/2014/09/30/2003600906.

Lin, Ching-Fu, Chien-Huei Wu, and Chuan-Feng Wu. 2020. "Reimagining the Administrative State in Times of Global Health Crisis: An Anatomy of Taiwan's Regulatory Actions in Response to the COVID-19 Pandemic." *European Journal of Risk Regulation* 11 (2): 256–72. https://doi.org/10.1017/err.2020.25.

Lin, Enru. 2016. "China Preparing to Cut No. of Tourists to Taiwan on 'Implicit Gov't Orders.'" *China Post*, March 5, 2016. http://www.chinapost.com.tw/taiwan-business/2016/03/05/459912/China-preparing.htm.

Lin, Fei-fan. 2014. "Today's Hong Kong, Today's Taiwan." *Foreign Policy*, October 1, 2014.

Lin, Rebecca. 2012a. "Spending Big, but to Whose Benefit?" *CommonWealth Magazine*, November 1, 2012. https://english.cw.com.tw/article/article.action?id=629.

——. 2012b. "Will Taiwan Go the Way of Hong Kong?" *CommonWealth Magazine*, November 8, 2012. https://english.cw.com.tw/article/article.action?id=626.

Lin, Syaru Shirley. 2016. *Taiwan's China Dilemma: Contested Identities and Multiple Interests in Taiwan's Cross-Strait Economic Policy*. Stanford, CA: Stanford University Press.

Lin, Thalia. 2014. "Don't Say Goodbye to Taiwan." *National Interest*, February 27, 2014. https://nationalinterest.org/commentary/dont-say-goodbye-taiwan-9966.

Lisle, Debbie. 2016. *Holidays in the Danger Zone: Entanglements of War and Tourism*. Minneapolis: University of Minnesota Press. http://www.jstor.org/stable/10.5749/j.ctt1ch7789.

Litvin, Stephen W. 1998. "Tourism: The World's Peace Industry?" *Journal of Travel Research* 37 (1): 63–66. https://doi.org/10.1177/004728759803700108.

Liu, Jiyan and Hejun Hou. 2017. "Guotaiban: Dalu Youke Bu Tai Lüyou Renshu Xiajiang Genben Yuanyin Zai Tai Dangju." *People.Cn*, February 8, 2017. http://tw.people.com.cn/n1/2017/0208/c14657-29066191.html.

Liu, John. 2013. "Taiwan Gender Equality Ranked 2nd Globally Due to Political Engagement: DGBAS." *China Post*, June 11, 2013.

Liu, Wei-Ting. 2009. "The Influence of and Debate about Chinese Tourists." *Taiwan Economic Research Monthly* 32 (8): 57–63.

Lo, Sonny Shiu-ling. 2008. *The Dynamics of Beijing-Hong Kong Relations: A Model for Taiwan?* Hong Kong: Hong Kong University Press.

——. 2011. "The Politics of Soft Power in Sino-Canadian Relations: Stephen Harper's Visit to China and the Neglected Hong Kong Factor." In *The China Challenge: Sino-Canadian Relations in the 21s Century*, edited by Huhua Cao and Vivienne Poy, 66–80. Ottawa: University of Ottawa Press.

Loa, Iok-sin. 2012. "London 2012 Olympics: ROC Flag Warning Sparks Outrage." *Taipei Times*, August 3, 2012. http://www.taipeitimes.com/News/front/archives/2012/08/03/2003539309.

Long, Tom, and Francisco Urdinez. 2021. "Status at the Margins: Why Paraguay Recognizes Taiwan and Shuns China." *Foreign Policy Analysis* 17 (1): 1–22. https://doi.org/10.1093/fpa/oraa002.

MacCannell, Dean. 1976. *The Tourist: A New Theory of the Leisure Class*. New York: Schocken Books.

Makeham, John, and A-chin Hsiau, eds. 2005. *Cultural, Ethnic, and Political Nationalism in Contemporary Taiwan: Bentuhua*. New York: Palgrave Macmillan.

Mälksoo, Maria. 2012. "The Challenge of Liminality for International Relations Theory." *Review of International Studies* 38 (2): 481–94. https://doi.org/10.1017/S02602 10511000829.

McDonald, Kate. 2017. *Placing Empire: Travel and the Social Imagination in Imperial Japan.* Oakland: University of California Press.

McKinlay, Alan. 2010. "Performativity: From J. L. Austin to Judith Butler." In *"The Leading Journal in the Field": Destabilizing Authority in the Social Sciences of Management,* edited by Peter Armstrong and Geoff Lightfoot, 119–142. London: MayFlyBooks.

Mckirdy, Euan. 2016. "Tourists Die in Taiwan Tour Bus Blaze." *CNN,* July 19, 2016. https://edition.cnn.com/2016/07/19/asia/taiwan-tour-bus-fire/.

Mengin, Françoise. 2008. "Taiwan as the Westphalian Society's Foucaldian Heterotopia." *Sociétés politiques comparées: Revue européenne d'analyse des sociétés politiques,* no. 7: 1–21.

Mezzadra, Sandro, and Brett Neilson. 2013. *Border as Method, or, the Multiplication of Labor.* Durham, NC: Duke University Press. https://doi.org/10.1215/9780822377542.

Miéville, China. 2009. *The City and the City.* London: Macmillan.

Mitchell, Timothy. 1991. "The Limits of the State: Beyond Statist Approaches and Their Critics." *American Political Science Review* 85 (1): 77–96. https://www.jstor.org/stable/1962879%0A.

Mok, Connie, and Agnes L. Defranco. 2000. "Chinese Cultural Values: Their Implications for Travel and Tourism Marketing." *Journal of Travel & Tourism Marketing* 8 (2): 99–114. https://doi.org/10.1300/J073v08n02_07.

Mostafanezhad, Mary. 2019. "Tourism Frontiers: Primitive Accumulation, and the 'Free Gifts' of (Human) Nature in the South China Sea and Myanmar." *Transactions of the Institute of British Geographers* 45 (2): 434–47. https://doi.org/10.1111/tran .12357.

National Chengchi University Election Study Center. 2019. "Changes in the Taiwanese/Chinese Identity of Taiwanese." National Chengchi University Election Study Center, Taipei.

Navaro-Yashin, Yael. 2012. *The Make-Believe Space: Affective Geography in a Postwar Polity.* Durham, NC: Duke University Press.

Newman, David. 1999. "Geopolitics Renaissant: Territory, Sovereignty and the World Political Map." In *Boundaries, Territory, and Postmodernity,* edited by David Newman, 1–16. London: Frank Cass.

Nyíri, Pál. 2006. *Scenic Spots: Chinese Tourism, the State, and Cultural Authority.* Seattle: University of Washington Press.

——. 2010. *Mobility and Cultural Authority in Contemporary China.* Seattle: University of Washington Press.

Oakes, Tim. 1998. *Tourism and Modernity in China.* London: Routledge. https://www .routledge.com/Tourism-and-Modernity-in-China/Oakes/p/book/9781138 863057.

——. 2011. "Touring Modernities: Disordered Tourism in China." In *Real Tourism: Practice, Care, and Politics in Contemporary Travel Culture,* edited by Claudio Minca and Tim Oakes, 103–122. London: Routledge.

Ong, Aihwa. 1999. *Flexible Citizenship: The Cultural Logics of Transnationality.* Durham, NC: Duke University Press.

Osnos, Evan. 2011. "The Grand Tour." *New Yorker,* April 18, 2011.

Ownby, David. 2003. "A History for Falun Gong: Popular Religion and the Chinese State since the Ming Dynasty." *Nova Religio* 6 (2): 223–43. https://doi.org/10.1525/nr .2003.6.2.223.

Paasi, Anssi. 1998. "Boundaries as Social Processes: Territoriality in the World of Flows." *Geopolitics* 3 (1): 69–88. https://doi.org/10.1080/14650049808407608.

———. 2000. "Territorial Identities as Social Constructs." *HAGAR: International Social Science Review* 1 (2): 91–113.

Painter, Joe. 2006. "Prosaic Geographies of Stateness." *Political Geography* 25 (7): 752–74. https://doi.org/10.1016/j.polgeo.2006.07.004.

Park, Christian J. 2005. "Politics of Geumgansan Tourism: Sovereignty in Contestation." *Korean Studies* 8 (3): 113–35.

Phillips, Steven E. 2003. *Between Assimilation and Independence: The Taiwanese Encounter Nationalist China, 1945–1950.* Stanford, CA: Stanford University Press.

Ramzy, Austin. 2014. "Tempest over a Chamber Pot as Taiwan Scrutinizes Chinese Tourists' Manners." *New York Times*, October 22, 2014.

Research Development and Evaluation Commission. 2009. "Poll on Issues Associated with the Third Chiang-Chen Talks and Mainland Tourists Visiting Taiwan." Republic of China Executive Yuan, May 18, 2009. http://www.rdec.gov.tw/redirect.asp?xItem=4163483&ctNode=12142&mp=100.

Rich, Timothy S. 2009. "Status for Sale: Taiwan and the Competition for Diplomatic Recognition." *Issues & Studies* 45 (4): 159–88.

Richardson, Tim. 2013. "Borders and Mobilities: Introduction to the Special Issue." *Mobilities* 8 (1): 1–6. https://doi.org/10.1080/17450101.2012.747747.

Richter, Linda K. 1983a. "Political Implications of Chinese Tourism Policy." *Annals of Tourism Research* 10 (3): 395–413. https://doi.org/10.1016/0160-7383(83)90064-6.

———. 1983b. "Tourism Politics and Political Science: A Case of Not So Benign Neglect." *Annals of Tourism Research* 10 (3): 313–35. https://doi.org/10.1016/0160-7383(83)90060-9.

Rickards, Jane. 2006. "Taipei Urges Beijing over Opening Island to Tourists." *China Post*, February 11, 2006.

Rigger, Shelley. 1999. *Politics in Taiwan: Voting for Democracy.* London: Routledge.

Romberg, Alan. 2004. "The Role of the United States in Seeking a Peaceful Solution." In *Peace and Security across the Taiwan Strait*, edited by Steve Tsang, 111–43. New York: Palgrave Macmillan.

Rose, Nikolas, and Peter Miller. 1992. "Political Power beyond the State: Problematics of Government." *British Journal of Sociology* 43 (2): 173–205. https://doi.org/10.2307/591464.

Rowen, Ian. 2015. "Inside Taiwan's Sunflower Movement: Twenty-Four Days in a Student-Occupied Parliament, and the Future of the Region." *Journal of Asian Studies* 74 (1): 5–21. https://doi.org/10.1017/S0021911814002174.

———. 2017. "Tourism as a Territorial Strategy in the South China Sea." In *Enterprises, Localities, People, and Policy in the South China Sea*, edited by Jonathan Spangler, Dean Karalekas, and Moises Lopes de Souza, 61–74. Cham: Palgrave Macmillan. https://doi.org/10.1007/978-3-319-62828-8_3.

———. 2020. "Crafting the Taiwan Model for COVID-19: An Exceptional State in Pandemic Territory." *Asia-Pacific Journal: Japan Focus* 18 (14).

———. 2021. "Tourism Studies Is a Geopolitical Instrument: Conferences, Confucius Institutes, and 'the Chinese Dream.'" *Tourism Geographies* 23 (4): 895–914. https://doi.org/10.1080/14616688.2019.1666912.

Rowen, Ian, and Jamie Rowen. 2017. "Taiwan's Truth and Reconciliation Committee: The Geopolitics of Transitional Justice in a Contested State." *International Journal of Transitional Justice* 11 (1): 92–112. https://doi.org/10.1093/ijtj/ijx001.

Sakai, Naoki. 2009. "Imperial Nationalism and the Comparative Perspective." *Positions: Asia Critique* 17 (1): 159–205. https://doi.org/10.1215/10679847-2008-029.

Salazar, Noel B. 2006. "Touristifying Tanzania. Local Guides, Global Discourse." *Annals of Tourism Research* 33 (3): 833–52. https://doi.org/10.1016/j.annals.2006.03.017.

Salter, Mark B. 2007. "Governmentalities of an Airport: Heterotopia and Confession." *International Political Sociology* 1 (1): 49–66. https://doi.org/10.1111/j.1749-5687.2007.00004.x.

——. 2013. "To Make Move and Let Stop: Mobility and the Assemblage of Circulation." *Mobilities* 8 (1): 7–19. https://doi.org/10.1080/17450101.2012.747779.

Satsuka, Shiho. 2015. *Nature in Translation: Japanese Tourism Encounters the Canadian Rockies*. Durham, NC: Duke University Press.

Saunders, Phillip C., and Scott L. Kastner. 2009. "Bridge over Troubled Water? Envisioning a China-Taiwan Peace Agreement." *International Security* 33 (4): 87–114.

Sautman, Barry. 1997. "Racial Nationalism and China's External Behavior." *World Affairs* 160 (2): 78–95.

Schafferer, Christian. 2002. "Taiwan: Municipal Elections 2002." *Journal of Contemporary Eastern Asia* 1 (2): 9–28. https://doi.org/10.17477/jcea.2002.1.2.009.

Schein, Louisa. 1997. "Gender and Internal Orientalism in China." *Modern China* 23 (1): 69–98. https://doi.org/10.1177/009770049702300103.

——. 2000. *Minority Rules: The Miao and the Feminine in China's Cultural Politics*. Durham, NC: Duke University Press.

Schubert, Gunter. 2020. "Taiwan Has Done Exceptionally Well in Fighting COVID-19—but Needs an 'Exit Strategy' as Well." *CommonWealth Magazine*, April 28, 2020.

Scott, Dylan. 2020. "Taiwan's Single-Payer Success Story—and Its Lessons for America." *Vox*, January 13, 2020. https://www.vox.com/health-care/2020/1/13/21028702/medicare-for-all-taiwan-health-insurance.

Shambaugh, David. 2004. "China Engages Asia: Reshaping the Regional Order." *International Security* 29 (3): 64–99. https://doi.org/10.1162/0162288043467496.

Shan, Shelley. 2009. "Average Cross-Strait Flight Occupancy Reaches 62.7%." *Taipei Times*, November 4, 2009. https://www.taipeitimes.com/News/taiwan/archives/2009/11/04/2003457576.

Sheller, Mimi, and John Urry. 2006. "The New Mobilities Paradigm." *Environment and Planning A: Economy and Space* 38 (2): 207–26. https://doi.org/10.1068/a37268.

Shen, Shiau-Chi, and Nai-teh Wu. 2008. "Ethnic and Civic Nationalisms: Two Roads to the Formation of a Taiwanese Nation." In *The "One China" Dilemma*, edited by Peter C. Y. Chow, 117–46. New York: Palgrave Macmillan.

Shepherd, John Robert. 1993. *Statecraft and Political Economy on the Taiwan Frontier, 1600–1800*. Stanford, CA: Stanford University Press.

Shih, Shu-mei. 1995. "The Trope of Mainland China in Taiwan's Media." *Positions: Asia Critique* 3 (1): 149–83. https://doi.org/10.1215/10679847-3-1-149.

Sim, Shuan. 2015. "Chinese Tourists in Hong Kong: Lawmakers to Call for Restriction of Visitors following Protests." *International Business Times*, March 4, 2015.

Siu, Grace, Louisa Y. S. Lee, and Daniel Leung. 2013. "Residents' Perceptions toward the 'Chinese Tourists' Wave' in Hong Kong: An Exploratory Study." *Asia Pacific Journal of Tourism Research* 18 (5): 446–63. https://doi.org/10.1080/10941665.2012.665062.

Smith, Valene L., ed. 1977. *Hosts and Guests: The Anthropology of Tourism*. Philadelphia: University of Pennsylvania Press.

Sofield, Trevor H. B. 2006. "Border Tourism and Border Communities: An Overview." *Tourism Geographies* 8 (2): 102–21. https://doi.org/10.1080/14616680600585489.

Stein, Rebecca L. 2008. *Itineraries in Conflict: Israelis, Palestinians, and the Political Lives of Tourism*. Durham, NC: Duke University Press.

Sutter, Karen M. 2002. "Business Dynamism across the Taiwan Strait: The Implications for Cross-Strait Relations." *Asian Survey* 42 (3): 522–40. https://doi.org/10.1525/as .2002.42.3.522.

Tan, Huileng. 2016. "China Holiday Season Starts but Taiwan Tourism Suffering amid One China Spat." *CNBC*, September 16, 2016. https://www.cnbc.com/2016/09/16 /china-holiday-season-starts-but-taiwan-tourism-suffering-amid-one-china -spat.html.

Taylor, Jeremy E. 2010. "*QuJianghua*: Disposing of and Re-appraising the Remnants of Chiang Kai-shek's Reign on Taiwan." *Journal of Contemporary History* 45 (1): 181– 96. https://doi.org/10.1177/0022009409348030.

Templeman, Kharis. 2019. "Taiwan's January 2020 Elections: Prospects and Implications for China and the United States." https://www.brookings.edu/research/taiwans -january-2020-elections-prospects-and-implications-for-china-and-the-united -states/.

Teng, Emma Jinhua. 2004. *Taiwan's Imagined Geography: Chinese Colonial Travel Writing and Pictures, 1683–1895*. Cambridge, MA: Harvard University Asia Center.

Teo, Peggy, and Sandra Leong. 2006. "A Postcolonial Analysis of Backpacking." *Annals of Tourism Research* 33 (1): 109–31. https://doi.org/10.1016/j.annals.2005.05.001.

Timothy, Dallen J. 1995. "Political Boundaries and Tourism: Borders as Tourist Attractions." *Tourism Management* 16 (7): 525–32. https://doi.org/10.1016/0261-5177 (95)00070-5.

——. 2001. *Tourism and Political Boundaries*. London: Routledge.

Tomba, L. 2009. "Of Quality, Harmony, and Community: Civilization and the Middle Class in Urban China." *Positions: Asia Critique* 17 (3): 591–616. https://doi.org /10.1215/10679847-2009-016.

Tong, Elson. 2017. "Not Just Officials: Taiwan Students Blocked from Visiting UN Public Gallery in Geneva." *Hong Kong Free Press*, June 15, 2017. https://www.hong kongfp.com/2017/06/15/not-just-officials-taiwan-students-blocked-visiting-un -public-gallery-geneva/.

Torpey, John. 2000. *The Invention of the Passport: Surveillance, Citizenship and the State*. Cambridge: Cambridge University Press.

Tsai, Shih-shan Henry. 2005. *Lee Teng-hui and Taiwan's Quest for Identity*. New York: Palgrave Macmillan. https://doi.org/10.1057/9781403977175.

Tsai, Ting-I. 2006. "Taiwanese Arms Open for Mainland Tourists." *Asia Times*, July 6, 2006.

Tsai, Tsung-hsien, and Jake Chung. 2014. "Chinese Tourists Shock Swimmers." *Taipei Times*, April 9, 2014.

Tsoi, Grace. 2014. "'Today's Hong Kong,' Tomorrow's Taiwan.'" *Foreign Policy*, August 19, 2014.

Tsoi, Grace, and Tessa Wong. 2016. "What Are Hong Kong's Localists Angry About?" *BBC*, February 11, 2016. https://www.bbc.com/news/world-asia-china-35547186

Tu, Weiming. 1996. "Cultural Identity and the Politics of Recognition in Contemporary Taiwan." *China Quarterly* 148: 1115–40. https://doi.org/10.1017/S0305741000050578.

United Daily News. 2009. "Mainland Tourist Numbers Collapse," June 24, 2009.

Urry, John, and Jonas Larsen. 2011. *The Tourist Gaze 3.0*. 3rd ed. London: SAGE Publications.

Veg, Sebastian. 2015. "Legalistic and Utopian: Hong Kong's Umbrella Movement." *New Left Review* 92: 55–73.

——. 2017. "The Rise of 'Localism' and Civic Identity in Post-Handover Hong Kong: Questioning the Chinese Nation-State." *China Quarterly* 230: 323–47. https://doi .org/10.1017/S0305741017000571.

Wainwright, Joel, and Morgan Robertson. 2003. "Territorialization, Science and the Colonial State: The Case of Highway 55 in Minnesota." *Cultural Geographies* 10 (2): 196–217. https://doi.org/10.1191/1474474003eu269oa.

Wang, Horng-luen. 2004. "Regulating Transnational Flows of People: An Institutional Analysis of Passports and Visas as a Regime of Mobility." *Identities: Global Studies in Culture and Power* 11 (3): 351–76. https://doi.org/10.1080/1070289049049 3536.

——. 2009. "How Are Taiwanese Shanghaied?" *Positions: Asia Critique* 17 (2): 321–46. https://doi.org/10.1215/10679847-2009-005.

Wang, Li Rong. 2011. "How Taiwan's Economy Benefits from Independent Chinese Tourists." *China Report* 6: 50–51.

Wang, Ning. 2006. "Itineraries and the Tourist Experience." In *Travels in Paradox: Remapping Tourism*, edited by Claudio Minca and Tim Oakes, 65–76. Lanham, MD: Rowman & Littlefield.

Watt, Louise. 2020. "Taiwan Says It Tried to Warn the World about Coronavirus. Here's What It Really Knew and When." *Time*, May 19, 2020.

Williams, Stephen. 1998. *Tourism Geography.* London and New York: Routledge.

Winter, Tim, Peggy Teo, and T. C. Chang, eds. 2009. *Asia on Tour: Exploring the Rise of Asian Tourism.* New York: Routledge.

Wong, Chun Han. 2014. "Pandas Behaving Badly Remind Chinese Tourists to Mind Their Manners." *Wall Street Journal*, October 16, 2014.

Wong, Simon, and Elaine Lau. 2001. "Understanding the Behavior of Hong Kong Chinese Tourists on Group Tour Packages." *Journal of Travel Research* 40 (1): 57–67. https://doi.org/10.1177/004728750104000108.

Woo, Chun-kai. 2011. "Tourism as the Cultural Governance: Jiang, Mainland Tourists and the (De)politicization of Cross-Strait Mobility." In *Proceedings of the Asian Conference on Cultural Studies*, 147–161. Osaka: International Academic Forum. https://www.wttc.org/-/media/files/reports/economic impact research/countries 2016/taiwan2016.pdf.

World Travel and Tourism Council. 2016. "Travel & Tourism: Economic Impact 2016 Taiwan."

Wu, Chang-hung, and Wei-han Chen. 2015. "Pro-Unification Advocates Threaten to Sue Police." *Taipei Times*, March 8, 2015. https://www.taipeitimes.com/News/front/archives/2015/03/08/2003613030.

Wu, Debbie. 2011. "Tourism Gain in Doubt as Polls Near." *Associated Press (Reprinted in Taipei Times)*, August 1, 2011. http://www.taipeitimes.com/News/taiwan/print/2011/08/01/2003509660.

Wu, Jieh-min. 2020. "Xiang Gang 'Bolin Weiji' xia de Taiwan duice." *The Reporter*, May 2020. https://www.twreporter.org/a/opinion-international-situation-after-hong-kong-national-security-law-draft-passed.

Wu, J. R. 2016. "Taiwan Says China Tourists Down 36.2 Percent amid Political Tension." *Reuters*, December 29, 2016. https://www.reuters.com/article/uk-taiwan-china-tourism-idUKKBN14I0U5.

Yang, Dominic Meng-Hsuan. 2020. *The Great Exodus from China: Trauma, Memory, and Identity in Modern Taiwan.* Cambridge: Cambridge University Press.

Hsin-hui, Yang, and Jake Chung. 2020. "China Skewed '1992 Consensus,' Ma Says." *Taipei Times*, January 19, 2020. http://www.taipeitimes.com/News/taiwan/archives/2020/01/19/2003729511.

Yeh, Sophia, Tseng Ying-yu, Lawrence Chiu, and Y. F. Low. 2015. "DPP Candidate: Quotas for Chinese Tourists Won't Be Cut If Elected." *CNA*, September 10, 2015. http://focustaiwan.tw/news/acs/201509100021.aspx.

Yu, Junwei. 2008. "China's Foreign Policy in Sport: The Primacy of National Security and Territorial Integrity concerning the Taiwan Question." *China Quarterly* 194: 294–308. https://doi.org/10.1017/S0305741008000386.

Yu, Larry. 1997. "Travel between Politically Divided China and Taiwan." *Asia Pacific Journal of Tourism Research* 2 (1): 19–30. https://doi.org/10.1080/10941669808721982.

Yu, Shuenn-Der. 2004. "Taiwan's Night Market Culture." In *The Minor Arts of Daily Life: Popular Culture in Taiwan*, edited by David K. Jordan, Andrew D. Morris, and Marc L. Moskowitz, 129–49. Honolulu: University of Hawaii Press.

Zhang, J. J. 2013. "Borders on the Move: Cross-Strait Tourists' Material Moments on 'the Other Side' in the Midst of Rapprochement between China and Taiwan." *Geoforum* 48: 94–101. https://doi.org/10.1016/j.geoforum.2013.04.014.

——. 2017. "Paying Homage to the 'Heavenly Mother': Cultural-Geopolitics of the Mazu Pilgrimage and Its Implications on Rapprochement between China and Taiwan." *Geoforum* 84: 32–41. https://doi.org/10.1016/j.geoforum.2017.05.012.

Zhao, Suisheng. 2013. "Foreign Policy Implications of Chinese Nationalism Revisited: The Strident Turn." *Journal of Contemporary China* 22 (82): 535–53. https://doi.org/10.1080/10670564.2013.766379.

Zheng, Liang. 2011. "'We Are More Chinese than You.'" *Journal of International Communication* 17 (2): 163–77. https://doi.org/10.1080/13216597.2011.589367.

Zhuang, Zhequan. 2013. "Shui Wang Shang Liu Sheli Pai Quanu Luke Liuyan." *China Times*, January 30, 2013. https://www.chinatimes.com/newspapers/20130130000702-260107?chdtv.

Index

Taiwan Independence Revolutionary Army
(TIRA), 64–66, 125, 146
Taiwan International Tour Manager
Development Association, 44
Taiwanization, as term, 155n5 (ch. 6)
"Taiwanization" initiatives, 25
Taiwan miracle, 22
Taiwan National Immigration Agency, 45
Taiwan Normal Country Promotion
Association, 49
Taiwan Post, 58
Taiwan Relations Act, 27
Taiwan Semiconductor Manufacturing
Company, 144
Taiwan Solidarity Union, 29
Taiwan Strait, 1
Taiwan Strait Tourism Association, 35, 40–41
Taiwan Think Tank, 135
Taiwan Tourism Bureau, 77
Taoyuan Airport, Taipei, 38, 41, 44, 56, 58, 60,
73, 124, 137
Taroko National Park, 89
taxation, 19
Teng, Teresa, 82, 99. *See also* Teresa Teng
Memorial Museum
Teresa Teng Memorial Museum, 75, 82.
See also Teng, Teresa
territoriality: defined, 5; Taiwan's shifting
designations of, 26–29; tourism industry
and, 2–6, 9–14, 52. *See also* boundaries;
heterotopia
territorial socialization, 5–6
territorial translation, 52–54, 94–96
Thailand, 37, 63
Thao tribe, 60, 62, 80
Tiananmen Square massacre (1989), 122
tianrandu, 29
Tien, Michael, 129
Time (publication), 134
TIRA. *See* Taiwan Independence Revolutionary Army (TIRA)
"Today Hong Kong, tomorrow Taiwan"
slogan, 119, 125, 129
tongbao, 37
tongwen, tongzhong, 51
tongzhong, tongyuan, 80
total-alter space, 48–49
tourism, 2–7, 9–14, 34–35, 142–47; COVID-19
effects on, 144–45, 147; currency and, 52,
53, 77, 84–85, 86, 94; in Hong Kong, 126–29;
identification and difference in, 7–8;
language and, 49; 1992 Consensus and loss
of, 137–41; opening of cross-strait, 39–45;

passports for, 16–17, 45–46, 72–73; revenue
statistics of, 43, 44; Sunflower Movement
and, 118–25; as tool of state power, 35–38;
tourist, defined, 153n1 (intro.); translation
of Taiwan for, 50–56; travel permits for, 3, 4,
36, 45–46, 58, 72, 75, 77, 115, 138, 154n3;
visitor statistics of, 39, 41, 42, 155n4 (ch. 6);
weaponization of, 130–37; youth music
culture and, 111–14. *See also* group tourism;
heterotopia; independent tourism;
mainland guests; Taiwan
Tourism Bureau, 11, 133
Tourism Industry Self-Help Association, 134
tourism research, 6–8, 9–10, 38
tourist, defined, 153n1 (intro.)
trade history, 18–19, 22
transgressions, 2
Travel Agent Association, 40, 45, 121, 132, 134,
136
travel permits, 3, 4, 36, 45–46, 58, 72, 75, 77,
115, 138, 154n3. *See also* passports; tourism
Travel Quality Assurance Association, 132
travel restrictions, 14, 21, 37–39. *See also*
tourism
Treaty of Shimonoseki (1895), 19, 26
Tsai, Morris, 144
Tsai Chi-chang, 134
Tsai Ing-wen, 12–13, 25, 118–19, 131–32,
134, 139
Tseng, Johnson, 40, 41, 44–45
TVBS, 123
228 Incident (1947), 21, 22, 79
228 Memorial Park, 84
two-state theory, 24
"two Taiwans," as concept, 3, 48–50, 141.
See also Taiwan

Umbrella Movement, 118, 119, 125–27, 128–30,
155n6 (ch. 6). *See also* protest
demonstrations
unification of China-Taiwan: bridge
symbolism of, 80; independent tourists on,
103–104; 1992 Consensus on, 11, 13, 34,
118–19, 137–38, 145; as "One China"
principle, 3, 27, 34, 62, 118–19, 124, 135; as
"One Country, Two Systems" scheme, 124,
125, 138, 146; as term, 1; threat of, as
political strategy, 2–3; Tsai on, 140–141. *See
also* self-determination of Taiwan
United Nations, 16, 18, 23, 27, 28, 109
United States, 2, 20, 24, 27, 110
Urry, John, 7
Uyighur people, 131

vaccines and vaccination programs, 144–45.
    See also global health management
veterans, 39, 89, 90, 91, 98, 129
Vigor Kobo shop, 91, 98, 99
visas. *See* travel permits
Voice of America Chinese, 132–33

waiguoren, 37
waishengren, 22, 54, 96, 153n1 (ch. 1)
Wall (music venue), 112
Wang, Ning, 74
Wang Dan, 122
Wang Jin-pyng, 123
Washington Post (publication), 134
Water Running Up (attraction), 56, 68–69,
    87–88, 103
weisheng, 55
Wen Jiabao, 77, 94
wenming, 55, 108
wenxin, 105, 108
When Heaven Burns (television show), 126
White Terror, 21–22, 79
"Winds of the Pacific" (Han), 100–101
Witch House (music venue), 111
Wong, Joshua, 145

World Bank, 27
World Health Assembly (WHA), 28, 156n1
World Health Organization (WHO), 14, 28,
    142–43, 156n1
World Trade Organization, 28, 120
Wu, Joseph, 40, 143
Wu'er Kaixi, 122
Wu Hung-yi, 45
Wu Jieh-min, 145
Wu Pi-lian, 132

xiaoqingxin, 104–6
Xi Jinping, 78, 124, 138
Xiziwan, 83–84, 85

Yao Ta-kuang, 45, 121
Yeh Kuang-Shih, 45
Yehliu Geopark, 91
"Yi shang cu zheng, yi min cu guan"
    (slogan), 35
youth music culture, 111–14

Zhongguo Guomindang. *See* Chinese
    Nationalist Party (KMT)
Zhou Yongkang, 78

Printed in the USA
CPSIA information can be obtained
at www.ICGtesting.com
LVHW091635250823
756268LV00004B/74

9 781501 766930